Credits

Author
Wojciech Kocjan

Reviewers
Péter Károly "Stone" Juhász

Emilien Kenler

Daniel Parraz

Pall Sigurdsson

Acquisition Editors
Anthony Albuquerque

Nikhil Chinnari

Content Development Editor
Chalini Victor

Technical Editors
Monica John

Akashdeep Kundu

Faisal Siddiqui

Copy Editors
Alisha Aranha

Roshni Banerjee

Brandt D'Mello

Deepa Nambiar

Project Coordinator
Kranti Berde

Proofreaders
Clyde Jenkins

Lucy Rowland

Indexer
Hemangini Bari

Graphics
Ronak Dhruv

Disha Haria

Yuvraj Mannari

Production Coordinator
Pooja Chiplunkar

Cover Work
Pooja Chiplunkar

About the Author

Wojciech Kocjan is a system administrator and programmer with 10 years of experience. His work experience includes several years of using Nagios for enterprise IT infrastructure monitoring. He also has experience in large variety of devices and servers, routers, Linux, Solaris, AIX servers and i5/OS mainframes. His programming experience includes multiple languages (such as Java, Ruby, Python, and Perl) and focuses on web applications as well as client-server solutions.

I'd like to thank my wife Joanna and my son Kacper for all of the help and support during the writing of this book.

About the Reviewers

Péter Károly "Stone" Juhász was born in 1980 in Hungary, where he lives with his family and their cat. He holds an MSc degree in Programmer Mathematics. At the very beginning of his career, he turned toward operations. Since 2004, he has been working as a general — mainly GNU/Linux — system administrator.

His average working day includes patching in the server room, installing servers, managing PBX, maintaining VMware vSphere infrastructure and servers at Amazon AWS, managing storage and backups, monitoring with Nagios, trying out new technology, and writing scripts to ease everyday work.

His interests in IT are Linux, server administration, virtualization, artificial intelligence, network security, and distributed systems. His hobbies include learning Chinese, program developing, reading, hiking, playing the game Go, listening to music and unicycling. For his contact information or to find out more about him, you can visit his website at `http://midway.hu`.

Emilien Kenler, after working on small web projects, began to focus on Game Development in 2008, when he was in high school. Until 2011, he worked for different groups and has specialized in system administration. In 2011, he founded a company, HostYourCreeper (`http://www.hostyourcreeper.com`) to sell Minecraft servers, while he was studying Computer Science Engineering. He created a lightweight IaaS based on new technologies such as Node.js and RabbitMQ.

Thereafter, he worked at TaDaweb as a system administrator, building its infrastructure and creating tools to manage deployments and monitoring. In 2014, he began a new adventure at Wizcorp, Tokyo. He will graduate at the end of the year from the University of Technology of Compiègne.

Daniel Parraz was raised in New Mexico and began using computer-type devices at an early age. After graduating from school, he found a technical support job and started to learn Linux. He has been administrating Linux/Unix systems since 2001 and has worked on large storage engineering and installations with Fortune 500 companies and start-ups. He currently lives in Albuquerque, New Mexico, with his family, and enjoys hiking, reading, and growing fruits and vegetables as a volunteer with an agriculture group supported by a local community.

Pall Sigurdsson is a lifelong open source geek with special interest in automation and monitoring. He is known for his work in developing Adagios, a modern web status, and a configuration interface to monitor systems that are compatible with Nagios.

Pall also maintains other projects such as Pynag (a high-level python API for Nagios configuration files) and okconfig (a set of preconfigured Nagios plugins and configuration templates).

www.PacktPub.com

Support files, eBooks, discount offers and more

You might want to visit www.PacktPub.com for support files and downloads related to your book.

Did you know that Packt offers eBook versions of every book published, with PDF and ePub files available? You can upgrade to the eBook version at www.PacktPub.com and as a print book customer, you are entitled to a discount on the eBook copy. Get in touch with us at service@packtpub.com for more details.

At www.PacktPub.com, you can also read a collection of free technical articles, sign up for a range of free newsletters and receive exclusive discounts and offers on Packt books and eBooks.

http://PacktLib.PacktPub.com

Do you need instant solutions to your IT questions? PacktLib is Packt's online digital book library. Here, you can access, read and search across Packt's entire library of books.

Why Subscribe?

- Fully searchable across every book published by Packt
- Copy and paste, print and bookmark content
- On demand and accessible via web browser

Free Access for Packt account holders

If you have an account with Packt at www.PacktPub.com, you can use this to access PacktLib today and view nine entirely free books. Simply use your login credentials for immediate access.

Table of Contents

Preface

The book is a practical guide to setting up Nagios 4, an open source network monitoring tool. It is a system that checks whether hosts and services are working properly and notifies users when problems occur. The book covers the installation and configuring of Nagios 4 on various operating systems, and it focuses on the Ubuntu Linux operating system.

The book takes the reader through all the steps of compiling Nagios from sources, installing, and configuring advanced features such as setting up redundant monitoring. It also mentions how to monitor various services such as e-mail, WWW, databases, and file sharing. The book describes what SNMP is and how it can be used to monitor various devices. It also gives the details of monitoring the Microsoft Windows computers. The book contains troubleshooting sections that aid the reader in case any problems arise while setting up the Nagios functionalities.

No previous experience with network monitoring is required, although it is assumed that the reader has a basic understanding of the Unix systems. It also mentions examples to extend Nagios in several languages such as Perl, Python, Tcl, and Java so that readers who are familiar with at least one of these technologies can benefit from extending Nagios. When you finish this book, you'll be able to set up Nagios to monitor your network and will have a good understanding of what can be monitored.

What this book covers

Chapter 1, Introducing Nagios, talks about Nagios and system monitoring in general. It shows the benefits of using system monitoring software and the advantages of Nagios in particular. It also introduces the basic concepts of Nagios.

Chapter 2, Installing Nagios 4, covers the installation of Nagios both when compiling from source code or using the prebuilt packages. Details on how to configure users, hosts, and services as well as information on how Nagios sends notifications to users are given in this chapter.

Chapter 3, Using the Nagios Web Interface, talks about how to set up and use the Nagios web interface. It describes the basic views for hosts and services and gives detailed information on each individual item. It also introduces some features such as adding comments, scheduled downtimes, viewing detailed information, and generating reports.

Chapter 4, Using the Nagios Plugins, goes through the standard set of Nagios plugins that allows you to perform checks of various services. It shows how you can check for standard services such as e-mail, Web, file, and database servers. It also describes how to monitor resources such as CPU usage, storage, and memory usage.

Chapter 5, Advanced Configuration, focuses on the efficient management of large configurations and the use of templates. It shows how dependencies between hosts and services can be defined and discusses custom variables and adaptive monitoring. It also introduces the concept of flapping and how it detects services that start and stop frequently.

Chapter 6, Notifications and Events, describes the notification system in more details. It focuses on effective ways of communicating problems to the users and how to set up problem escalations. It also describes how events work in Nagios and how they can be used to perform automatic recovery of services.

Chapter 7, Passive Checks and NSCA, focuses on cases where external processes send results to Nagios. It introduces the concept of passive check, which is not scheduled and run by Nagios, and gives practical examples of when and how it can be used. It also shows how to use Nagios Service Check Acceptor (NSCA) to send notifications.

Chapter 8, Monitoring Remote Hosts, covers how Nagios checks can be run on remote machines. It walks through details of deploying checks remotely over SSH using public key authentication. It also shows how Nagios Remote Plugin Executor (NRPE) can be used for deploying plugins remotely.

Chapter 9, Monitoring using SNMP, describes how the Simple Network Management Protocol (SNMP) can be used from Nagios. It provides an overview of SNMP and its versions. It explains the reading of SNMP values from the SNMP-aware devices and covers how that can then be used to perform checks from Nagios.

Chapter 10, Advanced Monitoring, focuses on how Nagios can be set up on multiple hosts and how that information could be gathered on a central server. It also covers how to monitor computers that run the Microsoft Windows operating system.

Chapter 11, Programming Nagios, shows how to extend Nagios. It explains how to write custom check commands, how to create custom ways of notifying users, and how passive checks and NSCA can be used to integrate your solutions with Nagios. The chapter covers many programming languages to show how Nagios can be integrated with them.

Chapter 12, Using the Query Handler, focuses on the use of the Nagios query handler to send commands to Nagios as well as receive results and notifications from these commands. It shows how the query handler can be used from multiple programming languages and how it can be used to build an application to display Nagios updates in real time.

What you need for this book

This book requires a Linux server. As all of the examples are created using Ubuntu Linux, it is recommended that you use this distribution. The book goes through the process of setting up Nagios, so installing it is not a prerequisite of this book.

The Nagios web interface requires a web server. *Chapter 3, Using the Nagios Web Interface,* provides a step-by-step instruction on how to set up an Apache web server and configure it so that it be used with Nagios.

Who this book is for

The target readers of this book are System Administrators who are interested in using Nagios. This book will introduce Nagios along with the new features of Version 4.

Conventions

In this book, you will find a number of styles of text that distinguish between different kinds of information. Here are some examples of these styles, and an explanation of their meaning.

Code words in text, object names, folder names, filenames, file extensions, pathnames, dummy URLs, user input, and Twitter handles are shown as follows: "This service group consists of the `mysql` and `pgsql` services on the `linuxbox01` host."

A block of code is set as follows:

```
define service{
    host_name                       linuxbox01
    service_description             mysql
    check_command                   check_ssh
    servicegroups                   databaseservices
    }
```

When we wish to draw your attention to a particular part of a code block, the relevant lines or items are set in bold:

```
define service{
    host_name                       linuxbox01
    service_description             mysql
    check_command                   check_ssh
    servicegroups                   databaseservices
    }
```

Any command-line input or output is written as follows:

```
# cp /usr/src/asterisk-addons/configs/cdr_mysql.conf.sample
    /etc/asterisk/cdr_mysql.conf
```

New terms and **important words** are shown in bold. Words that you see on the screen, in menus or dialog boxes for example, appear in the text like this: "You should start by downloading the source tarball of the latest Nagios 4.x branch. It is available under the **Get Nagios Core** section."

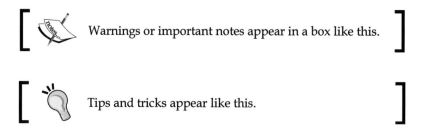

> Warnings or important notes appear in a box like this.

> Tips and tricks appear like this.

Reader feedback

Feedback from our readers is always welcome. Let us know what you think about this book—what you liked or may have disliked. Reader feedback is important for us to develop titles that you really get the most out of.

To send us general feedback, simply send an e-mail to feedback@packtpub.com, and mention the book title via the subject of your message.

If there is a topic that you have expertise in and you are interested in either writing or contributing to a book, see our author guide on www.packtpub.com/authors.

Customer support

Now that you are the proud owner of a Packt book, we have a number of things to help you to get the most from your purchase.

Downloading the example code

You can download the example code files for all Packt books you have purchased from your account at http://www.packtpub.com. If you purchased this book elsewhere, you can visit http://www.packtpub.com/support and register to have the files e-mailed directly to you.

Errata

Although we have taken every care to ensure the accuracy of our content, mistakes do happen. If you find a mistake in one of our books—maybe a mistake in the text or the code—we would be grateful if you would report this to us. By doing so, you can save other readers from frustration and help us improve subsequent versions of this book. If you find any errata, please report them by visiting http://www.packtpub.com/submit-errata, selecting your book, clicking on the **errata submission form** link, and entering the details of your errata. Once your errata are verified, your submission will be accepted and the errata will be uploaded on our website, or added to any list of existing errata, under the Errata section of that title. Any existing errata can be viewed by selecting your title from http://www.packtpub.com/support.

Piracy

Piracy of copyright material on the Internet is an ongoing problem across all media. At Packt, we take the protection of our copyright and licenses very seriously. If you come across any illegal copies of our works, in any form, on the Internet, please provide us with the location address or website name immediately so that we can pursue a remedy.

Please contact us at copyright@packtpub.com with a link to the suspected pirated material.

We appreciate your help in protecting our authors, and our ability to bring you valuable content.

Questions

You can contact us at questions@packtpub.com if you are having a problem with any aspect of the book, and we will do our best to address it.

1

Introducing Nagios

Imagine you're working as an administrator of a large IT infrastructure. You just started receiving e-mails that a web application just stopped working. When you try to access the same page, it just doesn't load. What are the possibilities? Is it the router? Is it the firewall? Perhaps the machine hosting the page is down? Before you even start thinking rationally on what to do, your boss calls about the critical situation and demands explanations. In all this panic, you'll probably start plugging everything in and out of the network, rebooting the machine…and that doesn't help.

After hours of nervous digging into the issue, you've finally found the solution: the web server was working properly, but it would time out communication with the database server. This was because the machine with the DB did not receive the correct IP as yet another box ran out of memory and killed the DHCP server on it. Imagine how much time it would take to find all that manually? It would be a nightmare if the database server was in another branch of the company or in a different time zone and perhaps guys over there were still sleeping.

But what if you had Nagios up and running across your entire company? You would just go to the web interface and see that there are no problems with the web server and the machine on which it is running. There would also be a list of issues — the machine serving IP addresses to the entire company does not do its job and the database is down. If the setup also monitored the DHCP server itself, you'd get a warning e-mail that little swap memory is available on it or too many processes are running. Maybe it would even have an event handler for such cases to just kill or restart noncritical processes. Also, Nagios will try to restart the *dhcpd* process over the network in case it is down.

In the worst case, Nagios would speed up hours of investigation to 10 minutes. In the best case, you would just get an e-mail that there was such a problem and another e-mail that it's already fixed. You would just disable a few services and increase the swap size for the DHCP machine and solve the problem once and for all. Nobody would even notice that there was such a problem.

Understanding the basics of Nagios

Nagios is a tool for system monitoring. It means that Nagios watches computers or devices on your network and ensures that they are working as they should. Nagios constantly checks if other machines are working properly. It also verifies that various services on those machines are working fine. In addition, Nagios accepts other processes or machines reporting their status, for example, a web server can directly report if it is not overloaded to Nagios.

The main purpose of system monitoring is to detect as soon as possible any system that is not working properly so that users of that system will not report the issue to you first.

System monitoring in Nagios is split into two categories of objects: hosts and services. Hosts represent a physical or virtual device on your network (servers, routers, workstations, printers, and so on). Services are particular functionalities, for example, a **Secure Shell (SSH)** server (*sshd* process on the machine) can be defined as a service to be monitored. Each service is associated with a host on which it is running. In addition, machines can be grouped into host groups.

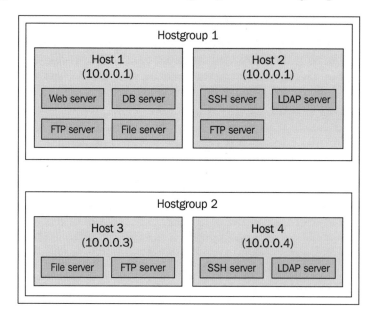

A major benefit of Nagios' performance checks is that it only uses four distinct states — **Ok**, **Warning**, **Critical**, and **Unknown**. It is also based on plugins — this means if you want to check something that's not yet possible to do, you just need to write a simple piece of code, and that's it!

The approach to only offer three states allows administrators to ignore monitoring values themselves and just decide on what the warning/critical limits are. This is a proven concept, and is far more efficient than monitoring graphs and analyzing trends. For example, system administrators tend to ignore things such as gradually declining storage space. People often simply ignore the process until a critical process runs out of disk space. Having a strict limit to watch is much better, because you always catch a problem regardless of whether it turns from warning to critical in 15 minutes or in a week. This is exactly what Nagios does. Each check performed by Nagios is turned from numeric values (such as the amount of disk space or CPU usage) to one of the three possible states.

Another benefit is a report stating that X services are up and running, Y are in warning state, and Z are currently critical, which is much more readable than a matrix of values. It saves you the time of analyzing what's working and what's failing. It can also help prioritize what needs to be handled first, and which problems can be handled later.

Nagios performs all of its checks using plugins. These are external components for which Nagios passes information on what should be checked and what the warning and critical limits are. Plugins are responsible for performing the checks and analyzing results. The output from such a check is the status (**working**, **questionable**, or **failure**) and additional text describing information on the service in details. This text is mainly intended for system administrators to be able to read the detailed status of a service.

Nagios comes with a set of standard plugins that allow performance checks for almost all services your company might offer. See *Chapter 4, Using the Nagios Plugins*, for detailed information on plugins that are developed along with Nagios. Moreover, if you need to perform a specific check (for example, connect to a Web service and invoke methods), it is very easy to write your own plugins. And that's not all—they can be written in any language and it takes less than 15 minutes to write a complete check command! *Chapter 11, Programming Nagios*, talks about that ability in more detail.

The benefits of monitoring resources

There are many reasons for you to ensure that all your resources are working as expected. If you're still not convinced after reading the introduction to this chapter, here are a few important points why it is important to monitor your infrastructure.

The main reason is quality improvement. If your IT staff can notice failures quicker by using a monitoring tool, they will also be able to respond to them much faster. Sometimes it takes hours or days to get the first report of a failure even if many users bump into errors. Nagios ensures that if something is not working, you'll know about it. In some cases, event handling can even be done so that Nagios can switch to the backup solution until the primary process is fixed. A typical case would be to start a dial-up connection and use it as a primary connection in cases when the company VPN is down.

Another reason is much better problem determination. Very often what the users report as a failure is far from the root cause of the problem, such as an email system is down due to the LDAP service not working correctly. If you define dependencies between hosts correctly, then Nagios will point out that the POP3 e-mail server is assumed to be "not working" because the LDAP service that it depends upon has a problem. Nagios will start checking the e-mail server as soon as the problem with LDAP has been resolved.

Nagios is also very flexible when it comes down to notifying people of what isn't functioning correctly. In most cases, your company has a large IT team or multiple teams. Usually, you want some people to handle servers, others to handle network switches/routers/modems. There might also be a team responsible for network printers or a division is made based on geographical locations. You can instruct Nagios on who is responsible for particular machines or groups of machines, so that when something is wrong, the right people will get to know of it. You can also use Nagios' web interface to manage who is working on what issue.

Monitoring resources not only is useful for finding problems, but also saves you from having them—Nagios handles warnings and critical situations differently. This means that it's possible to be aware of situations that may become problems really soon. For example, if your disk storage on an e-mail server is running out, it's better to be aware of this situation before it becomes a critical issue.

Monitoring can also be set up on multiple machines across various locations. These machines will then communicate all their results to a central Nagios server so that information on all hosts and services in your system can be accessed from a single machine. This gives you a more accurate picture of your IT infrastructure, as well as allows testing more complex systems such as firewalls. For example, it is vital that a testing environment is accessible from a production environment, but not the other way around.

It is also possible to set up a Nagios server outside the company's intranet (for example, over a dedicated DSL) to make sure that traffic from the Internet is properly blocked. It can be used to check if only certain services are available, for example, verify that only SSH and **Hypertext Transfer Protocol (HTTP)** are accessible from external IP addresses, and that services such as databases are inaccessible to users.

Main features

Nagios' main strength is flexibility — it can be configured to monitor your IT infrastructure in the way you want it. It also has a mechanism to react automatically to problems and has a powerful notification system. All of this is based on a clear object definition system, which in turn is based on a few types of objects, shown as follows:

- **Commands**: These are definitions of how Nagios should perform particular types of checks. They are an abstraction layer on top of actual plugins that allow you to group similar types of operations.

- **Time periods**: These are date and time spans at which an operation should or should not be performed. For example, Monday–Friday, 09:00–17:00.

- **Hosts and host groups**: These are devices along with the possibility to group hosts. A single host might be a member of more than one group.

- **Services**: These are various functionalities or resources to monitor on a specific host. For example, CPU usage, storage space, or Web server.

- **Contacts and contact groups**: These are people that should be notified with information on how and when they should be contacted; contacts can be grouped, and a single contact might be a member of more than one group.

- **Notifications**: These define who should be notified of what, for example, all errors for the *linux-servers* host group should go to the *linux-admins* contact group during working hours and to the *critsit-team* contact group outside of working hours. Notifications are not strictly an object, but a combination of all the preceding objects and are an essential part of Nagios.

- **Escalations**: These are an extension to notifications; they define that after an object is in same state for specific period of time, other people should get notified of certain events — for example, a critical server being down for more than 4 hours should alert IT management so that they track the issue.

A beneficial feature of using Nagios is that it is a mature dependency system. For any administrator, it is obvious that if your router is down, then all machines accessed via it will fail. Some systems don't take that into account, and in such cases, you get a list of several failing machines and services. Nagios allows you to define dependencies between hosts to reflect actual network topology. For example, if a router that connects you to the rest of your network is down, Nagios will not perform checks for the subsequent parts and machines that are dependent on the router. This is illustrated in the following figure:

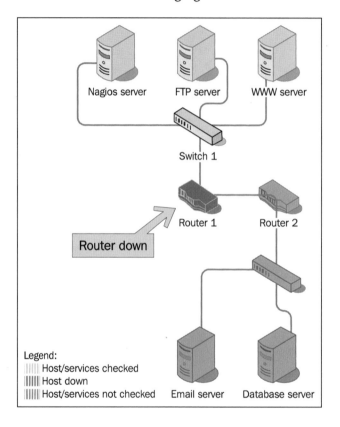

You can also define that a particular service depends on another service, either on the same host or a different host. In case one of the dependent services is down, a check for a service is not even performed.

For example, in order for your company's intranet application to function properly, both an underlying Web server and database server must be running properly. So, if a database service is not working properly, Nagios will not perform checks and/or not send notifications that your application is not working, because the root cause of the problem is that the database is not working properly. The database server might be on the same host or a different host. If the database is not working properly, if the dependent machine is down or not accessible, all services dependent on the database service will not be checked as well.

Nagios offers a consistent system of macro definitions. These are variables that can be put into all object definitions and depend on the context. They can be put inside commands, and depending on the host, service, and many other parameters, macro definitions are substituted accordingly. For example, a command definition might use an IP address of the host it is currently checking in all remote tests. It also makes it possible to put information such as the previous and current status of a service in a notification e-mail. Nagios 3 also offers various extensions to macro definitions, which make it an even more powerful mechanism.

Nagios also offers mechanism for scheduling planned downtimes. This is mainly used when maintenance of the IT infrastructure is to be carried out, and servers and/or services they provide are out of order for a period of time. You can let Nagios know that such an event will occur, and it will not send notifications about problems with hosts and/or services that have a scheduled downtime. In such cases, dependencies are also taken into consideration—if a database has a scheduled downtime, notifications for the services that depend on it will not be sent out. Nagios can also notify people of planned downtimes automatically. This allows creating an integrated process of scheduling downtimes that will also handle informing users.

Soft and hard states

Nagios works by checking if a particular host or service is working correctly and storing its status. Because the status of a service is only one of our possible values, it is crucial that it actually reflects what the current status is. In order to avoid detecting random and temporary failures, Nagios uses soft and hard states to describe what the current status is for a host or service.

Imagine that an administrator is restarting a Web server, and this operation makes connecting to the webpages unavailable for 5 seconds. Since such restarts are usually done at night to lower the number of users affected, this is an acceptable period of time. However, a problem might be that Nagios will try to connect to the server and notice it is actually down. If it would only rely on a single result, Nagios could trigger an alert that a Web server is down. It would actually be up and running again in a few seconds, but it could take a couple of minutes for Nagios to find that out.

To handle situations where a service is down for a very short time, or the test has temporarily failed, soft states were introduced. When a previous status of a check is unknown or is different from the previous one, Nagios will re-test the host or service a couple of times to make sure the change is permanent. Nagios assumes that the new result is a soft state. After additional tests have verified that the new state is permanent, it is considered a hard state.

Each host and service check defines the number of retries to perform before assuming a change is permanent. This allows more flexibility over how many failures should be treated as an actual problem instead of a temporary one. Setting the number of checks to 1 will cause all changes to be treated as hard instantly. The following figure is an illustration of soft and hard state changes, assuming that number of checks to be performed is set to 3:

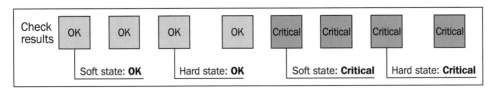

This feature is very useful for checks that should skip short outages of a service or use a protocol that might fail in case of extensive traffic — such as ICMP or UDP. Monitoring devices over SNMP is also an example of a check that can fail in cases where a single check fails; nevertheless, the check will eventually succeed during the second or third check.

> The following section is mainly intended for people already familiar with Nagios' functionality and who only want to know what's been added to the new version.
>
> If you are not experienced with Nagios, you may skip this section, because the features are described throughout the book.

What's new in Nagios 4.0

The 4.0 version of Nagios is a major release, and many changes have been made since the release of Nagios 3 in 2008. This version contains both new features and multiple improvements to existing functionality.

Nagios has also changed its name — it is now called Nagios Core, which is used to indicate the core, open source project for monitoring. This was also needed as more commercial solutions using Nagios were introduced. However, Nagios Core is still often referred to as simply Nagios, and throughout this book, any reference to Nagios indicates Nagios Core.

This release introduces a new element of Nagios—`libnagios`. It provides many data structures and algorithms that Nagios has already been using and allows using it in third-party applications and add-ons. This is especially useful for plugins and applications that communicate with Nagios, because they can depend on the library already being installed and can benefit from implementations optimized for performance. This functionality is described in more detail in *Chapter 11, Programming Nagios*, and *Chapter 12, Using the Query Handler*.

Another new feature is the query handler—it is a generic mechanism for communicating between the Nagios service and add-ons. It is a two-way communication protocol using Unix sockets for sending and receiving data.

It can be used to communicate with various parts of Nagios and allows easy integration with third-party solutions, such as allowing an application to run checks instead of a plugin. It can be used also for retrieving updates from service or host checks, and allows registering an application as the handler for a check or notification. The **Nagios Event Radio Dispatcher (NERD)**, which works on top of the query handler, also allows subscribing to host and service status changes and updates.

Chapter 12, Using the Query Handler, talks about the query handler and NERD in more detail, as well as shows actual examples of using it.

Nagios 4 has introduced several minor features and improvements. Nagios 4 handling for hosts and services has been combined—this means that performing checks, sending notifications, and running events works the same for both types of objects. It is also possible to specify a parent service, which indicates dependencies between services, similar to how it works now for hosts.

An important goal of the Nagios 4 release is to improve Nagios' stability and scalability. Many parts of the Nagios internals have been optimized in terms of CPU and memory usage.

Previous versions of Nagios (up to 3.x) have worked as a single Nagios process, starting child processes to perform checks, notifications, and event handlers. This becomes an issue when running a large number of child processes because of how Unix operating systems create child processes—a process using a lot of memory consumes more resources to start a child process. Nagios 4 uses its main process for scheduling events and multiple worker processes for running the child processes. The workers do not use many resources, and are able to spawn child processes much faster.

Multiple components of Nagios were also optimized for performance. The event processing, macro expansion, and configuration parsing are now much faster, which improves startup time for Nagios as well as regular operations.

Nagios 4 also introduces a few backward incompatibilities. First, embedded Perl has been removed. This includes the Perl support, as well as all options related to it. The main reason was that this feature has caused many problems related to memory leaks, and disabling it has improved Nagios performance. This is also related to the new approach that Nagios worker processes mentioned earlier in the chapter.

It is no longer possible to define groups that include each other, that is, `hostgroup1` including `hostgroup2` and vice versa. This used to work in previous Nagios versions, but generates an error in Nagios 4.

The `obsess_over_host` and `obsess_over_service` options were merged as the `obsess` option. In Nagios 4, they are defined as aliases and will be removed in future versions of Nagios. Also, setting host and service obsess to different values is no longer possible.

All of the changes mentioned earlier in this section make Nagios 4 much less resource intensive. This allows monitoring more services and hosts without additional investment in servers. Thus, you should consider upgrading your Nagios setup even if you do not plan on using any of the new features.

Summary

In this chapter, we learned the basics of Nagios as a tool for performing system monitoring. It can be used to ensure that services are working correctly, problems are detected earlier, and appropriate people are aware when something's wrong.

We learned the basic types of objects in Nagios — commands, hosts, services, time periods, contacts, as well as object grouping. We have also found out about notifications and escalations, which can be used to notify administrators about problems.

The chapter also introduced the concept of dependencies that helps in understanding the root cause of complex problems.

We also learned the most important changes that Nagios 4 brings and how they can be used.

The next chapter will guide us through the process of setting up and configuring Nagios and the standard Nagios plugins.

2
Installing Nagios 4

The previous chapter has described what Nagios is, the basic concepts of monitoring, and types of objects in Nagios. This chapter describes how to install Nagios and the standard Nagios plugins. The process described here does not take advantage of any packaging systems that are currently available on the majority of operating systems.

In this chapter, we will cover the following points:

- How to upgrade Nagios from a previous version
- Installing Nagios prerequisites (software, users, and groups)
- Obtaining and compiling Nagios from source
- Installing Nagios and setting up a system service
- Configuring Nagios with a basic set of objects
- Setting up basic notifications
- Using templates and object inheritance

Installation

Nagios can be installed in two ways. The first one is to install Nagios from your Linux distribution's binary packages, which has the upside that the packages are updated in terms of security issues by your Linux distribution automatically or by running updates manually. The downside is that for many distributions, Nagios 4 may not be available for some time, such as long term support distributions that may be providing the Nagios 3.x version.

Another option is to compile and install Nagios manually. Manual installation is recommended for system administrators who want more power where their software is installed, and want to manage software upgrades and configuration on their own. It also allows updating to latest version of Nagios faster; binary distributions may not always have the latest versions.

This section discusses the installation of Nagios 4. It focuses on Ubuntu Linux distribution, but the commands for Ubuntu are also valid for Debian Linux distribution. This chapter also has guides for RedHat and CentOS Linux distributions. If you are using a different Linux distribution, the commands may be slightly different.

Upgrading from previous versions

If you already have Nagios setup, it is worth upgrading to Nagios 4, either to take advantage of the new features or performance improvements that the latest version offers. While upgrading, you should proceed with the same steps as when performing a fresh installation. You need to use the same username, groups, and directories that you have used for the previous Nagios installation. It is also needed to stop all Nagios processes before performing an upgrade. This can usually be done by invoking the following command:

```
service nagios stop
```

The preceding command works on all modern Linux distributions and supports services installed as SysVinit (in /etc/init.d or /etc/rc.d/init.d) and Upstart services (added in /etc/init and using a different format of the service file definition).

If the preceding command did not work properly, running the init.d script directly should work:

```
service nagios stop
```

It is recommended to stop Nagios while compiling and installing a new version. You should then proceed with the installation steps described in the next sections. Almost all of Nagios 4 configuration parameters are backward compatible, so your current configuration will work fine after upgrading. Backward incompatibilities between Nagios 4 and 3 are mentioned in *Chapter 1, Introducing Nagios*. Once the new version of Nagios is installed, it is recommended to check the Nagios configuration with the new version to ensure there are no incompatibilities:

```
/opt/nagios/bin/nagios -v /etc/nagios/nagios.cfg
```

We can now simply run the command:

```
service nagios start
```

If the preceding command did not work properly, run the following init.d script, and the upgrade process should be complete:

```
/etc/init.d/nagios start
```

Installing prerequisites

This section applies for people compiling Nagios from sources and manually installing them. Almost all modern Linux distributions include Nagios in their packages. Nagios website also offers instructions for automated installation on several operating systems. In such cases, all related packages will be installed by the underlying system (such as APT in Debian and Ubuntu systems and Yum for RedHat and CentOS systems). Usually, a system with a set of development packages installed already contains all the packages needed to build Nagios.

Building Nagios from sources requires having a C compiler, standard C library development files, and the make/imake command. Additionally, development files for OpenSSL should be installed so that network-based plugins will be able to communicate over an SSL layer. MySQL and PostgreSQL development packages should also be installed so that database checks can be run.

First of all, if we're planning to build the Nagios system, a compiler along with several build tools will be required. These are gcc, make, cpp, and binutils. It also needs standard C library development files. All those packages are often already installed, but make sure they are present, as they are needed before any compilation.

Nagios by itself does not have a large number of packages that need to be installed on your system in order for it to offer the basic functionality. However, if we want to use all functionalities that Nagios can offer, it is required to install an additional software.

If we want to use the Nagios web interface, a web server capable of serving CGI scripts is required. Apache web is the recommended and also the most popular web server on a Linux installation. Even though Nagios should work with any web server supporting CGI and PHP, the book covers configuring Apache.

Additionally, several plugins from the Nagios standard distribution are written in Perl and will not work if Perl is not installed. Some plugins also need Perl's Net::Snmp package to communicate with devices over the SNMP protocol.

Also, the GD graphics library is needed for the Nagios web interface to create status map and trends images. We will also install libraries for JPEG and PNG images so that GD can create images in these formats.

All of the packages mentioned earlier are usually installed with many operating systems and most of them are already available for almost any Unix-based platform.

Throughout this chapter, we will use the Ubuntu Linux 12.04 Precise distribution as it is very popular. All newer Ubuntu platforms use the same package names, so the following commands will work without any problem.

We will also install Apache 2 and Perl from Ubuntu packages. For different operating systems, the package names might be different but should be similar. A command to install all the packages for our chosen distribution is as follows:

```
apt-get install gcc make binutils cpp \
                libpq-dev libmysqlclient-dev \
                libssl1.0.0 libssl-dev pkg-config \
                libgd2-xpm libgd2-xpm-dev libgd-tools \
                perl libperl-dev libnet-snmp-perl snmp \
                apache2 libapache2-mod-php5
```

Downloading the example code

You can download the example code files for all Packt books you have purchased from your account from http://www.packtpub.com. If you purchased this book elsewhere, you can visit http://www.packtpub.com/support and register to have the files e-mailed directly to you.

Package names might be different for other operating systems and distributions. The command to install corresponding packages might also be different. For RPM packages, the naming convention is a bit different development; packages have devel suffix. Libraries themselves are also named slightly differently.

For Red Hat Enterprise Linux, CentOS and Fedora Core operating systems with yum installed, the command to install all prerequisites would be as follows:

```
yum install gcc make imake binutils cpp \
            postgresql-devel mysql-libs mysql-devel \
            openssl openssl-devel pkgconfig \
            gd gd-devel gd-progs libpng libpng-devel \
            libjpeg libjpeg-devel perl perl-devel \
            net-snmp net-snmp-devel net-snmp-perl net-snmp-utils \
            httpd php
```

The preceding command is for the CentOS 6 Linux distribution. Package names may vary slightly depending on your system's distribution and version. The packages include tools for compiling applications, various libraries, and their development packages. Apache and PHP5 are needed for the web interface, which is described in more detail in *Chapter 3, Using the Nagios Web Interface*. Usually a system with a set of development packages installed already contains all of the packages needed to build Nagios.

Obtaining Nagios

Nagios is an open source application, which means that source code of all Nagios components is freely available from the Nagios home page. Nagios is distributed under **GNU GPL (General Public License)** Version 2 (visit http://www.gnu.org/licenses/old-licenses/gpl-2.0.html for more details), which means that the Nagios source code can be redistributed and modified almost freely under the condition that all changes are also distributed as source code. Nagios also has a standard set of plugins, named Nagios plugins, which are developed independently as SourceForge project available at http://sourceforge.net/projects/nagiosplug/ and are distributed under the GPL Version 3 license, which can be found at http://www.gnu.org/licenses/gpl.html.

First of all, many operating systems already have binary distributions of Nagios. If you are not an IT expert and just want to try out or learn Nagios in your environment, it is best to use binary distributions instead of compiling Nagios by yourself. Therefore, it is recommended to check if your distribution does not contain a compiled version of Nagios 4. For RedHat and Fedora Linux systems, Nagios download page (available at http://www.nagios.org/download/) contains RPMs that can be simply installed onto your system. For other distributions, their package repository might contain binary Nagios packages. The NagiosExchange website (http://exchange.nagios.org/) also hosts Nagios builds for various platforms, such as AIX or SUSE Linux. All binary distributions of Nagios are split into packages (the rpm, dpkg, pkg, or bin file) that contain the Nagios daemon. It is usually called Nagios, and the standard set of plugins is usually named **Nagios plugins**.

If you are an experienced user and want to control software installed on your machines, it's recommended to install Nagios from sources. In that case, you should also download sources of both Nagios and its plugins. In order to download the Nagios source packages, please go to the Nagios download page, available at `http://www.nagios.org/download/`. All Nagios downloads are hosted on SourceForge, so the download links will redirect you to the SourceForge download page. The download process should begin automatically.

You should start by downloading the source tarball of the latest Nagios 4.x branch. It is available under the **Get Nagios Core** section. When asked about Nagios software editions, please choose the free version of Nagios. The filename of the source tarball should be similar to `nagios-4.0.tar.gz`, depending on what is the exact version of latest stable release.

You should also download the source tarball of the latest Nagios plugins from the same download page. It is available under the **Get Nagios Plugins** page. The filename for the plugins should be similar to `nagios-plugins-1.4.16.tar.gz`, also depending on which the exact version of latest stable release is.

To unpack both the files, we first need to create a source directory; we will use `/usr/src/nagios4` throughout the chapter, but the path can be any location. To create it and unpack both files, we should execute the following commands:

```
mkdir /usr/src/nagios4
cd /usr/src/nagios4
tar -xzf /path/to/nagios-4.0.tar.gz
tar -xzf /path/to/nagios-plugins-1.4.16.tar.gz
```

Setting up users and groups

This section describes how to do a compilation and installation of Nagios and standard Nagios plugins from source tarballs. If you plan on installing Nagios from binary distributions, you should skip this section and proceed to the next section that describes the exact Nagios configurations. You might also need to adjust parameters mentioned in the book to use directories that your Nagios installation uses. If you are upgrading from a previous Nagios version, then you already have all users and groups properly set up. In such cases, you should proceed to the next section.

The first thing that needs to be done is to decide where to install Nagios. In this section, we'll install Nagios binaries into the /opt/nagios directory and all configuration files will be based on these locations. This is a location for all Nagios binaries, plugins, and additional files. The Nagios data will be stored in the /var/nagios directory. This is where the status of everything is kept. It can be a part of the Nagios binaries installation directory or a separate directory, as in our case. The Nagios configuration will be put into /etc/nagios. These directories will be created as part of the Nagios installation process.

After we have decided on our directory structure, we need to set up the users and groups for Nagios data. We'll also create a system user and a group named nagios, which will be used by the daemon. We'll also set up the nagioscmd group that can communicate with the daemon. The Nagios user will be a member of the nagios and nagioscmd groups. The following commands will create the groups and users:

```
groupadd nagios
groupadd nagioscmd
useradd -g nagios -G nagioscmd -d /opt/nagios nagios
```

The reason for creating additional users in the system is that Nagios uses a separate user. This increases security and allows a more flexible setup. Nagios also communicates with external components over a Unix socket. This is a socket that works similar to a file on your file system. All commands are passed to Nagios via the pipe, and therefore, if you want your processes to be able to send reports or changes to Nagios, you need to make sure they have access to the socket. One of typical uses for this is that the Nagios web interface needs to be able to send commands to the monitoring process.

If you want to use the web interface, it is necessary to add the user that your web server runs at to the nagioscmd group. This will allow the web interface to send commands to Nagios. The user that the web server is working as is usually www-data, apache, or httpd. It can be checked with a simple grep command:

```
root@ubuntu:~# grep -r ^User /etc/apache* /etc/httpd*
/etc/apache2/apache2.conf:User www-data
```

For our preceding example, we now know the user name is www-data.

Sometimes on Ubuntu, the setting is slightly different, as shown in the following command:

```
root@ubuntu:~# grep -r ^User /etc/apache* /etc/httpd*
/etc/apache2/apache2.conf:User ${APACHE_RUN_USER}
```

In that case, the value is defined in the `/etc/apache2/envvars` file:

```
# grep APACHE_RUN_USER /etc/apache2/envvars
/etc/apache2/envvars:export APACHE_RUN_USER=www-data
```

In this case, the user name is also www-data.

Now we will add this user to the nagioscmd group. This requires a simple command to be run:

```
usermod -G nagioscmd www-data
```

Compiling and installing Nagios

The next step is to set up the Nagios destination directories and change their owners accordingly. The following commands will create the directories and change their owner user and group to nagios.

```
mkdir -p /opt/nagios /etc/nagios /var/nagios
chown nagios:nagios /opt/nagios /etc/nagios /var/nagios
```

We will now create a source directory, where all of our builds will take place. For the purpose of this book, it will be /usr/src/nagios4. We need to extract our Nagios and standard plugins into that directory. The extraction will create nagios-4.0 and nagios-plugins-1.4.16 subdirectories (or similar ones, depending on your source versions).

Now lets go to the directory where Nagios sources are located; in our case it is /usr/src/nagios4/nagios-4.0. We'll configure Nagios parameters for the directories, we plan to install it by running the configure script. Some of the options that the script accepts are described in the following table:

Option	Description
--prefix=<dir>	Specifies the main directory in which all Nagios binaries are installed; this defaults to /usr/local/nagios
--sysconfdir=<dir>	Specifies the directory where all Nagios configurations will be stored; this defaults to [PREFIX]/etc
--localstatedir=<dir>	Specifies the directory where all Nagios status and other information will be kept; this defaults to [PREFIX]/var
--with-nagios-user=<user>	Specifies the Unix user to be used by the Nagios daemon; this defaults to nagios
--with-nagios-group=<grp>	Specifies the Unix group to use for the Nagios daemon; this defaults to nagios

Option	Description
`--with-mail=<path>`	Specifies the path to the `mail` program used for sending e-mails
`--with-httpd-conf=<path>`	Specifies the path to the Apache configuration directory; this can be used to generate Apache configuration files
`--with-init-dir=<path>`	Specifies the directory where all scripts required for setting up a system service should be installed; this defaults to `/etc/rc.d/init.d`

For the directory structure that was described earlier in this section, the following configure script should be used:

```
sh configure \
    --prefix=/opt/nagios \
    --sysconfdir=/etc/nagios \
    --localstatedir=/var/nagios \
    --libexecdir=/opt/nagios/plugins \
    --with-command-group=nagioscmd
```

The script might take time to complete as it will try to guess the configuration of your machine and verify how to build Nagios. If the `configure` script fails, the most probable reason is that one or more prerequisites are missing. At that point, you will need to analyze which test failed and install or configure additional packages. Most of the times, the output is quite clear, and it is easy to understand what went wrong.

Assuming the `configure` command worked, we now need to build Nagios. The build process uses the `make` command, similar to almost all Unix programs. The following commands can be used to build or install Nagios:

Command	Description
`make all`	Compiles Nagios; this is the first thing you should be doing
`make install`	Installs the main program, CGI, and HTML files
`make install-commandmode`	Installs and configures the external command file
`make install-config`	Installs the sample Nagios configuration; this target should only be used for fresh installations
`make install-init`	Installs scripts to set up Nagios as a system service

First, we'll need to build every module within Nagios. To do this, simply run the following command:

```
make all
```

If an error occurs, it is probably due to some header files missing or a development package not installed. The following is a sample output from a successful Nagios build. It finishes with a friendly message saying that it has completed successfully.

```
cd ./base && make
make[1]: Entering directory '/usr/src/nagios4/base'
[...]
*** Compile finished ***
[...]
***************************************************************
Enjoy.
```

If an error occurs during the build, information about it is also shown. For example, the following is a sample output from the build:

```
[...]
In file included from checks.c:40:
../include/config.h:163:18: error: ssl.h: No such file or directory
[...]
make[1]: *** [checks.o] Error 1
make[1]: Leaving directory '/usr/src/nagios4/base'
make: *** [all] Error 2
```

If this or a similar error occurs, please make sure that you have all the prerequisites mentioned earlier installed. Also, please make sure that you have enough memory and storage space during compilation as this might also cause unexpected crashes during builds.

On Ubuntu systems, it is possible to look for development packages using the apt-cache search command; for example, apt-cache search ssl will find all packages related to OpenSSL. Development packages always have the -dev suffix in their package name—in this case, it would be the libssl-dev package. Combined with the grep command to filter only development packages, for SSL it would be the following command:

```
apt-cache search ssl | grep -- -dev
```

On RedHat Enterprise Linux, CentOS and Fedora Core, it is possible to look for development packages using the yum search command:

```
yum search ssl | grep -- -devel
```

Now, we need to install Nagios by running the following commands:

```
make install
make install-commandmode
```

For a fresh install, it is recommended to also install sample configuration files that will be used later for configuring Nagios:

```
make install-config
```

At this point Nagios is installed. It is recommended to keep all of your Nagios sources, as well as prepare dedicated scripts that install Nagios. This is just in case you decide to enable/disable specific options and don't want to guess how exactly Nagios was configured to build the last time it was installed.

Compiling and installing Nagios plugins

The next step that should be carried out is compile Nagios Plugins package. Similar to Nagios, we can both install packages from binary distributions or compile the standard plugins from source code. To install the plugins on an Ubuntu Linux distribution, we can run the following command:

```
apt-get install nagios-plugins-basic nagios-plugins-standard
```

And for RedHat Enterprise Linux and CentOS, we need to run the following command:

```
yum -y install nagios-plugins-all
```

If you choose to install the Nagios plugins manually you may continue to the next section and skip the manual installation process. In order to compile Nagios plugins manually, first let's go to the directory where Nagios plugins source code is located, in our case it is `/usr/src/nagios4/nagios-plugins-1.4.16`. We'll configure Nagios plugins parameters for the directories, we plan to install it by running the `configure` script. Some of the options that the script accepts are described in the following table:

Option	Description
`--prefix=<dir>`	Specifies the main directory in which all Nagios binaries are installed; defaults to `/usr/local/nagios`
`--sysconfdir=<dir>`	Specifies the directory where all Nagios configurations will be stored; defaults to `[PREFIX]/etc`
`--libexecdir=<dir>`	Specifies the directory where all Nagios plugins will be installed; defaults to `[PREFIX]/libexec`
`--localstatedir=<dir>`	Specifies the directory where all Nagios status and other information will be kept; defaults to `[PREFIX]/var`
`--enable-perl-modules`	Installs the `Nagios::Plugin` package along with all dependant packages
`--with-nagios-user=<user>`	Specifies the Unix user used by the Nagios daemon; defaults to `nagios`
`--with-nagios-group=<grp>`	Specifies the Unix group to use for the Nagios daemon; defaults to `nagios`
`--with-pgsql=<path>`	Specifies path to PostgreSQL installation; required for building of PostgreSQL testing plugins
`--with-mysql=<path>`	Specifies the path to the MySQL installation; required for building of MySQL testing plugins
`--with-openssl=<path>`	Specifies the path to the OpenSSL installation; can be specified if OpenSSL is installed in a non-standard location (such as `/opt/nagios/openssl`)
`--with-perl=<path>`	Specifies the path to Perl installation; can be specified if Perl is installed in a non-standard location (such as `/opt/nagios/perl`)

The `--enable-perl-modules` option enables installing additional Perl modules (`Nagios::Plugin` and its dependencies) that aid in developing your own Nagios plugins in Perl. It is useful to enable this option if you are familiar with Perl.

The `--with-pgsql` and `--with-mysql` options allow us to specify locations for the installations of PostgreSQL and/or MySQL databases. It is used to create plugins for monitoring PostgreSQL and/or MySQL. If not specified, the build process will look for the development files for these databases in their default locations. Installing development files for these databases is described in the *Prerequisites* section. For the directory structure that was described earlier in this section, the following `configure` script should be used:

```
sh configure \
    --prefix=/opt/nagios \
    --sysconfdir=/etc/nagios \
    --localstatedir=/var/nagios \
    --libexecdir=/opt/nagios/plugins
```

The script should run for some time and succeed, assuming that all prerequisites are installed. If not, the script should indicate what the missing component is. The build process also uses the `make` command similar to how Nagios is compiled. In this case, only `all` and `install` targets will be used. Therefore, the next step is to run the `make` commands as shown here:

```
make all
make install
```

If any of these steps fail, an investigation on what exactly has failed is needed, and if it is due to a missing library or a development package, please install those and try again. If all of the preceding commands succeeded, then you now have a fully installed Nagios setup. Congratulations!

The next step is to make sure that Nagios is working properly after being set up. To do this, we can simply run Nagios with the sample configuration that was created by `install-config`.

We should run it as a `nagios` user, since the process will be run as normally only as a `nagios` user. We will use the `su` command to switch the user and run the specified command:

```
# su -c '/opt/nagios/bin/nagios /etc/nagios/nagios.cfg' nagios
Nagios Core 4.0.0
Copyright (c) 2009-present Nagios Core Development Team and Community
Contributors
Copyright (c) 1999-2009 Ethan Galstad
Last Modified: 05-24-2013
License: GPL


Website: http://www.nagios.org
Nagios 4.0.0 starting... (PID=1302)
Local time is Fri Aug 30 21:01:59 CEST 2013
nerd: Channel hostchecks registered successfully
nerd: Channel servicechecks registered successfully
nerd: Channel opathchecks registered successfully
nerd: Fully initialized and ready to rock!
wproc: Successfully registered manager as @wproc with query handler
wproc: Registry request: name=Core Worker 1304;pid=1304
wproc: Registry request: name=Core Worker 1303;pid=1303
wproc: Registry request: name=Core Worker 1306;pid=1306
wproc: Registry request: name=Core Worker 1305;pid=1305
Successfully launched command file worker with pid 1307
```

This message indicates that the process was successfully started. After we have verified that Nagios has started successfully, we now need to press *Ctrl + C* to stop the Nagios process.

Setting up Nagios as a system service

After installing Nagios, it is worth making sure the daemon will be running as a system service, and will properly start up during system boot. In order to do this, go to the sources directory; in our case it is `/usr/src/nagios4/ nagios-4.0`. Then, run the following command:

```
make install-init
```

This will install a script in our `init.d` directory (this usually is `/etc/init.d` or `/etc/rc.d/init.d`). The script is automatically created, and will contain usernames and paths that were put when the `configure` script was run. To check it, simply run the following command:

```
# /etc/init.d/nagios start
```

In Nagios 4.0.0, the `/etc/init.d/nagios` script shipped with the source code does not work properly on Ubuntu Linux. If running the preceding command failed, a solution can be found in the next section. The next step is to set up a system to stop and start this service automatically. For Ubuntu Linux distributions, the command is:

```
update-rc.d nagios defaults
```

For RedHat Enterprise Linux and CentOS, the command is:

```
chkconfig --add nagios ; chkconfig nagios on
```

After Nagios has been set up as a system service, it is recommended to reboot to verify that it is actually starting. After your system has been fully restarted, make sure that Nagios is running. This can be done by checking the process list as follows:

```
root@ubuntu:~# ps -ef|grep ^nagios
nagios 796 1  0 00:00:00 /opt/nagios/bin/nagios -d /etc/nagios/nagios.cfg
```

If at least one process is found, it means that Nagios has been properly started. If not, please read the Nagios log file (which has the name `/var/nagios/nagios.log` assuming the Nagios installed using the method described earlier) and see why exactly it was failing. This usually relates to incorrect permissions. In such case, you should perform all steps mentioned in previous sections and reinstall Nagios from the beginning.

The result of the startup is mentioned at the end of the log file and an error indication should also be present of what the issue might be. For example, a part of the log for an error related to incorrect permissions is as follows:

```
 [1377937468] Nagios 4.0.0 starting... (PID=1403)
[1377937468] Local time is Sat Aug 31 10:24:28 CEST 2013
[1377937468] LOG VERSION: 2.0
[1377937468] qh: Socket '/var/nagios/rw/nagios.qh' successfully
initialized
[1377937468] qh: core query handler registered
[1377937468] nerd: Channel hostchecks registered successfully
```

```
[1377937468] nerd: Channel servicechecks registered successfully
[1377937468] nerd: Channel opathchecks registered successfully
[1377937468] nerd: Fully initialized and ready to rock!
[1377937468] wproc: Successfully registered manager as @wproc with query
handler
[1377937468] wproc: Registry request: name=Core Worker 1407;pid=1407
[1377937468] wproc: Registry request: name=Core Worker 1405;pid=1405
[1377937468] wproc: Registry request: name=Core Worker 1404;pid=1404
[1377937468] wproc: Registry request: name=Core Worker 1406;pid=1406
[1377937468] Successfully launched command file worker with pid 1408
[1377937468] Error: Could not open external command file for reading via
open(): (13) -> Permission denied
```

By default, Nagios also sends its logs to syslog daemon. So if the Nagios log file does not exist, looking into system log (usually `/var/log/messages` or `/var/log/syslog`) might provide some information on the problem. If you wish to start or stop Nagios manually, please run the `nagios` script from the `init.d` directory with one of the parameters:

```
/etc/init.d/nagios stop|start|restart
```

Please note that path to the `init.d` directory might be different for your operating system.

Resolving errors with script for Nagios system service

This section is mainly meant to provide a solution if the `/etc/init.d/nagios` script that was installed in the previous section does not work. If creating the service worked for you and Nagios has started properly, you should skip this section and continue on to the next one.

If the `/etc/init.d/nagios` script installed by the Nagios `make install-init` command is working properly, the following is a minimal version of the script that works on all modern Linux systems. Before starting, we should first create a backup of the original file by executing the following command:

```
cp /etc/init.d/nagios /etc/init.d/nagios.bak
```

Next, we can create a new `/etc/init.d/nagios` file using the following code:

```sh
#!/bin/sh

BINARY=/opt/nagios/bin/nagios
CONFIG=/etc/nagios/nagios.cfg

is_running ()
{
  pgrep -U nagios nagios >/dev/null 2>&1
}

case "$1" in
  start)
    if is_running ; then
      echo "Nagios is already running"
    else
      echo "StartingStartingStartingStartingt Nagios"
      su -c "$BINARY -d $CONFIG" nagios
    fi
    ;;
  stop)
    if is_running ; then
      echo "Stopping Nagios"
      pkill -U nagios nagios >/dev/null 2>&1
    else
      echo "Nagios is not running"
    fi
    ;;
  restart|force-reload|reload)
    $0 stop
    Sleep 5
    $0 start
    ;;
  *)
    echo "Usage: $0 start|stop|restart"
    ;;
esac
```

Next, make sure that the file can be run as a script by changing the permissions to `0755` and restart the Nagios service:

```
chmod 0755 /etc/init.d/nagios
service nagios restart
```

The command does not make use of distribution-specific commands (such as daemon or start-stop-daemon tools) and only uses the `pgrep` and `pkill` commands available on all recent Linux distributions.

> This script does not make use of all Nagios features (such as pre-cached objects) and should only be used in case of running into errors with the script bundled with the Nagios source code.

Configuring Nagios

Nagios stores it's configuration in a separate directory. Usually it's either in `/etc/nagios` or `/usr/local/etc/nagios`. If you followed the steps for manual installation, it's in `/etc/nagios`. We will now configure Nagios so that it is ready for use. While it will not be easy to check the results right away, we will verify that the configuration itself is valid. *Chapter 3, Using the Nagios Web Interface*, talks about setting up the Nagios web interface, which will allow us to check the status of the host and services that we will create in this section.

Creating the main configuration file

The main configuration file is called `nagios.cfg`, and it is the main file that is loaded during Nagios startup. Its syntax is simple, a line beginning with # is a comment, and all lines in the form of `<parameter>=<value>` set a value. In some cases, a value might be repeated (like specifying additional files/directories to read). The following is a sample of the Nagios main configuration file:

```
# log file to use
log_file=/var/nagios/nagios.log
# object configuration directory
cfg_dir=/etc/nagios/objects
# storage information
resource_file=/etc/nagios/resource.cfg
status_file=/var/nagios/status.dat
status_update_interval=10
(...)
```

The main configuration file needs to define a log file to use, and that has to be passed as the first option in the file. It also configures various Nagios parameters that allow tuning its behavior and performance. The following are some of the commonly changed options:

Option	Description
log_file	Specifies the log file to use; defaults to [localstatedir]/nagios.log
cfg_file	Specifies the configuration file to read for object definitions; might be specified multiple times
cfg_dir	Specifies the configuration directory where all files in it should be read for object definitions; might be specified multiple times
resource_file	File that stores additional macro definitions; [sysconfdir]/resource.cfg
temp_file	Path to a temporary file that is used for temporary data; defaults to [localstatedir]/nagios.tmp
lock_file	Path to a file that is used for synchronization; defaults to [localstatedir]/nagios.lock
temp_path	Path to where Nagios can create temporary files; defaults to /tmp
status_file	Path to a file that stores the current status of all hosts and services; defaults to [localstatedir]/status.dat
status_update_interval	Specifies how often (in seconds) the status file should be updated; defaults to 10 (seconds)
nagios_user	User to run the daemon
nagios_group	Group to run the daemon
command_file	It specifies the path to the external command line that is used by other processes to control the Nagios daemon; defaults to [localstatedir]/rw/nagios.cmd
use_syslog	Whether Nagios should log messages to syslog as well as to the Nagios log file; defaults to 1 (enabled)
state_retention_file	Path to a file that stores state information across shutdowns; defaults to [localstatedir]/retention.dat
retention_update_interval	How often (in seconds) the retention file should be updated; defaults to 60 (seconds)
service_check_timeout	After how many seconds should a service check be assumed that it has failed; defaults to 60 (seconds)

Option	Description
`host_check_timeout`	After how many seconds should a host check be assumed that it has failed; defaults to `30` (seconds)
`event_handler_timeout`	After how many seconds should an event handler be terminated; defaults to `30` (seconds)
`notification_timeout`	After how many seconds should a notification attempt be assumed that it has failed; defaults to `30` (seconds)
`enable_environment_ macros`	Whether Nagios should pass all macros to plugins as environment variables; defaults to `1` (enabled)
`interval_length`	Specifies the number of seconds a "unit interval" is; this defaults to `60`, which means that an interval is one minute; it is not recommended to change the option in any way, as it might end with undesirable behavior

For a complete list of accepted parameters, please consult with the Nagios documentation available at `http://library.nagios.com/library/products/ nagioscore/manuals/`.

The Nagios option `resource_file` defines a file to store user variables. This file can be used to store additional information that can be accessed in all object definitions. These usually contain sensitive data as they can only be used in object definitions and it is not possible to read their values from the web interface. This makes it possible to hide passwords to various sensitive services from Nagios administrators without proper privileges. There can be up to 32 macros, named $USER1$, $USER2$ ... $USER32$. The Macro definition $USER1$ defines the path to Nagios plugins and is commonly used in check command definitions.

The `cfg_file` and `cfg_dir` options are used to specify files that should be read for object definitions. The first option specifies a single file to read and second specifies the directory to read all files with the `.cfg` extension in the directory and all child directories. Each file may contain different types of objects. The next section describes each type of definitions that Nagios uses.

One of the first things that needs to be planned is how your Nagios configuration should be stored. In order to create a configuration that will be maintainable as your IT infrastructure changes, it is worth investing some time to plan out how you want your host definitions set up and how that could be easily placed in a configuration file structure. Throughout this book, various approaches on how to make your configuration maintainable are discussed. It's also recommended to set up a small Nagios system to get a better understanding of the Nagios configuration before proceeding to larger setups.

Sometimes, it is best to have the configuration grouped into directories by locations in which hosts and/or services are. In other cases, it might be best to keep definitions of all servers with a similar functionality in one directory.

A good directory layout makes it much easier to control the Nagios configuration; for example, massively disable all objects related to a particular part of the IT infrastructure Even though it is recommended to use downtimes, it is sometimes useful to just remove all entries from the Nagios configuration.

Throughout all configuration examples in this book, we will use the directory structure. A separate directory is used for each object type and similar objects are grouped within a single file. For example, all command definitions are to be stored in the commands/ subdirectory. All host definitions are stored in the hosts/<hostname>.cfg file.

For Nagios to read the configuration from these directories, edit your main Nagios configuration file (/etc/nagios/nagios.cfg), remove all the cfg_file and cfg_dir entries, and add the following ones:

```
cfg_dir=/etc/nagios/commands
cfg_dir=/etc/nagios/timeperiods
cfg_dir=/etc/nagios/contacts
cfg_dir=/etc/nagios/contactgroups
cfg_dir=/etc/nagios/hosts
cfg_dir=/etc/nagios/hostgroups
cfg_dir=/etc/nagios/services
cfg_dir=/etc/nagios/servicegroups
```

The next step is to create the directories by executing the following commands:

```
root@ubuntu:~# cd /etc/nagios
root@ubuntu:/etc/nagios# mkdir commands timeperiods \
  contacts contactgroups hosts hostgroups services servicegroups
```

In order to use default Nagios plugins, copy the default Nagios command definition file /etc/nagios/objects/commands.cfg to /etc/nagios/commands/default.cfg. Also, make sure that the following options are set as follows in your nagios.cfg file:

```
check_external_commands=1
interval_length=60
accept_passive_service_checks=1
accept_passive_host_checks=1
```

If any of the options is set to a different value, please change it and add it at the end of the file if they are not currently present. After such changes in the Nagios setup, you can now move on to next sections and prepare a working configuration for your Nagios installation.

Understanding macro definitions

The ability to use macro definitions is one of the key features of Nagios. They offer a lot of flexibility in object and command definitions. Nagios also provides custom macro definitions, which give you greater possibility to use object templates for specifying parameters common to a group of similar objects.

All command definitions can use macros. Macro definitions allow parameters from other objects, such as hosts, services, and contacts to be referenced so that a command does not need to have everything passed as an argument. Each macro invocation begins and ends with a $ sign.

A typical example is a HOSTADDRESS macro, which references the address field from the host object. All host definitions provide the value of the address parameter. The following is a host and command definition:

```
define host{
  host_name      somemachine
  address        10.0.0.1
  check_command check-host-alive
  }


define command{
  command_name   check-host-alive
  command_line   $USER1$/check_ping -H $HOSTADDRESS$
                 -w 3000.0,80% -c 5000.0,100% -p 5
  }
```

The following command will be invoked:

```
/opt/nagios/plugins/check_ping -H 10.0.0.1 -w 3000.0,80% -c 5000.0,
100% -p 5
```

Also, please note that the USER1 macro was also used and expanded as a path to the Nagios plugins directory. This is a macro definition that references the data contained in a file that is passed as the resource_file configuration directive. Even though it is not required for the USER1 macro to point to the plugins directory, all standard command definitions that come with Nagios use this macro, so it is not recommended to change it. Some of the macro definitions are listed in the following table:

Macro	Description
HOSTNAME	Short, unique name of the host; maps to the host_name directive in the host object
HOSTADDRESS	The IP or hostname of the host; maps to the address directive in the host object
HOSTDISPLAYNAME	Description of the host; maps to the alias directive in the host object
HOSTSTATE	The current state of the host (one of UP, DOWN, UNREACHABLE)
HOSTGROUPNAMES	Short names of all host groups a host belongs, separated by a comma
LASTHOSTCHECK	The date and time of last check of the host, in Unix timestamp (number of seconds since 1970-01-01)
LASTHOSTSTATE	The last known state of the host (one of UP, DOWN, UNREACHABLE)
SERVICEDESC	Description of the service; maps to the description directive in the service object
SERVICESTATE	The current state of the service (one of OK, WARNING, UNKNOWN, CRITICAL)
SERVICEGROUPNAMES	Short names of all service groups a service belongs, separated by a comma
CONTACTNAME	Short, unique name of the contact; maps to the contact_name directive in the contact object
CONTACTALIAS	Description of the contact; maps to the alias directive in the contact object
CONTACTEMAIL	The e-mail address of the contact; maps to the email directive in the contact object
CONTACTGROUPNAMES	Short names of all contact groups a contact belongs, separated by a comma

This table is not complete and only covers commonly used macro definitions. A complete list of available macros can be found in the Nagios documentation available at http://library.nagios.com/library/products/nagioscore/manuals/. Also, please remember that all macro definitions need to be prefixed and suffixed with a $ sign, for example, $HOSTADDRESS$ maps to the HOSTADDRESS macro definition.

An additional functionality is **on-demand macro definitions**. These are macros that are not defined, not exported as environment variables, but if found in a command definition, will be parsed and substituted accordingly. These macros accept one or more arguments inside the macro definition name, each passed after a colon. This is mainly used to read specific values, not related to the current object. In order to read the contact e-mail for the user `jdoe`, regardless of who the current contact person is, the macro would be as follows: `$CONTACTEMAIL:jdoe$` which means getting a `CONTACTEMAIL` macro definition in the context of the `jdoe` contact.

Nagios also offers custom macro definitions. This works in a way that administrators can define additional attributes in each type of an object and that macro can then be used inside a command. This is used to store additional parameters related to an object; for example, you can store a MAC address in a host definition and use it in certain types of host checks.

It works in such a way that an object has a directive that starts with an underscore and is written in uppercase. It is referenced in one of the following ways, based on the object type it is defined in:

`$_HOST<variable>$` - for directives defined within a host object

`$_SERVICE<variable>$` - for directives defined within a service object

`$_CONTACT<variable>$` - for directives defined within a contact object

A sample host definition that includes an additional directive with a MAC address would be as follows:

```
define host{
    host_name       somemachine
    address         10.0.0.1
    _MAC            12:12:12:12:12:12
    check_command   check-host-by-mac
    }
```

A corresponding check command that uses this attribute inside a check is as follows:

```
define command{
    command_name    check-host-by-mac
    command_line    $USER1$/check_hostmac -H $HOSTADDRESS$ -m $_HOSTMAC$
    }
```

A majority of standard macro definitions are exported to check commands as environment variables. The environment variable names are the same as macros, but are prefixed with `NAGIOS_`; for example, `HOSTADDRESS` is passed as the `NAGIOS_HOSTADDRESS` variable. Variables are not made available on demand. For security reasons, the `$USERn$` variables are also not passed to commands as environment variables.

Configuring hosts

Hosts are objects that describe machines that should be monitored—either physical hardware or virtual machines. A host consists of a short name, descriptive name, and an IP address or host name. It also tells Nagios when and how the system should be monitored as well as who shall be contacted with regards to any problems related to this host. It also specifies how often the host should be checked, how retrying the checks should be handled, and how often should a notification about problems be sent out. A sample definition of a host is as follows:

```
define host{
    host_name                   linuxbox01
    hostgroups                  linuxservers
    alias                       Linux Server 01
    address                     10.0.2.15
    check_command               check-host-alive
    check_interval              5
    retry_interval              1
    max_check_attempts          5
    check_period                24x7
    contact_groups              linux-admins
    notification_interval       30
    notification_period         24x7
    notification_options        d,u,r
    }
```

It defines a Linux box that will use the `check-host-alive` command to make sure it is up and running. The test will be performed every 5 minutes, and after 5 failed tests, it will assume the host is down. If it is down, a notification will be sent out every 30 minutes. The following is a table of common directives that can be used to describe hosts. Items in bold are required when specifying a host.

Option	Description
host_name	The Short, unique name of the host
alias	The descriptive name of the host
address	An IP address or fully qualified domain name of the host; It is recommended to use an IP address as all tests will fail if DNS servers are down
parents	The list of all parent hosts on which this host depends, separated by a comma; this is usually one or more switch and router to which this host is directly connected
hostgroups	The list of all hostgroups this host should be a member of; separated by a comma

Option	Description
check_command	The short name of the command that should be used to test if the host is alive; if a command returns an OK state, the host is assumed to be up. is assumed to be down otherwise
check_interval	Specifies how often a check should be performed; the value is in minutes
retry_interval	Specifies how many minutes to wait before retesting if the host is up
max_check_attempts	Specifies how many times a test needs to report that a host is down before it is assumed to be down by Nagios
check_period	Specifies the name of the time period that should be used to determine times during which tests if the host is up should be performed
contacts	The list of all contacts to which should receive notifications related to host state changes be sent; separated by a comma; at least one contact or contact group needs to be specified for each host
contact_groups	List of all contacts groups that should receive notifications related to host state changes be sent to; separated by a comma; at least one contact or contact group needs to be specified for each host
first_notification_delay	Specifies the number of minutes before the first notification related to a host being down is sent out
notification_interval	Specifies the number of minutes before each next notification related to a host being down is sent out
notification_period	Specifies time periods during which notifications related to host states should be sent out
notification_options	Specifies which notification types for host states should be sent, separated by a comma; should be one or more of the following: d: the host DOWN state
	u: the host UNREACHABLE state
	r: host recovery (UP state)
	f: the host starts and stops flapping
	s: notify when scheduled downtime starts or ends

For a complete list of accepted parameters, please consult with the Nagios documentation. By default, Nagios assumes all host states to be up. If the check_ command option is not specified for a host, then its state will always be set to up. When the command to perform host checks is specified, then regularly scheduled checks will take place, and the host state will be monitored using the value of check_ interval as number of minutes between checks.

Nagios uses a soft and hard state logic to handle host states. Therefore, if a host state has changed from UP to DOWN since last hard state, then Nagios assumes that the host is soft DOWN state and performs retries of the test, waiting `retry_interval` minutes between each test. Once the result is the same after `max_check_attempts` number of times, Nagios assumes that the DOWN state is a hard state. The same mechanisms apply for DOWN to UP transitions. Notifications are also only sent if a host is in a hard state. This means that a temporary failure that only occurred for a single test will not cause a notification to be sent if `max_check_attempts` was set to a number higher than 1.

The host object `parents` directive is used to define the topology of the network. Usually, this directive points to a switch, router, or any other device that is responsible for forwarding network packets. The host is assumed to be unreachable if the parent host is currently in hard DOWN state. For example, if a router is down, then all machines accessed via it are considered unreachable and no tests will be performed on these hosts.

If your network consists of servers connected via switches and routers to a different network, then the parent for all servers in the local network as well as the router would be the switch. The parent of the router on the other side of the link would be the local router. The following diagram shows the actual network infrastructure and how Nagios hosts should be configured in terms of parents for each element of the network:

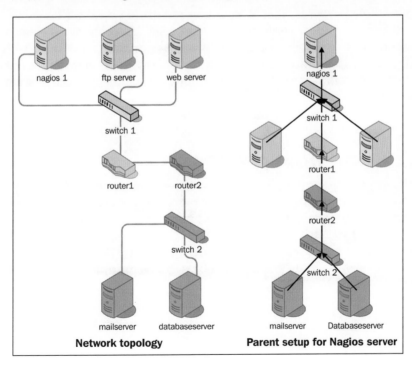

Network topology   **Parent setup for Nagios server**

The actual network topology is shown on the left, and parent hosts setup for each of the machine are shown on the right. Each arrow represents mapping from a host to a parent host. There is no need to define a parent for hosts that are directly on the network with your Nagios server. So in this case, `switch1` should not have a parent host set.

Even though some devices such as switches cannot be easily checked if they are down, it is still a good idea to describe them as part of your topology. In that case, you might use functionality, such as scheduled downtime, to keep track of when the device is going to be offline or mark it as down manually. This helps in determining other problems—Nagios will not scan any hosts that have the router somewhere along the path that is currently scheduled for downtime. This way you won't be flooded with notifications on actually unreachable hosts being down.

Check and notification periods specify the time periods during which checks for host state and notifications are to be performed. These can be specified so that different hosts can be monitored at different times.

It is also possible to set up where information that a host is down is kept, but nobody should be notified about it. This can be done by specifying `notification_period` that will tell Nagios when a notification should be sent out. No notifications will be sent out outside this time period.

A typical example is a server that is only required during business hours and has a daily maintenance window between 10PM and 4AM. You can set up Nagios so as to not monitor host availability outside of business hours, or you can make Nagios monitor it but without notifying that it is actually down. If monitoring is not done at all, then Nagios will perform fewer operations during this period. In second case, it is possible to gather statistics on how much of the maintenance window is used, which can be used if changes to the window need to be made.

Configuring host groups

Nagios allows grouping multiple hosts in order to manage them effectively. In order to do that, Nagios offers the `hostgroup` objects that are a group of one or more machines. A host might be a member of more than one host group. Usually, grouping is done by type of machines, location they are in, and the role of the machine. Each host group has a unique short name that it is identified, a descriptive name, and one or more hosts that are members of this group.

The following are the examples of host group definitions that define groups of hosts and a group that combines both groups:

```
define hostgroup{
    hostgroup_name                 linux-servers
    alias                          Linux servers
    members                        linuxbox01,linuxbox02
    }

define hostgroup{
    hostgroup_name                 aix-servers
    alias                          AIX servers
    members                        aixbox1,aixbox2
    }

define hostgroup{
    hostgroup_name                 unix-servers
    alias                          UNIX servers servers
    hostgroup_members              linux-servers,aix-servers
    }
```

The following table is of directives that can be used to describe host groups. Items in bold are required when specifying a host group.

Option	Description
hostgroup_name	The short, unique name of the host group
alias	The descriptive name of the host group
members	The list of all hosts that should be a member of this group; separated by a comma
hostgroup_members	The list of all other host groups whose all members should also be members of this group; separated by a comma

Host groups can also be used when defining services or dependencies. For example, it is possible to tell Nagios that all Linux servers should have their SSH service monitored, and all AIX servers should have a telnet accepting connections.

It is also possible to define dependencies between hosts. They are, in a way, similar to the parent-host relationship, but dependencies offer more complex configuration options. Nagios will only issue host and service checks if all dependent hosts are currently up. More details on dependencies can be found in *Chapter 5, Advanced Configuration*.

For the purpose of this book, we will define at least one host in our Nagios configuration directory structure. To be able to monitor a local server that the Nagios installation is running, we will need to add its definition into the `/etc/nagios/hosts/localhost.cfg` file:

```
define host{
    host_name                       localhost
    alias                           Localhost
    address                         127.0.0.1
    check_command                   check-host-alive
    check_interval                  5
    retry_interval                  1
    max_check_attempts              5
    check_period                    24x7
    contact_groups                  admins
    notification_interval           60
    notification_period             24x7
    notification_options            d,u,r
    }
```

Although Nagios does not require a naming convention, it is a good practice to use the hostname as name of the file. To make sure Nagios monitoring works, it is also a good idea to set the `address` to a valid IP address of local machine, such as `127.0.0.1`, as stated in the preceding code or the IP address in your network if it is static.

If you are planning on monitoring other servers as well, you will want to add them — the recommended approach is to define a single object definition in a single file.

Configuring services

Services are objects that describe a functionality that a particular host is offering. This can be virtually anything — network servers such as FTP, resources such as storage space, or CPU load.

A service is always tied to a host that it is running. It is also identified by its description, which needs to be unique within a particular host. A service also defines when and how Nagios should check if it is running properly and how to notify people responsible for this service. A short example of a web server that is defined on the `localhost` machine created earlier is as follows:

```
define service{
    host_name                    localhost
    service_description          www
    check_command                check_http
    check_interval               10
    check_period                 24x7
    retry_interval               3
    max_check_attempts           3
    notification_interval        30
    notification_period          24x7
    notification_options         w,c,u,r
    contact_groups               admins
}
```

This definition tells Nagios to monitor that the web server is working correctly every 10 minutes. The recommended file for this definition is /etc/nagios/ services/localhost-www.cfg—with services, a good approach is to use <host>- <servicename> as the name of the file if a single host or host group is being set up for monitoring. The following table is about the common directives that can be used to describe service. Items in bold are required when specifying a service:

Option	Description
host_name	The short name of the host on which the service is running; separated by a comma
hostgroup_name	The short name of the host groups that the service is running on; separated by a comma
service_description	The description of the service that is used to uniquely identify services running on a host
servicegroups	The list of all service groups of which this service should be a member; separated by a comma
check_command	The short name of the command that should be used to test if the service is running
check_interval	Specifies how often a check should be performed; the value is in minutes
retry_interval	Specifies how many minutes to wait before retesting whether the service is working
max_check_attempts	Specifies how many times a test needs to report that a service is down before it is assumed to be down by Nagios
check_period	Specifies the name of the time period that should be used to determine the time during which tests should be performed if the service is working

Option	Description
contacts	The list of all contacts that should receive notifications related to service state changes; separated by a comma; at least one contact or contact group needs to be specified for each service
contact_groups	The list of all contacts groups that should receive notifications related to service state changes, separated by a comma. At least one contact or contact group needs to be specified for each service
first_notification_delay	Specifies the number of minutes before the first notification related to a service state change is sent out
notification_interval	Specifies the number of minutes before each next notification related to a service not working correctly is sent out
notification_period	Specifies time periods during which notifications related to service states should be sent out
notification_options	Specifies which notification types for service states should be sent, separated by a comma; should be one or more of the following:
	w: the service WARNING state
	u: the service UNKNOWN state
	c: the service CRITICAL state
	r: the service recovery (back to OK) state
	f: the host starts and stops flapping
	s: notify when the scheduled downtime starts or ends

For a complete list of accepted parameters, please consult with the Nagios documentation. Nagios requires that at least one service should be defined for every host, and requires that at least one service is defined for it to run. That is why we will now create a sample service in our configuration directory structure. For this purpose, we'll monitor the secure shell protocol.

In order to monitor whether SSH server is running on the Nagios installation, we will need to add its definition into the /etc/nagios/services/localhost-ssh. cfg file:

```
define service{
    host_name                localhost
    service_description      ssh
    check_command            check_ssh
    check_interval           5
    retry_interval           1
    max_check_attempts       3
```

```
    check_period                    24x7
    contact_groups                  admins
    notification_interval           60
    notification_period             24x7
    notification_options            w,c,u,r
    }
```

If you are planning on monitoring other services as well, you will want to add a definition as well.

Very often, the same service is being offered by more than one host. In such cases, it is possible to specify a service that will be used by multiple machines or even specify host groups for which all hosts will be checked. It is also possible to specify hosts for which checks will not be performed; for example, if a service is present on all hosts in a group except for a specific box. To do that, exclamation needs to be added before a host name or host group name. To tell Nagios that SSH should be checked on all Linux servers except for linux01 and the aix01 machine, a service definition similar to the following has to be created:

```
    define service{
        hostgroup_name              linux-servers
        host_name                   !linuxbox01,aix01
        service_description         SSH
        check_command               check_ssh
        check_interval              10
        check_period                24x7
        retry_interval              2
        max_check_attempts          3
        notification_interval       30
        notification_period         24x7
        notification_options        w,c,r
        contact_groups              linux-admins
    }
```

Services may be configured to be dependent on one another similar to hosts. In this case, Nagios will only perform checks on a service if all dependent services are working correctly. More details on dependencies can be found in *Chapter 5, Advanced Configuration*.

Configuring service groups

Services can be grouped similar to host objects. This can be used to manage services more conveniently. It also aids in viewing service reports on the Nagios web interface. Service groups are also used to configure dependencies in a more convenient way. The following table describes attributes that can be used to define a group. Items in bold are required when specifying a service group.

Option	Description
servicegroup_name	The short, unique name of the service group
alias	The descriptive name of the service group
members	The list of all hosts and services that should be a member of this group; separated by a comma
servicegroup_members	The list of all other service groups whose all members should also be members of this group; separated by a comma

The format of the members directive of service group object is one or more `<host>,<service>` pair.

An example of a service group is shown:

```
define servicegroup{
   servicegroup_name   databaseservices
   alias               All services related to databases
   members             linuxbox01,mysql,linuxbox01,pgsql,aix01,db2
   }
```

This service group consists of the mysql and pgsql services on a linuxbox01 host and db2 on the aix01 machine. It is uniquely identified by its name databaseservices. It is also possible to specify groups that a service should be member of inside the service definition itself. To do this, add groups so that it will be a member of in servicegroups directive in the service definition. It is also possible to define an empty service group and have the service definitions specify to which groups they belong, for example:

```
define servicegroup{
   servicegroup_name   databaseservices
   alias               All services related to databases
   }

define service{
   host_name                    linuxbox01
   service_description          mysql
   check_command                check_ssh
   servicegroups databaseservices
   }
```

Configuring commands

Command definitions describe how host/service checks should be done. They can also define how notifications about problems or event handlers should work. Commands defined in Nagios tell how it can perform checks, such as what commands to run to check if a database is working properly; how to check if SSH, SMTP, or FTP server is properly working, or if DHCP server is assigning IP addresses correctly. Commands are also run to let users know of issues, or try to recover a problem automatically.

Nagios makes no distinction between commands provided by Nagios plugins project and custom commands, either created by a third party or written by you, and since its interface is very straight forward, it is very easy to create your own checks. *Chapter 11, Programming Nagios,* talks about writing custom commands to perform things such as monitoring custom protocols or communicating with installed applications.

Commands are defined in a manner similar to other objects in Nagios. A command definition has two parameters: name and command line. The first parameter is a name that is then used for defining checks and notifications. The second parameter is an actual command that will be run along with all parameters.

Commands are used by hosts and services. They define which system command to execute when making sure a host or service is working properly. A check command is identified by its unique name.

When used with other object definitions, it can also have additional arguments and uses exclamation mark as a delimiter. Commands with parameters have the following syntax: command_name[!arg1][!arg2][!arg3][...].

A command name is often the same as the plugin that it runs, but it can be different. The command line includes macro definitions (such as $HOSTADDRESS$). Check commands also use macros $ARG1$, $ARG2$ ... $ARG32$ if a check command for a host or service passed additional arguments. The following is an example that defines a command to ping a host to make sure it is working properly. It does not use any arguments.

```
define command{
  command_name   check-host-alive
  command_line   $USER1$/check_ping -H $HOSTADDRESS$
                 -w 3000.0,80% -c 5000.0,100% -p 5
}
```

A very short host definition that would use this check command could be similar to the one shown here:

```
define host{
   host_name      somemachine
   address        10.0.0.1
   check_command  check-host-alive
   }
```

Such a check is usually done as part of the host checks. This allows Nagios to make sure that a machine is working properly if it responds to ICMP requests. Commands allow passing arguments as it offers a more flexible way of defining checks. So, a definition accepting parameters would be as follows:

```
define command{
   command_name  check-host-alive-limits
   command_line  $USER1$/check_ping -H $HOSTADDRESS$
                 -w $ARG1$ -c $ARG2$ -p 5
   }
```

The corresponding host definition is as follows:

```
define host{
   host_name      othermachine
   address        10.0.0.2
   check_command  check-host-alive-limits!3000.0,80%!5000.0,100%
   }
```

The following is another example that sets up a check command for a previously-defined service:

```
define command{
   command_name  check_http
   command_line  $USER1$/check_http -H $HOSTADDRESS$
   }
```

This check can be used when defining a service to be monitored by Nagios. Our Nagios configuration includes the default Nagios plugins definitions that we have previously copied as /etc/nagios/commands/default.cfg. *Chapter 4, Using the Nagios Plugins*, covers standard Nagios plugins along with sample command definitions.

Configuring time periods

Time periods are definitions of dates and times during which an action should be performed or specified people should be notified. They describe ranges of days and times and can be reused across various operations. A time period definition consists of a name that uniquely identifies it in Nagios. It also contains a description. It contains one or more days or dates, along with time spans as well.

A typical example of a time period would be working hours, which defines that a valid time to perform an action is from Monday to Friday during business hours. Another definition of a time period can be weekends which mean Saturday and Sunday, all day long. The following is a sample time period for working hours:

```
define timeperiod{
  timeperiod_name   workinghours
  alias             Working Hours, from Monday to Friday
  monday            09:00-17:00
  tuesday           09:00-17:00
  wednesday         09:00-17:00
  thursday          09:00-17:00
  friday            09:00-17:00
  }
```

This particular example tells Nagios that a good time to perform something is from Monday to Friday between 9 AM and 5 PM. Each entry in a time period contains information on date or weekday. It also contains a range of hours. Nagios first checks if current date matches any of the dates specified. If it does, then it compares whether current time matches time ranges specified for particular date.

There are multiple ways a date can be specified. Depending on what type of date it is, one definition might take precedence over another. For example, a definition for December 24th is more important than a generic definition that every weekday an action should be performed between 9AM to 5PM.

Possible date types are mentioned here:

- **Calendar date**: For example, 2009-11-01 which means November 1st, year 2009; Nagios accepts dates in the YYYY-MM-DD format
- **Date recurring every year**: For example, July 4 which means 4th of July
- **Specific day within a month**: For example, day 14 which means 14th of every month
- **Specific weekday along with offset in a month**: For example, Monday 1 September which means the first Monday in September; Monday -1 would mean last Monday in May

- **Specific weekday in all months**: For example, Monday 1, which means every 1st Monday in a month
- **Weekday**: For example, Monday which means all Mondays

It lists all types by order in which Nagios uses different date types. This means that a date recurring every year will always be used prior to an entry describing what should be done every Monday.

In order to be able to correctly configure all objects, we will now create some standard time periods that will be used in the configuration. The following example periods will be used by the remaining sections of this chapter, and it is recommended to put them in the /etc/nagios/timeperiods/default.cfg file:

```
define timeperiod{
  timeperiod_name   workinghours
  alias             Working Hours, from Monday to Friday
  monday            09:00-17:00
  tuesday           09:00-17:00
  wednesday         09:00-17:00
  thursday          09:00-17:00
  friday            09:00-17:00
  }

define timeperiod{
  timeperiod_name   weekends
  alias             Weekends all day long
  saturday          00:00-24:00
  sunday            00:00-24:00
  }

define timeperiod{
  timeperiod_name   24x7
  alias             24 hours a day 7 days a week
  monday            00:00-24:00
  tuesday           00:00-24:00
  wednesday         00:00-24:00
  thursday          00:00-24:00
  friday            00:00-24:00
  saturday          00:00-24:00
  sunday            00:00-24:00
  }
```

The last time period is also used by the SSH service defined earlier. This way, monitoring the SSH server will be done all the time.

Configuring contacts

Contacts define people who can be either owners of specific machines, or people who should be contacted in case of problems. Depending on how your organization might contact people in case of problems, a definition of a contact may vary a lot. A contact consists of a unique name, a descriptive name, one or more e-mail addresses, and pager numbers. Contact definitions can also contain additional data specific to how a person can be contacted.

A basic contact definition is shown here, and specifies the unique contact name, an alias, and the contact information. It also specifies event types that the person should receive and time periods during which notifications should be sent.

```
define contact{
    contact_name                    jdoe
    alias                           John Doe
    email                           john.doe@yourcompany.com
    contactgroups                   admins,nagiosadmin
    host_notification_period        workinghours
    service_notification_period     workinghours
    host_notification_options       d,u,r
    service_notification_options    w,u,c,r
    host_notification_commands      notify-host-by-email
    service_notification_commands   notify-service-by-email
    }
```

The `contactgroups` line defines that this user is a member of groups admins, which is defined later in this chapter. We will now create a similar file in /etc/nagios/ contacts, setting values for `contact_name`, `alias`, and `email` based on your username, full name, and e-mail address. The recommended name for the file is based on `contact_name`.

The following table describes all available directives when defining a contact. Items in bold are required when specifying a contact.

Option	Description
contact_name	The short, unique name of the contact
alias	The descriptive name of the contact; usually this is the full name of the person
contactgroups	The list of all contact groups of which this user should be a member; separated by a comma
host_notifications_enabled	This specifies whether this person should receive notifications regarding host state

Option	Description
host_notification_period	This specifies the name of the time period that should be used to determine time during which a person should receive notifications regarding the host state
host_notification_commands	Specifies one or more commands that should be used to notify the person of a host state; separated by a comma
host_notification_options	Specifies host states about which the user should be notified, separated by a comma; should be one or more of the following:
	d: the host DOWN state
	u: the host UNREACHABLE state
	r: the host recovery (UP state)
	f: the host starts and stops flapping
	s: notify when scheduled downtime starts or ends
	n: the person will not receive any service notifications
service_notifications_enabled	Specifies whether this person should receive notifications regarding the service state
service_notification_period	Specifies name of the time period that should be used to determine time during which a person should receive notifications regarding the service state
service_notification_commands	Specifies one or more commands that should be used to notify the person of a service state; separated by a comma
service_notification_options	Specifies service states about which that the user should be notified, separated by a comma; should be one or more of the following:
	w: the service WARNING state
	u: the service UNKNOWN state
	c: the service CRITICAL state
	r: the service recovery (OK state)
	f: the service starts and stops flapping
	n: the person will not receive any service notifications
email	Specifies the e-mail address of the contact

Option	Description
pager	Specifies the pager number for the contact. It can also be an e-mail to the pager gateway
address1 ... address6	Additional six addresses that can be specified for the contact; these can be anything, based on how the notification commands will use these fields
can_submit_commands	Specifies whether the user is allowed to execute commands from Nagios web interface
retain_status_information	Specifies whether the status-related information about this person is retained across restarts
retain_nonstatus_information	Specifies whether the non-status information about this person should be retained across restarts

Contacts are also mapped to users that log into the Nagios web interface. This means that all operations done via the interface will be logged as that particular user and that the web interface will use the access granted to particular contact objects when evaluating if an operation should be allowed. The contact_name field from a contact object maps to user names in the Nagios web interface.

Configuring contact groups

Contacts can be grouped. Usually, grouping is used to keep a list of which users are responsible for which tasks, and maps to job responsibilities for particular people. It also makes it possible to define people that should be responsible for handling problems at specific time periods, and Nagios will automatically contact the right people for a particular time a problem has occurred. A sample definition of a contact group is as follows:

```
define contactgroup{
   contactgroup_name              linux-admins
   alias                          Linux Administrators
   members                        jdoe,asmith
   }
```

This group is also used when defining the linuxbox01 and www service contacts. This means that both the jdoe and asmith contacts will receive information on status of this host and service.

The following table is a complete list of directives that can be used to describe contact groups. Items in bold are required when specifying a contact group.

Option	Description
contactgroup_name	The short, unique name of the contact group
alias	The descriptive name of the contact group
members	The list of all contacts that should be a member of this group; separated by a comma
contactgroup_members	The list of all other contact groups whose all members should also be members of this group; separated by a comma

Members of a contact group can either be specified in the contact group definition or using the contactgroups directive in a contact definition. It is also possible to combine both methods—some of the members can be specified in the contact group definition and others can be specified in their contact object definition.

Contacts are used to specify who shall be contacted if a status changes for one or more hosts or services. Nagios accepts both contacts and contact groups in their object definitions. This allows making either specific people or entire groups responsible for particular machines or services.

It is also possible to specify different people or groups for handling host-related problems and service related problems—for example, hardware administrators for handling host problems and system administrators for handling service issues.

In order for our previously created user jdoe to work properly, we need to define the admins and nagiosadmin groups in the /etc/nagios/contactgroups/admins.cfg file:

```
define contactgroup{
  contactgroup_name         admins
  alias                     System administrators
}

define contactgroup{
  contactgroup_name         nagiosadmin
  alias                     Nagios administrators
  }
```

Verifying the configuration

At this point, our configuration file should be ready for use. We can now verify that all of the configuration statements are correct and that Nagios would start correctly with our configuration. We can do this by running the `nagios` command with the `-v` option. For example:

```
root@ubuntu:~# /opt/nagios/bin/nagios -v /etc/nagios/nagios.cfg


Nagios Core 4.0.0

Copyright (c) 2009-present Nagios Core Development Team and Community
Contributors

Copyright (c) 1999-2009 Ethan Galstad

Last Modified: 05-24-2013

License: GPL


Website: http://www.nagios.org

Reading configuration data...

    Read main config file okay...

    Read object config files okay...


Running pre-flight check on configuration data...


Checking services...

        Checked 1 services.

Checking hosts...

        Checked 1 hosts.

Checking host groups...

        Checked 1 host groups.

Checking service groups...

        Checked 1 service groups.

Checking contacts...

        Checked 1 contacts.

Checking contact groups...

        Checked 1 contact groups.

Checking commands...

        Checked 24 commands.
```

```
Checking time periods...
        Checked 3 time periods.
Checking for circular paths...
        Checked 1 hosts
        Checked 0 service dependencies
        Checked 0 host dependencies
        Checked 3 timeperiods
Checking global event handlers...
Checking obsessive compulsive processor commands...
Checking misc settings...


Total Warnings: 0
Total Errors:   0


Things look okay - No serious problems were detected during the pre-
flight check
```

The preceding command indicates a correct configuration file. If there are errors, the message will indicate the problem, as shown in the following command:

```
root@ubuntu:~# /opt/nagios/bin/nagios -v /etc/nagios/nagios.cfg


Nagios Core 4.0.0
Copyright (c) 2009-present Nagios Core Development Team and Community
Contributors
Copyright (c) 1999-2009 Ethan Galstad
Last Modified: 05-24-2013
License: GPL


Website: http://www.nagios.org
Reading configuration data...
    Read main config file okay...
Error: Contactgroup 'admin' is not defined anywhere
Error: Could not add contactgroup 'admin' to service (config file '/etc/
nagios/services/localhost-www.cfg', starting on line 1)
    Error processing object config files!
```

```
***> One or more problems was encountered while processing the config
files...

      Check your configuration file(s) to ensure that they contain valid
      directives and data defintions.  If you are upgrading from a
previous
      version of Nagios, you should be aware that some variables/
definitions
      may have been removed or modified in this version.  Make sure to
read
      the HTML documentation regarding the config files, as well as the
      'Whats New' section to find out what has changed.
```

The preceding example indicates the `contactgroup` value admin is not valid for a service defined in `/etc/nagios/services/localhost-www.cfg` file.

It is always recommended to verify the Nagios configuration file after making changes to ensure it does not prevent Nagios from functioning properly.

Even if the `/etc/init.d/nagios` script prevents restarting when the configuration is incorrect, this would cause Nagios not to start after a system restart.

Understanding notifications

Notifications is Nagios' way of letting people know that something is either wrong or has returned to the normal way of functioning. This is a very important functionality in Nagios, and configuring notifications correctly might seem a bit tricky in the beginning.

When and how notifications are sent out is configured as part of the contact configuration. Each contact has configuration directives for when notifications can be sent out and how he/she wants to be contacted. Contacts also contain information about contact details, such as telephone number, e-mail address, and Jabber/MSN address. Each host and service is configured with when information about it should be sent, and who should be contacted. Nagios then combines all this information in order to notify people of changes in the status.

Notifications may be sent out in one of the following situations:

- The host has changed its state to the DOWN or UNREACHABLE state; a notification is sent out after `first_notification_delay` number of minutes specified in the corresponding host object
- The host remains in the DOWN or UNREACHABLE state; a notification is sent out every `notification_interval` number of minutes specified in the corresponding host object
- The host recovers to an UP state; a notification is sent out immediately and only once
- The host starts or stops flapping; a notification is sent out immediately
- The host remains flapping; a notification is sent out every `notification_interval` number of minutes specified in the corresponding host object
- The service has changed its state to the WARNING, CRITICAL or UNKNOWN state; a notification is sent out after `first_notification_delay` number of minutes specified in the corresponding service object
- The service remains in the WARNING, CRITICAL or UNKNOWN state; a notification is sent out every `notification_interval` number of minutes specified in the corresponding service object
- The service recovers to an OK state; a notification is sent out immediately and only once
- The service starts or stops flapping; a notification is sent out immediately
- The service remains flapping; a notification is sent out every `notification_interval` number of minutes specified in the corresponding service object

If one of these conditions occurs, Nagios starts evaluating whether information about it should be sent out and to whom.

First of all, the current date and time is checked against the notification time period. The time period is taken from the `notification_timeperiod` field from the current host or the service definition. Only if the time period includes the current time will a notification be sent out.

Next, a list of users based on the `contacts` and `contact_groups` fields is created. Based on all members of all groups and included groups, as well as all contacts directly bound with the current host or service, a complete list of users is made.

Each of matched users is checked whether they should be notified about the current event. In this case, each user's time period is also checked whether it includes the current date and time. The `host_notification_period` or `service_notification_period` directive is used, depending on whether the notification is for the host or the service.

For host notifications, the `host_notification_options` directive for each contact is also used to determine whether that particular person should be contacted; for example, different users might be contacted about an unreachable host if the host is actually down. For service notifications, the `service_notification_options` parameter is used to check every user if they should be notified about this issue. The section on hosts and services configuration described what values these directives take.

If all of these criteria have been met, then Nagios will send a notification to this user. It will now use commands specified in the `host_notification_commands` and `service_notification_commands` directives.

It is possible to specify multiple commands that will be used for notifications, so it is possible to set up Nagios so that it sends both e-mail as well as a message on an instant messaging system.

Nagios also offers escalations which allow sending e-mails to other people when a problem has not been resolved for too long. This can be used to propagate problems to the higher management or teams that might be affected by unresolved problems. It is a very powerful mechanism and is split between the host and service-based escalations. This functionality is described in more detail in *Chapter 6, Notifications and Events*.

Templates and object inheritance

In order to allow flexible configuration of machines, Nagios offers a powerful inheritance engine. The main concept is that administrators can set up templates that define common parameters and re-use them in actual host or service definitions. The mechanism even offers the possibility to create templates that inherit parameters from other templates.

This mechanisms works in a way that templates are plain Nagios objects that specify the `register` directive and set it to `0`. This means that they will not be registered as an actual host or service that need to be monitored. Objects that inherit parameters from a template or another host should have a `use` directive pointing to the short name of the template object they are using.

When defining a template, its name is always specified using the `name` directive. This is slightly different from how typical hosts and services are registered, as they require the `host_name` and/or `service_description` parameters.

Inheritance can be used to define a template for basic host checks with only basic parameters such as IP address being defined for each particular host, and the following code is an example of this:

```
define host{
    name                        generic-server
    check_command               check-host-alive
    check_interval              5
    retry_interval              1
    max_check_attempts          5
    check_period                24x7
    notification_interval       30
    notification_period         24x7
    notification_options        d,u,r
    register                    0
}

define host{
    use                         generic-server
    name                        linuxbox01
    alias                       Linux Server 01
    address                     10.0.2.1
    contact_groups              linux-admins
}
```

It is possible to inherit from multiple templates. To do this, simply put multiple names in the use directive, separated by a comma. This allows an object to use several templates which define a part or all directives that it will use. If multiple templates specify the same parameters, the value from the first template specifying it will be used. The following is an example code:

```
define service{
    name                        generic-service
    check_interval              10
    retry_interval              2
    max_check_attempts          3
    check_period                24x7
    register                    0
}

define service{
    host_name                   workinghours-service
    check_period                workinghours
    notification_interval       30
```

```
        notification_period          workinghours
        notification_options         w,c,u,r
        register                     0
    }

    define service{
        use                          workinghours-service,generic-service
        contact_groups               linux-admins
        host_name                    linuxbox01
        service_description          SSH
        check_command                check_ssh
        }
```

In this case, values from both templates will be used. The value of workinghours will be used for the check_period directive as it was first specified in the workinghours-service template. Changing the order in use directive to generic-service,workinghours-service would cause value of the check_period parameter to be 24x7.

Nagios also accepts creating multiple levels of templates. For example, you can set up a generic service template, and inherit it to create templates for various types of checks, such as local services, resource sensitive checks, and template for passive-only checks. Let's consider the following object and template structure:

```
define host{
    host_name       linuxserver1
    use             generic-linux,template-chicago
    .....
    }
define host{
    register        0
    name            generic-linux
    use             generic-server
    .....
    }
define host{
    register        0
    name            generic-server
    use             generic-host
    .....
    }
define host{
    register        0
    name            template-chicago
    use             contacts-chicago,misc-chicago
    .....
    }
```

The following diagram shows how Nagios will look for values for all directives:

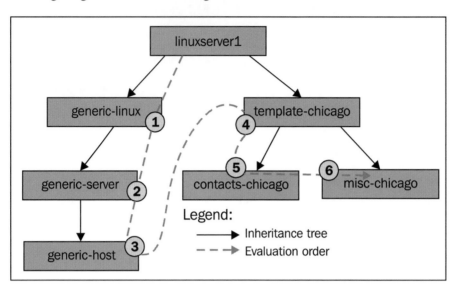

When looking for parameters, Nagios will first look for the value in the linuxserver1 object definition. Next, it will use the following templates, in this order: generic-linux, generic-server, generic-host, template-chicago, contacts-chicago, and misc-chicago in the end.

It is also possible to set up host or service dependencies that will be inherited from a template. In that case, the dependent hosts or services can't be templates themselves, and need to be registered as an object that will be monitored by the Nagios daemon.

Summary

Our Nagios setup is now complete and ready to be started! We took the road from source code into a working application. We have also configured it so that it monitors the machine it is running on from scratch, and it took very little time and effort to do this.

Our Nagios installation now uses three directories:`/opt/nagios` for binaries, `/etc/nagios` for the configuration, and `/var/nagios` for storing the data. All object definitions are stored in a categorized way as subdirectories `/etc/nagios`. This allows a much easier management of Nagios objects.

We have configured the server on which Nagios is running to be monitored. You might want to add more servers just to see how it all works. We told Nagios to monitor the SSH server, but most probably you'll also want to monitor other things such as a web server or an e-mail.

Chapter 4, Using the Nagios Plugins will help when it comes to setting up various types of checks. Make sure to also read the `/etc/nagios/commands/default.cfg` file to see with which commands Nagios was already configured. Sometimes, it will also be needed to set up your own check commands—either custom scripts or using Nagios plugins in a different way than the default command set.

You'll also want to set up other users if you are working as part of a larger team. It'll definitely help everyone in your team if you tell Nagios who is taking care of which parts of the infrastructure!

All that should be a good start for making sure everything works fine in your company. Of course, configuring Nagios for your needs might take a lot of time, but starting with monitoring just the essentials is a good thing. You'll learn how it works and increase the number of objects that are monitored over time.

The next step is to set up the web interface so that you'll be able to see things from your favorite browser or even put them on your desktop. The next chapter provides essential information on how to install, configure, and use the web interface.

3
Using the Nagios Web Interface

The previous chapter has described how to set up and configure Nagios. Now that our Nagios system is up and running, it will also send out notifications to people if something goes wrong. What we need now is a way to view current and historical information on which hosts and services are failing. Nagios offers just that! It comes with a web interface that can be used to view the status of all hosts and services, read logs, generate reports, and so on. And that's just a small part of its functionality.

Using any browser, you can access almost any information Nagios stores, such as status, performance data, history, and logs. You can check all of your hosts and services to find out whether they are working correctly with just a few clicks. The interface also offers the ability to change parts of configuration on the fly.

The ability to check the status of all the hosts and services is a very valuable functionality. Usually, a notification that shows something is wrong should just be a trigger to investigate the problem. Being able to see the big picture via various views of the web interface is very useful. You can use different detailed views and see what is not working properly.

Nagios can also show you a tree of your infrastructure that includes parent-host mappings. It's a great way to see which machines are down and which are assumed to be unreachable. In larger systems, where there are lots of dependencies, being able to see it clearly is very useful.

In this chapter, we will cover the following items:

- Setting up the web interface using Apache 2 server
- Checking the overall status with tactical overview
- Managing hosts and services
- Scheduling downtimes and adding comments
- Viewing Nagios information and generating reports
- Customizing the Nagios web interface and using third-party Nagios web interfaces

Setting up the web interface

The Nagios web interface is part of main Nagios sources and binary distributions. Therefore, if you installed Nagios, you will also have the web interface files. The only thing that you need is a web server with CGI and PHP support; in our case, this will be Apache 2 (visit `http://httpd.apache.org/` for more details).

Nagios web interface uses **CGI (Common Gateway Interface)**, a standard to generate dynamic websites (visit `http://httpd.apache.org/docs/current/howto/cgi.html` for more details), to work as it is the most commonly offered way to run applications. It also allows a flexible setup in terms of security as CGI binaries can be run as different users from the one the web server is running as.

Nagios web interface also uses additional files such as many static HTML pages and CSS and images. Starting with Nagios 4, **PHP (PHP: Hypertext Preprocessor)**, a scripting language for web development (see `http://php.net/` for more details), is used to aid in configuring the web interface HTML pages.

As described in the previous chapter, Nagios CGI scripts need to be able to write to the Nagios external command pipe. If you have followed the installation instructions contained in *Chapter 2, Installing Nagios 4*, your Apache server already has the correct access rights. If you set up Nagios on your own, you need to make sure your web server can write to the Nagios pipe. Please check your external command pipe permissions and make sure, for our installation parameters, the file is called `/var/nagios/rw/nagios.cmd` and is writable by the `nagioscmd` group. It needs to be writable by the user your web server is running as, so it is best to add your web server user to the group owning the file.

Configuring the web server

By default, all Nagios HTML and other static files that are used by the web interface are copied into the `share` subdirectory of the Nagios installation and all CGI binaries go into the `sbin` subdirectory. Assuming Nagios has been configured using the default directories used in the previous chapter, the files paths would be `/opt/nagios/share` and `/opt/nagios/sbin` respectively.

Nagios uses PHP files for static pages. PHP is mainly used for formatting HTML pages and Nagios uses PHP to allow configuring Nagios file and script locations such as the paths to the Nagios configuration file, the status file, and CGI configuration file and the URL to CGI files.

In order to run the web interface, PHP has to be enabled on the web server. In case of Apache running on Ubuntu or CentOS, installing the PHP package automatically will enable PHP on the web server.

If you're using other distributions, have installed Apache manually, or are using another web server, please make sure that PHP is enabled. It needs to be enabled either globally or for the virtual host that the Nagios web interface will be used for. The PHP documentation (visit `http://php.net/manual/en/install.php` for more details) describes enabling PHP for various operating systems and servers in detail.

If you installed Nagios from a binary distribution, it may have configured a web server so that it is accessible. In that case, the package management should have asked you for a password to access the Nagios web interface. You should start by trying to access `http://127.0.0.1/nagios/` from the machine that has Nagios installed. It should prompt you for a username and password. The main Nagios administrator is called `nagiosadmin` and the password will be the one you supplied during package installation. You should skip this section and proceed to the next ones that describe how Nagios web interface works.

If you have followed steps in the previous chapter to install Nagios, all that's needed is to configure Apache to use proper aliasing and create a valid user that will be able to access Nagios.

The following instructions assume that your Apache configuration is under `/etc/apache2` and that your web server will read all configuration files under `/etc/apache2/conf.d`. In case your paths are different, please modify paths in the following examples accordingly.

The first thing that we will do is create a configuration file called /etc/apache2/ conf.d/nagios. We will need to add an alias to the folder /nagios that will point to /opt/nagios/share and add CGI scripts under /nagios/cgi-bin to point to /opt/ nagios/sbin:

```
ScriptAlias /nagios/cgi-bin /opt/nagios/sbin
Alias /nagios /opt/nagios/share
```

Next, we need to set up password protection for the Nagios web interface. We can also limit IP addresses able to access the site. To do this, add the following directives to the nagios file located in /etc/apache2/conf.d/:

```
<DirectoryMatch /opt/nagios/share>
        Options FollowSymLinks
        AllowOverride AuthConfig
        Order Allow,Deny
        Allow From All
        AuthName "Nagios Access"
        AuthType Basic
        AuthUserFile /etc/nagios/htpasswd.users
        AuthGroupFile /etc/nagios/htpasswd.groups
        require valid-user
</DirectoryMatch>

<DirectoryMatch /opt/nagios/sbin>
        Options ExecCGI
        AllowOverride AuthConfig
        Order Allow,Deny
        Allow From All
        AuthName "Nagios Access"
        AuthType Basic
        AuthUserFile /etc/nagios/htpasswd.users
        AuthGroupFile /etc/nagios/htpasswd.groups
        require valid-user
</DirectoryMatch>
```

If you want to limit hosts that will be able to access the Nagios web interface, you can replace the Order and Allow directives in both DirectoryMatch definitions as follows:

```
Order Deny,Allow
Deny From All
Allow From 192.168.0.0/16
```

This will only allow access to Nagios website from IP addresses starting with 192.168.

Creating an administrative user for Nagios

We now need to add an administrative user for the web interface. We must also add this user to Nagios configuration as the authorized username will be used by the web interface to check permissions and perform actions as this user.

By default, Nagios configuration specifies `nagiosadmin` as a user who is authorized to access all parts of the Nagios web interface. Therefore, we will now create such a user in the `nagiosadmin.cfg` file located in `/etc/nagios/contacts/`:

```
define contact{
   contact_name                    nagiosadmin
   alias                           Nagios Administrator
   contactgroups                   admins
   email                           youremail@yourcompany.com
   host_notification_period        24x7
   service_notification_period     24x7
   host_notification_options       n
   service_notification_options    n
   host_notification_commands      notify-host-by-email
   service_notification_commands   notify-service-by-email
   }
```

Even though notifications have been disabled for this user, we should also set the `email` field to a valid e-mail address.

The configuration for the user authorized to perform all actions is stored in the `cgi.cfg` file in `/etc/nagios`. This file was created when we were installing Nagios by the `make install-config` command. Nagios CGI uses the configuration file.

The following lines in the file define an administrative user:

```
authorized_for_system_information=nagiosadmin
authorized_for_configuration_information=nagiosadmin
authorized_for_system_commands=nagiosadmin
authorized_for_all_services=nagiosadmin
authorized_for_all_hosts=nagiosadmin
authorized_for_all_service_commands=nagiosadmin
authorized_for_all_host_commands=nagiosadmin
```

This can be used to define one or more users that have full access to the configuration. Multiple users can be specified, separating each user with a comma in this manner: `jdoe,nagiosadmin`.

We should now create the files that will be used by the web server for authorization. We will need to run the following commands to set these up:

```
# cp /dev/null /etc/nagios/htpasswd.groups
# htpasswd -c /etc/nagios/htpasswd.users nagiosadmin
```

When prompted for the password, please specify the password you want to use.

We now need to set the ownership of the file appropriately so that it can only be read by the web server, not regular users. For an installation made according to instructions in the second step, the user that the web server runs is already added to the nagioscmd group, so we can simply set the owning group to nagioscmd and make it readable for the group. For example:

```
# chown root:nagioscmd /etc/nagios/htpasswd.*
# chmod 0640 /etc/nagios/htpasswd.*
```

The last thing that needs to be done is to restart Apache and Nagios by invoking the following commands:

```
root@ubuntu:~# service apache2 restart
root@ubuntu:~# service nagios restart
```

These commands will restart both services. The Nagios restart was required because we created a new user in the Nagios configuration.

Accessing the web interface

After restarting the web server, we can access the Nagios web interface by going to `http://127.0.0.1/nagios/` from the machine Nagios is running on. It will prompt for a username and password; use the credentials from the previous example. After a successful login, you should see a welcome screen similar to this one:

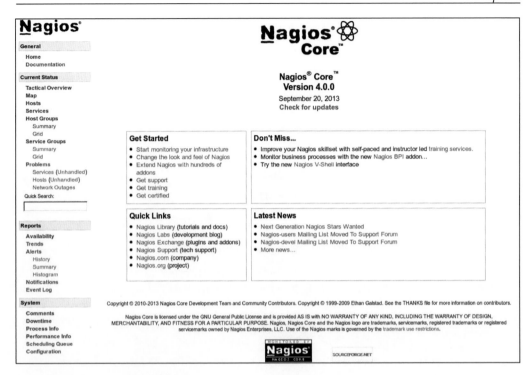

Troubleshooting

There might be cases where accessing the Nagios URL shows an error instead of showing the welcome screen. If this happens, it can be due to many things: the web server may not be started, the Nagios-related configuration setup may have been incorrect, incorrect permissions may have been set on directories, and so on.

The first thing that we should check is whether Apache is working properly. We can manually run the check_http plugin from Nagios. If the web server is up and running, we should see something similar to the following output:

```
# /opt/nagios/plugins/check_http -H 127.0.0.1
HTTP OK HTTP/1.1 200 OK - 296 bytes in 0.006 seconds
```

Likewise, if Apache is not currently running, the plugin will report an error similar to this:

```
# /opt/nagios/plugins/check_http -H 127.0.0.1
HTTP CRITICAL - Unable to open TCP socket
```

If Apache was stopped, start it by running the following command:

```
root@ubuntu:~# service apache2 start
```

The next step is to check whether the URL http://127.0.0.1/nagios/ is working properly. We can also use the same plugin for this. The -u argument can specify an exact link to access, and -a allows specifying the username and password to authorize. It is passed in the form <username>:<password>.

```
# /opt/nagios/plugins/check_http -H 127.0.0.1 \
    -u /nagios/ -a nagiosadmin:<yourpassword>
HTTP OK HTTP/1.1 200 OK - 979 bytes in 0.019 seconds
```

We can also check actual CGI scripts by passing a URL to one of the scripts:

```
# /opt/nagios/plugins/check_http -H 127.0.0.1 \
    -u /nagios/cgi-bin/tac.cgi -a nagiosadmin:<yourpassword>
HTTP OK HTTP/1.1 200 OK - 979 bytes in 0.019 seconds
```

If any of these checks returned any other HTTP code than 200, it means that there is a problem.

If the code is 500, it means that Apache is incorrectly configured. In such cases, the Apache error log contains useful information about any potential problems. On most systems, including Ubuntu Linux, the file is /var/log/apache2/error.log. An example error log could be:

```
[error] [client 127.0.0.1] need AuthName: /nagios/cgi-bin/tac.cgi
```

In this particular case, the problem is the missing AuthName directive for CGI scripts.

Internal errors can usually be resolved by making sure that the Nagios-related Apache configuration is correct. If you followed installation steps from this and the previous chapter, the Apache configuration should be exactly the same as in the previous examples.

If this does not help, it is worth checking other parts of the configuration, especially those related to virtual hosts and CGI configuration. Commenting out parts of the configuration can help to determine which parts of the configuration are causing problems.

Another possibility is that either checks for /nagios/ or /nagios/cgi-bin/tac.cgi, URL returned code 404. This code means that the page was not found. In this case, please make sure that Apache is configured according to the previous steps.

If it is, then it is a good idea to enable more verbose debugging to a custom file. The following Apache 2 directives can be added to either /etc/apache2/conf.d/nagios or any other file in the Apache configuration:

```
LogFormat "%h %l %u \"%r\" %>s %b %{Host}e %f" debuglog
CustomLog /var/log/apache2/access-debug.log debuglog
```

The first entry defines a custom logging format that also logs exact paths to files. The second one enables logging, with this format, to a dedicated file. An example entry in such a log would be as follows:

```
127.0.0.1 - - "GET /nagios/ HTTP/1.1" 404 481 127.0.0.1
/var/www/nagios
```

This log entry tells us that http://127.0.0.1/nagios/ was incorrectly expanded to /var/www/nagios. In this case, the Alias directive describing the /nagios/ prefix is missing. Making sure that the actual configuration matches the one provided in the previous section will also resolve this issue.

Another error that you can get is 403, which indicates that Apache was unable to access either CGI scripts in /opt/nagios/sbin or Nagios static pages in /opt/nagios/share. In this case, you need to make sure that these directories are readable by the user running Apache.

It might also be related to the folders above /opt/nagios or /opt in the folder tree. One of these might also be inaccessible to the user running Apache, which will also cause the same error to occur.

If you run into any other problems, it is best to start with making sure that the Nagios-related configuration matches the examples from the previous section. It is also a good idea to reduce the number of enabled features and virtual hosts in your Apache configuration.

Using the web interface

The Nagios web interface always offers a menu in the left-hand frame, and current information is shown in the remaining area. You can easily access all views from the left-hand menu.

In case you want to replace the standard Nagios welcome screen with your own, all that's needed is to change the /opt/nagios/share/main.php file. As this page is shown to everyone after they log in correctly, it can be used to provide administrators with some guidelines on how Nagios monitoring is used within their company and what should be done in certain circumstances. It can also be used to define links to commonly checked hosts or commonly accessed services.

It is also possible to extend the left-hand menu, which is defined in the `side.php` file located at `/opt/nagios/share/`. This way, quick links can be added to the menu and/or unused functionalities can be removed from it.

Throughout the rest of this chapter, we will use configuration that is far more complex than the one we created in the previous chapter. This will allow us to show more functionality in Nagios and its web interface.

Checking the tactical overview

Nagios offers a panel that shows an overall status of all hosts, services, and other features. It can be accessed by clicking on the **Tactical Overview** link in the left-hand menu. You can easily assess the scale of problems — the number of hosts and services failing, flapping and pending checks, and so on. It also shows how many hosts are unreachable due to other hosts being down.

The following is a screenshot of the **Tactical Monitoring Overview** page:

Tactical Monitoring Overview
Last Updated: Sun Oct 6 16:28:29 CEST 2013
Updated every 90 seconds
Nagios® Core™ 4.0.0 - www.nagios.org
Logged in as *nagiosadmin*

Monitoring Performance

Service Check Execution Time:	0.00 / 5.01 / 1.592 sec
Service Check Latency:	0.00 / 0.00 / 0.000 sec
Host Check Execution Time:	4.00 / 4.03 / 4.019 sec
Host Check Latency:	0.00 / 0.00 / 0.000 sec
# Active Host / Service Checks:	5 / 11
# Passive Host / Service Checks:	0 / 0

Network Outages

0 Outages

Network Health

Host Health:

Service Health:

Hosts

0 Down	0 Unreachable	5 Up	0 Pending

Services

0 Critical	0 Warning	0 Unknown	11 Ok	0 Pending

Monitoring Features

Flap Detection	Notifications	Event Handlers	Active Checks	Passive Checks
✓ All Services Enabled	✓ All Services Enabled	✓ All Services Enabled	✓ All Services Enabled	✓ All Services Enabled
No Services Flapping	All Hosts Enabled	All Hosts Enabled	All Hosts Enabled	All Hosts Enabled
All Hosts Enabled				
No Hosts Flapping				

Tactical overview presents you with overall information on Nagios and monitoring. The page reports on host and service conditions. It shows how many hosts and services are in which status. It also shows if any hosts and services have their checks, notifications, or event handlers disabled.

The top-right corner shows performance information. It shows details on checks that have been performed and reports latencies when performing checks and the average time that it takes to perform checks. These values are pretty important because if there are too many checks scheduled, Nagios might not be able to perform some of them. Usually, you should tweak your Nagios installation in cases where the latency is more than a couple of seconds.

Below the performance information is a status showing host and service health, as in the previous screenshot. It contains bars showing the number of hosts and services that are in the **Ok** state. Since all services are currently working properly, the bar spans to full width and is green. If some hosts or services are not working, the color of the bar changes to yellow or red accordingly.

Tactical overview can also be used to view the hosts or services lists filtered to only specific criteria. Clicking on any status-count text in the **Network Outages**, **Hosts**, or **Services** sections will show a list of hosts or services with the specified status. If we click on **11 Ok** in the **Services** section, it will show a list of all services with the status **Ok**.

Viewing the status map

Nagios allows showing a graphical map of host parent-child relations along with statuses. It can be accessed by clicking on the **Map** link in the left-hand menu. This can be used to keep track of hosts along with their statuses so that you can see how a host being down causes other parts of your network to be unreachable.

The following is a screenshot of a status page:

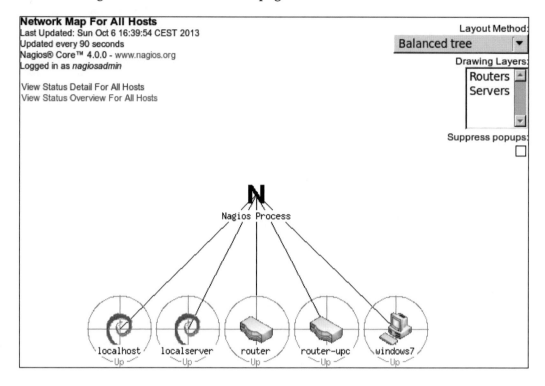

The status page can be shown in many ways. The preceding screenshot shows a circular tree of all hosts. It is possible to also display a top-down tree of all hosts.

Managing hosts

Nagios offers several pages that can be used to view and modify host information. The Nagios web interface offers a view of all defined hosts, their statuses, and basic information. These can be used to determine the statuses of hosts. Hostgroup-related views also show the statuses for services bound to hosts. Host information pages also offer modifying several parameters related to host configuration.

Checking statuses

Nagios offers a panel that shows all hosts along with their statuses. It can be accessed by clicking on the **Hosts** link in the left-hand menu.

The following screenshot reports five hosts, all of which are currently up:

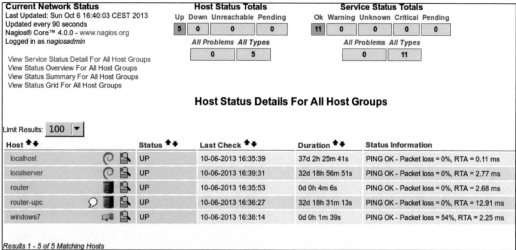

The page shows a list of all hosts, their statuses, and basic information, such as when the host was last checked and when the status last changed. It also shows the information text response from the check. The order of how the table is shown can be changed by using the arrow buttons next to each column's header.

As with the tactical overview page, the totals on the top of the page can be used to filter hosts or services to only display those with specific statuses. After clicking on any status type in the **Host Status Totals** table, the list of hosts is filtered down to only the ones that currently have that status. Clicking on any status type in **Service Status Totals** will show a list of services filtered only to the ones that currently have that specified status.

There is also a quick jump menu on the left that allows you to move to a list of all services and views related to host groups.

Nagios also offers three views that show the statuses of all host groups. One of these views is the status grid, which shows host groups along with hosts in them, and each service for that host along with its status. It can be accessed by clicking on the **Grid** option under the **View Status Grid For All Host Groups** link in the left-hand menu.

The following is a screenshot of such a status grid view:

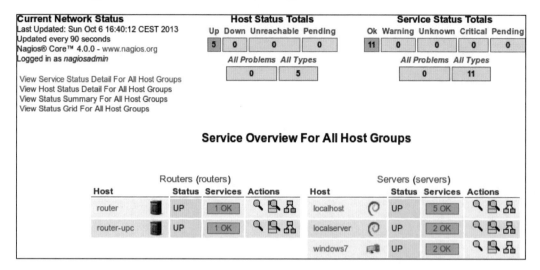

As with the previous view, clicking on the **Host Status Totals** or **Service Status Totals** table options will cause Nagios to filter results according to the specified criteria. The page also contains a quick jump menu on the left that can be used to change the currently selected view.

Clicking on any host group description will display a list of all services on all hosts within that group.

Clicking on a host group name, which is specified in brackets, will show a host group menu that allows modifying attributes for all hosts or services related to that host group.

Clicking on a host name in any host- or service-related view will cause Nagios to show detailed information about the chosen host.

Viewing host information

Clicking on a host in any view of the web interface will take you to the host information page. It contains details on current host status, a list of comments, and a commands panel that allows modifying host configuration, scheduling checks, or sending custom notifications.

The following is a screenshot of the host information page:

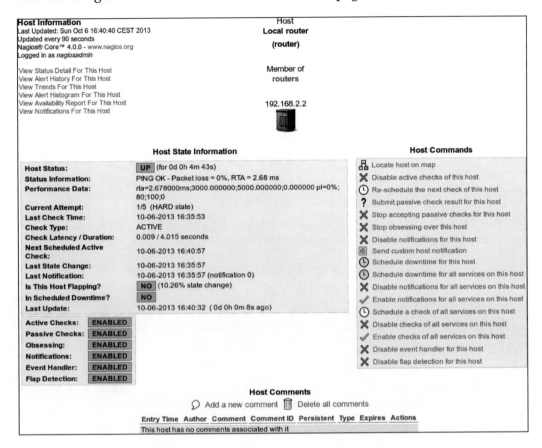

This page contains detailed information on the selected host. It shows the current status and host checks that have been or will be performed. It also contains information on what functionality is enabled or disabled for the specified host, whether the host is flapping along with flapping threshold value.

The menu on the right can be used to perform operations related to this host. It allows toggling between whether active checks should be performed, whether Nagios should accept passive check results, and whether it should detect flapping. You can also configure whether Nagios should obsess over a host or send notifications and events. It is also possible to view options for all services bound to this host. There is also an option to schedule checks for a host or all services bound to this host. You can also submit passive check results over the web interface.

The host information page also allows reading and modifying all comments related to this host. All current comments are listed under the **Host Comments** section. Clicking on the trash icon under the **Actions** column will delete a comment. You can also delete all comments and add a new comment bound to this host.

Managing services

As with host-related information and operations, Nagios has panels for working with services. It consists of several service and service-group views that allow you to view detailed information on each service and modify its parameters.

Checking statuses

The Nagios web interface offers a view of all defined services, their statuses, and basic information. It can be accessed by clicking on the **Services** link in the left-hand menu.

The following is a screenshot reporting 11 services, all of which are currently working correctly:

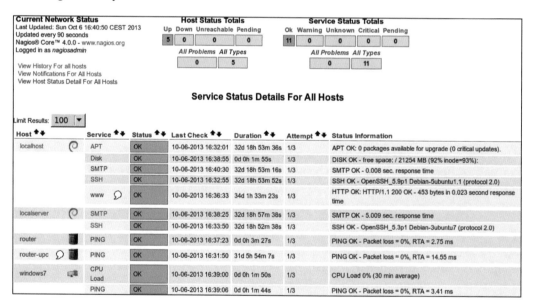

The main part of the page is the table showing all services along with their statuses and detailed information on the output from checks.

The default order by which the table is sorted is that all services are grouped by the hosts they are configured for, and they are sorted by service description. It is possible to sort the table according to your needs by clicking on the arrows in the headers for any column of the table.

Above the table, there are total values for each host and service status. You can also filter the service table using these values to only show specific statuses or services for hosts with a specific status.

The page also contains a quick menu that allows navigation to commonly used views. It allows jumping to history and the notification log, as well as navigating to a list of all hosts along with their detailed statuses.

Clicking on any host will take you to a host information page for the selected object. Similarly, clicking on any service will display a detailed information page for that object.

Another interesting view is a summary of all the services specified for each service group. It can be accessed by clicking on the **View Service Status Grid For All Service Groups** option on the left-hand menu.

The following is a screenshot of the page:

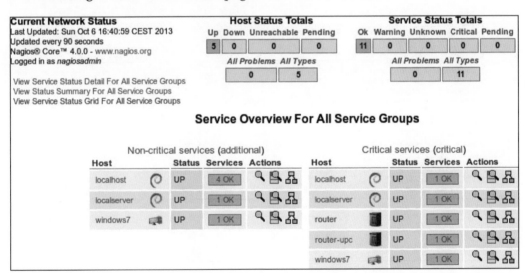

It shows each service group along with the count of all the services for each status. The page contains a status summary for all services that are members of a specific service group. It also shows a status summary for all hosts that have at least one service configured.

Clicking on any status summary column will show a list of all the services in that group along with detailed information about them. Clicking on a service group will show an overview of services split into individual hosts.

Viewing service information

Clicking on a service in any view of the web interface will take you to the service information page. It contains details on the current service status, a list of comments, and a commands panel that allows modifying service configuration, scheduling checks, or sending custom notifications.

The following is a screenshot of the service information page:

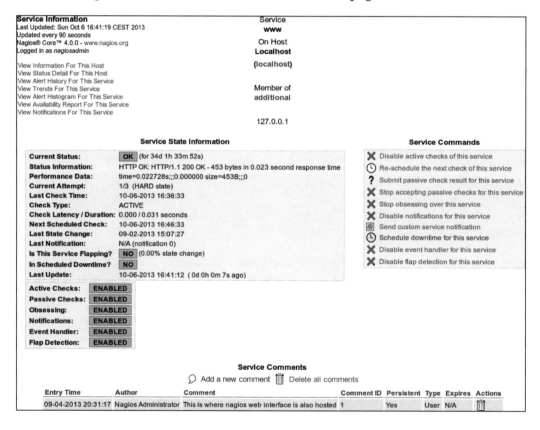

The main table on the left shows detailed information on the service, such as current status, output from the check, and detailed information on the last and next planned check. The page also shows whether the service is flapping along with the flapping threshold and when the last notification was sent out.

The menu on the right allows modifying whether checks should be performed, whether notifications and events should be done, and whether Nagios should obsess over this service. There is also an option to schedule when the next check is to be performed.

On the bottom, there is a **Service Comments** section containing a table that shows all existing comments related to this service. This is similar to the host information page. It is also possible to add a comment and delete a single comment or all comments related to this service.

Managing downtime

Nagios allows using the web interface to manage scheduled downtimes for hosts and services. This includes listing, adding, and deleting downtimes for both hosts and services.

Checking downtime statuses

The Nagios web interface allows listing all scheduled downtimes. This page can be accessed by clicking on the **Downtime** link on the left-hand menu. The following is a screenshot of the page:

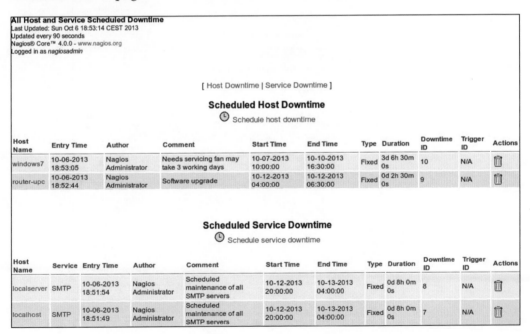

The page consists of two pages of all scheduled downtimes, for hosts and services separately. You can delete a downtime by clicking on the trash icon on the right, in the row that describes this particular downtime entry.

Downtimes can be triggered by other downtimes. When a host downtime is scheduled, Nagios automatically adds downtimes for all child hosts.

Scheduling downtime

In order to schedule a downtime, open a host or service information page and use the **Schedule downtime for this host** or **Schedule downtime for this service** options. It is also possible to use the downtime page to schedule downtimes directly. In that case, you will need to know the host name and service description of the service you want to disable, as Nagios will not fill these in automatically.

The following is a screenshot of scheduling downtime for a service:

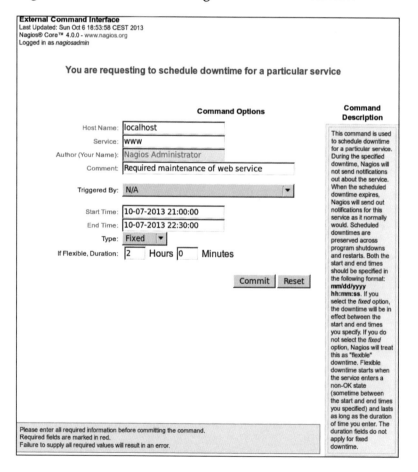

The form consists of fields for the host and service names, a comment, and an optional drop-down list to choose a downtime that triggered this host/service. When specifying the time during which a downtime should be scheduled, it is possible to fill the **Start Time** and **End Time** fields or use the **Duration** field. If you want to specify how long the duration will be, choose **Flexible** in the **Type** field. Otherwise, choose **Fixed** to specify start and end time.

Scheduling downtime for a host is very similar. The only differences are that the **Service** field is missing and the **Child Hosts** drop-down list is added to specify how child hosts should be handled.

Nagios can automatically schedule downtimes for child hosts. When scheduling host downtime, an additional option is present to specify whether child hosts should also be scheduled for downtime, and set to be triggered by this downtime.

Managing comments

Nagios allows inserting one or more comments associated with a host or a service. These can be anything from "third machine from top on the left shelf" to "reset button not working". Nagios also adds comments automatically in several cases; for example, when an object is scheduled for downtime, a comment is placed about it.

Comments associated with a specific object are shown on the host and service detail information pages. It can also be added and removed from these very pages.

Nagios also offers a page that allows managing comments for all hosts and services, which is similar to managing scheduled downtimes. It allows adding and deleting comments for all hosts. You can also navigate to the detailed information page for hosts and services by clicking on an object name. The page can be accessed via the **Comments** link on the left-hand menu.

The following is a screenshot of the comments page:

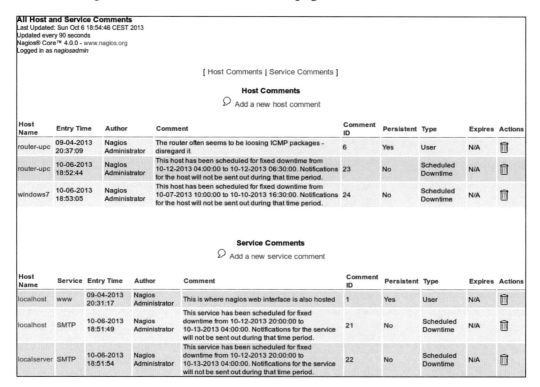

Clicking on the trash icon next to any comment will delete it. Adding a comment can be done by clicking on a host or service name and then doing so from the detailed information page, or by clicking on **Add a new service comment** above the table with comments. In the latter case, you will need to specify host name and service description yourself in the add comment form.

Nagios information

The web interface allows checking the Nagios daemon status along with general information on features enabled and disabled. It also allows checking performance information related to Nagios. This can be used to make sure that your Nagios interface is not overloaded with checks to perform, as well as seeing how long the checks take and how often they're performed.

Viewing process information

The **Nagios Process Information** page shows generic information about Nagios processes. It also allows performing several actions from the **Process Commands** panel. The following page can be accessed via the **Process Info** link on the left-hand menu:

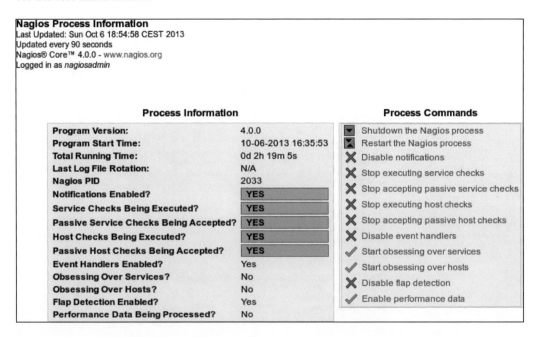

The page contains information on the Nagios version, process ID, status, and log rotation. It also shows whether checks, notifications, and many other functions are enabled.

The menu on the right allows stopping and restarting the Nagios daemon. It also offers the ability to enable and disable performing checks and sending notifications. Flap detection and performance data processing can also be turned on or off from this page.

Checking performance information

The **Program-Wide Performance Information** page shows information about the performance and load of Nagios processes. This page can be accessed via the **Performance Info** link on the left-hand menu.

The following is a screenshot of the page:

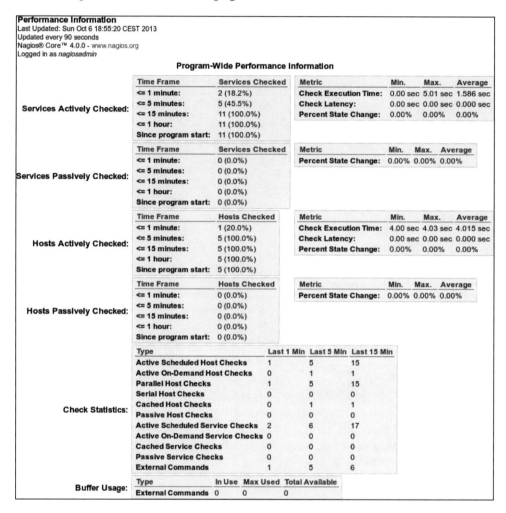

The page contains information on the number of host and service checks performed within various periods of time, as well as the number of reports received from external applications. It also contains the number of commands received from external applications–this usually means the web interface.

The page also contains information on average check execution times as well as latencies. This information is useful to determine whether the Nagios process is overloaded. If the average latency is above 60 seconds or is constantly growing, it means that Nagios is not able to perform all of the checks. In such cases, it is a good idea to increase check or notification intervals so that the number of commands Nagios runs is lower.

Generating reports

One of the most important features of the web interface is the ability to create reports. Many larger companies need those to make decisions at a higher management level, smaller ones can benefit from it. Reporting functionality can also be used to browse historical notifications and alerts and see complete logs from a specified period.

Nagios offers the following types of reports:

- **Trend reporting for hosts or services**: This report shows state history changes for a single object along with status information from performed checks.

- **Availability report for hosts or services**: This report shows how much time an object has spent in a particular status. It can report all objects or a single object and can also generate reports for host groups and service groups

- **Alert histogram**: This report shows the number of alerts that have occurred over a period of time for a particular host or service.

In addition, Nagios can report a history of alerts, notifications, or all events. This can be considered reading Nagios logs in a more convenient way. It allows reading the history either for all hosts and/or services, or for a specific object. The logs are also formatted in a more readable way.

Generating most reports begins with choosing the report type and then the object type—host, host group, and service, or service group. Then, either all objects or a specific object may be chosen for which the report will be generated.

Next, you will get a form for specifying the period for which a report should be generated along with many additional options, which can be dependent on the type of report that you want to generate. Additionally, a time period can be specified so that the report only includes specific time periods, such as working hours.

The following is a screenshot of a sample form for specifying parameters for a report. Actual fields might vary depending on the type of report you want to generate.

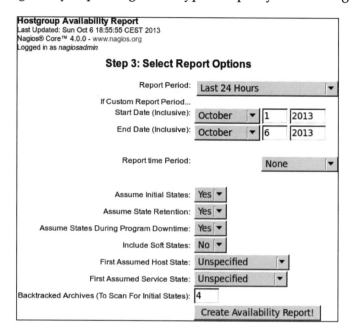

After you specify parameters in the form and submit it, the web interface will generate a report matching your criteria. Some types of reports also allow exporting information in CSV format for further analysis. For trend history reports, it is also possible to zoom in or out, in order to customize the period for which the report is generated.

The following is a screenshot of a report displaying the availability of all hosts. It shows how much time all hosts have been up, down, or unreachable, due to parent machines not being up.

Hostgroup Availability Report Last Updated: Sun Oct 6 18:56:05 CEST 2013 Nagios® Core™ 4.0.0 - www.nagios.org Logged in as *nagiosadmin*	**All Hostgroups** 10-05-2013 18:56:05 to 10-06-2013 18:56:05 Duration: 1d 0h 0m 0s	First assumed host state: First assumed service state state Unspecified ▼ Unspecified ▼ ▼ Report period: Backtracked archives: ives: Last 24 Hours ▼ 4 Update te *[Availability report completed in 0 min 0 sec]* sec]

Hostgroup 'routers' Host State Breakdowns:

Host	% Time Up	% Time Down	% Time Unreachable	% Time Undetermined
router	0.000% (0.000%)	0.000% (0.000%)	0.000% (0.000%)	100.000%
router-upc	0.000% (0.000%)	0.000% (0.000%)	0.000% (0.000%)	100.000%
Average	0.000% (0.000%)	0.000% (0.000%)	0.000% (0.000%)	100.000%

Hostgroup 'servers' Host State Breakdowns:

Host	% Time Up	% Time Down	% Time Unreachable	% Time Undetermined
localhost	0.000% (0.000%)	0.000% (0.000%)	0.000% (0.000%)	100.000%
localserver	0.000% (0.000%)	0.000% (0.000%)	0.000% (0.000%)	100.000%
windows7	11.148% (40.493%)	16.383% (59.507%)	0.000% (0.000%)	72.469%
Average	3.716% (13.498%)	5.461% (19.836%)	0.000% (0.000%)	90.823%

The report shows information for all hosts as a table, along with the summary of overall availability.

It is possible to change the parameters of a report even after it has been generated, for example, if you want to modify the reported period, or other such information.

Changing the look of the Nagios web interface

The Nagios source code comes with two themes—exfoliation and classical. So far, all of the screenshots in this chapter have been of the exfoliation theme, which has been the default theme for Nagios since Version 3.3.1.

The classical theme was the default for all Nagios versions up to 3.2.3. To install the classical theme, we need to run the following command from the Nagios source code directory:

```
make install-classicui
```

This command will install the classical theme and overwrite the theme currently installed for the Nagios web interface. After the command succeeds, the interface will look more familiar to those people that use, or have used, Nagios Version 3.2.3 or older.

Depending on preference, you may choose to use the new default theme, or use the classical one. Aside from a different look and feel, there is no difference in the Nagios UI features or behavior. The GUI has the exact same left-hand menu as the theme installed by default, and all of the operations such as scheduling downtime, managing comments, or generating reports, are performed in the same way.

The tactical overview page of the classical theme looks significantly different from the one in the exfoliation theme:

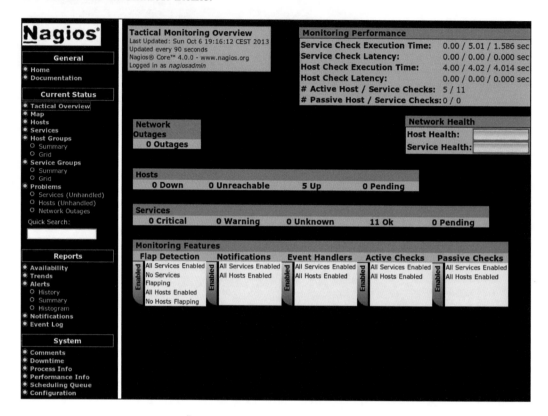

Also, the status pages for services and hosts look different from the ones shown earlier. The following screenshot is of the classic UI theme, showing service status:

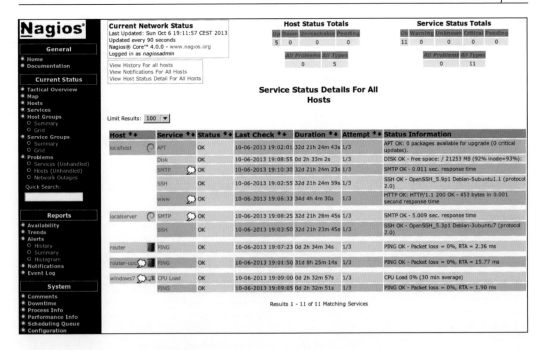

In order to install the exfoliation theme again, all that you need to run is the following command from the Nagios source code repository:

```
make install-exfoliation
```

This will restore the exfoliation theme that is installed by default with Nagios 4. The GUI will now look the same as it did before you installed the classical theme.

Several additional themes are available on Nagios Exchange at `http://exchange.nagios.org/directory/Addons/Frontends-(GUIs-and-CLIs)/Web-Interfaces/Themes-and-Skins`. When you choose a theme, please be sure to verify that it is compatible with your version of Nagios.

One of the themes that work properly with Nagios 4 is the Arana Theme. It is listed on Nagios Exchange and available directly from SourceForge at `http://sourceforge.net/projects/arana-nagios/`.

The first thing we should do is back up our Nagios web interface directory—`/opt/nagios/share`—before installing Nagios. Refer to the steps documented in *Chapter 2, Installing Nagios 4*.

This can be done using the following command:

```
cp -pfR /opt/nagios/share /opt/nagios/share-backup
```

First, we need to download and unpack the theme. The link to download the theme can be found both on Nagios Exchange and on the SourceForge `arana-nagios` project. We'll need to download the archive and unpack it anywhere on the local disk.

Next, copy the entire contents of the directory containing the unpacked Arana theme archive to `/opt/nagios/share`.

After this step, the theme should get properly installed and the Nagios page should look similar to the following screenshot:

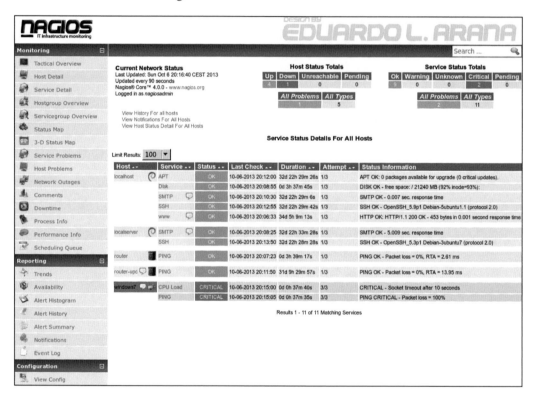

For most themes, the installation should be the same: extract the archive and copy its contents to the directory containing the Nagios web interface files.

Themes also usually come with `readme` or `install` text files that document the exact installation process. When you install a theme for the first time, it is recommended that you start by reading these files.

The Nagios 4 web interface uses PHP for formatting the templates, while previous versions used static HTML pages. Many themes created for Nagios 3 will work with Nagios 4; however, switching to PHP may cause some of the themes designed for Nagios 3 or older to not work properly with Nagios 4, without slight modifications to the themes.

Third-party Nagios web interfaces

There are also multiple web interfaces available on the Internet in addition to the GUI that comes with Nagios itself. A wide choice of additional web interfaces can be found on Nagios Exchange at `http://exchange.nagios.org/directory/Addons/Frontends-(GUIs-and-CLIs)/Web-Interfaces`.

Many of the GUIs available on Nagios Exchange are dashboards. These show statuses for hosts, services, and errors. The dashboards are often displayed on a large display, such as TV, so that the IT department can easily monitor the status of the infrastructure and identify problems that need to be fixed.

One example of such an interface is called **Nagios Dashboard**. It is a small PHP script that shows the statuses of hosts and services, starting with those that have an error status. The plugin can be found on Nagios Exchange at `http://exchange.nagios.org/directory/Addons/Frontends-%28GUIs-and-CLIs%29/Web-Interfaces/Nagios-Dashboard--2D-PHP/details`.

The entire interface is a single file. To install it, we simply need to unpack and copy the `nagios.php` file to any location, such as to `/opt/nagios/share`.

Next, if Nagios was installed according to the steps documented in *Chapter 2, Installing Nagios 4*, we need to change the path to the `status.dat` file to point to our location, which is `/var/nagios/`. To do this, we need to edit the file and change the third line to this:

```
$file = fopen("/var/nagios/status.dat", "r") or exit("Unable
to open file!"); //path to nagios file
```

We can then check the report by going to the appropriate URL; if the file was copied to `/opt/nagios/share`, it will be available at `http://localhost/nagios/nagios.php`:

Blue - Down		- Warning	Green - UP/OK	Grey - Disabled
Last Checked	**Host**		**Status Info**	**Service**
2013-10-06 19:42:00	windows7		CRITICAL - Socket timeout after 10 seconds	CPU Load
2013-10-06 19:42:05	windows7		PING CRITICAL - Packet loss = 100%	PING
2013-10-06 19:42:10	windows7		PING CRITICAL - Packet loss = 100%	HOST PING
2013-10-06 19:43:07	localhost		PING OK - Packet loss = 0%, RTA = 0.12 ms	HOST PING
2013-10-06 19:41:55	localserver		PING OK - Packet loss = 0%, RTA = 1.61 ms	HOST PING
2013-10-06 19:43:24	router		PING OK - Packet loss = 0%, RTA = 2.34 ms	HOST PING
2013-10-06 19:39:33	router-upc		PING WARNING - Packet loss = 93%, RTA = 13.09 ms	HOST PING
2013-10-06 19:42:01	localhost		APT OK: 0 packages available for upgrade (0 critical updates).	APT
2013-10-06 19:38:55	localhost		DISK OK - free space: / 21253 MB (92% inode=93%):	Disk
2013-10-06 19:40:30	localhost		SMTP OK - 0.003 sec. response time	SMTP
2013-10-06 19:42:55	localhost		SSH OK - OpenSSH_5.9p1 Debian-5ubuntu1.1 (protocol 2.0)	SSH
2013-10-06 19:36:33	localhost		HTTP OK: HTTP/1.1 200 OK - 453 bytes in 0.001 second response time	WWW
2013-10-06 19:38:25	localserver		SMTP OK - 5.009 sec. response time	SMTP
2013-10-06 19:43:50	localserver		SSH OK - OpenSSH_5.3p1 Debian-3ubuntu7 (protocol 2.0)	SSH
2013-10-06 19:37:23	router		PING OK - Packet loss = 0%, RTA = 2.20 ms	PING
2013-10-06 19:41:50	router-upc		PING OK - Packet loss = 0%, RTA = 12.45 ms	PING

This dashboard is freeware and may be customized if desired.
Currently in use on Nagios 3.0.3
October 2008.

There are many other dashboards for Nagios available at Nagios Exchange, such as **Nagios Dash**, which is a project based on Nagios Dashboard and they are quite similar.

Another example is **NagiosTV**, which is also a dashboard project for Nagios. It is best to check out a few of the projects and find the one that best suits your needs.

There are also projects offering a more complete web interface, meant to complement or replace the Nagios web interface. A good example of such a project is **Nagios V-Shell**. It is a web interface that provides most of the features of the original Nagios GUI.

It is created in PHP, is designed to be lightweight, and does not use frames, which makes it more convenient to use on mobile devices. It is available for download on Nagios Exchange at `http://exchange.nagios.org/directory/Addons/Frontends-%28GUIs-and-CLIs%29/Web-Interfaces/Nagios-V-2DShell/details`.

It requires Apache and PHP, which we have already set up for the Nagios web interface. It also requires **APC**, a caching mechanism for PHP. The `php-cli` command is also required to run the installation script for V-Shell.

To install the required dependencies, simply run the following command for Ubuntu:

```
# apt-get install php-apc php-cli
```

Use the following command for RedHat/CentOS:

```
# yum install php-pecl-apc php-cli
```

The installation of V-Shell itself is very simple. After downloading and unpacking the archive, we need to edit the `config/vshell.conf` and `config/vshell_apache.conf` configuration files.

For Nagios installation according to steps documented in *Chapter 2, Installing Nagios 4*, the `config/vshell.conf` file should have the following values set for each of the variables in the file:

```
STATUSFILE = "/var/nagios/status.dat"
OBJECTSFILE = "/var/nagios/objects.cache"
CGICFG = "/etc/nagios/cgi.cfg"
NAGCMD = "/var/nagios/rw/nagios.cmd"
NAGLOCK = "/var/nagios/nagios.lock"
```

We also need to change the location of the `htpasswd.users` file in `config/vshell_apache.conf`. It should be as follows:

```
AuthUserFile /etc/nagios/htpasswd.users
```

Finally, we should edit the `install.php` script if we're running on an Ubuntu system. The `APACHECONF` constant has to be changed to `/etc/apache2/conf.d` in this case:

```
define('APACHECONF',"/etc/httpd/conf.d");
```

The default value for `APACHECONF` is suitable for RedHat and CentOS and does not need to be changed in this case.

By default, the package will install itself to `/usr/local/vshell`. This can be changed by editing the `install.php` and `config/vshell_apache.conf` files. They have hardcoded locations of the files and require changing in case we want to install in a different location. For example, you can use the following code to change the location:

```
define('TARGETDIR',"/opt/nagios/vshell");
```

In the `config/vshell_apache.conf` file, change the first lines to:

```
Alias /vshell "/opt/nagios/vshell"

<Directory "/opt/nagios/vshell">
(...)
```

We can now install V-Shell by running the following command:

```
# php-cli install.php
```

This will run the installation script. It will automatically copy all of the files and add the Apache configuration file to the appropriate directory.

After that, it is recommended that you restart Apache by running the following command:

```
# service apache2 restart
```

And now, V-Shell should be available at `http://127.0.0.1/vshell/`:

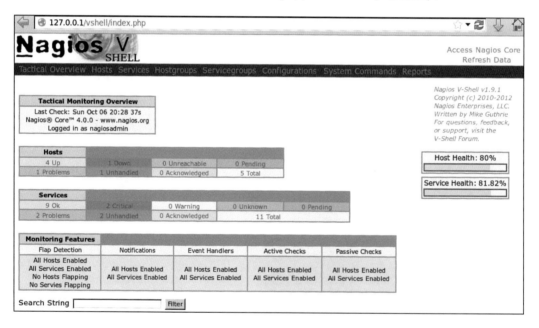

The V-Shell interface is very similar to Nagios' web interface; the main differences are that it does not use frames, and the menu is shown on top rather than on the left. The menu is also a drop-down menu, and hovering over one of the menu items shows a list of available elements.

V-Shell offers most of the views available in the standard web interface for Nagios, such as showing host details, and all of the information related to host management.

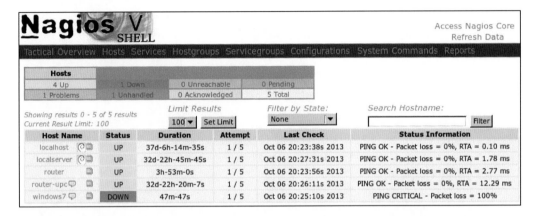

Similarly, the **Services** views also strongly resemble the original Nagios web interface.

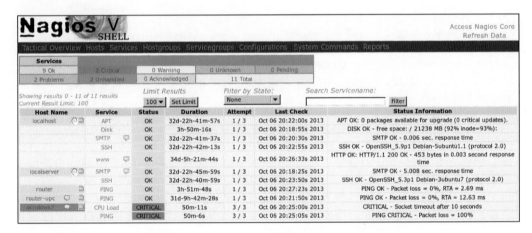

Nagios V-Shell provides views for most of the options available in the standard web interface. It also uses JavaScript for many operations, which makes it faster than the standard web interface. This is especially important for mobile devices that often have slower network connectivity.

Summary

Being able to view the status of your infrastructure from a web browser is a great functionality. Combined with an SSL-enabled web server or using VPN, it can allow people in your company to check the status of the entire network from any location in the world.

A large number of views can aid you in finding out what the root cause of your problem is. You can view objects by their groups as well as individual hosts and services.

There are also views for problems related to hosts and services that only show direct causes of problems, and skip issues that arose due to problems with other hosts or services.

The web interface also allows you to modify how Nagios behaves. It can also be used to configure individual hosts and services. You can also schedule host and service checks at a specified time. For example, you can use this to check whether the changes that your team has performed will resolve current problems.

The web interface also allows scheduling and managing host and service downtimes. You can also read, place, and manage comments associated with all objects.

The look and feel of the web UI can be customized to suit the needs of you and your company; different themes can be applied, and the company logo (and many other aspects of it) can be changed.

There are also several alternative web interfaces available to Nagios, providing dashboards for clear reporting of statuses and more complex and complete alternatives to the standard Nagios interface. Dashboards can be shown on large screens, such as HD TVs, to have a convenient view of the IT infrastructure. The alternatives to Nagios can replace the web interface or provide a better experience on mobile devices.

Getting to know the web interface is really essential in order to use Nagios effectively, and it is recommended that you spend some time getting familiar with it.

Now that we have learned both the Nagios service and its web interface, we can move on to set up a more complete monitoring system. The next chapter provides an overview of the standard Nagios plugins and how they can be used to monitor various types of hosts and services.

Using the Nagios Plugins

4

The previous chapter discussed the basic configuration of host and service checking. Nagios can be set up to check if your services are up and running. This chapter describes in detail how these checks work. It also introduces some of the Nagios plugins that are developed as a part of Nagios and as a part of the Nagios plugins project.

Nagios' strength comes from its ability to monitor servers and the services that they offer in a large number of ways. What's more interesting is that all of these ways make sure that your services are functional, external plugins, and work in quite an easy way. Many of these are even shipped with Nagios, as we mentioned in *Chapter 2, Installing Nagios 4*. Therefore, it is possible to either existing plugins or write your own. In this chapter, we will learn the checks that can be made using the Nagios plugins project, and we will cover the following:

- Using the standard checks for the host that is alive, and basic TCP/UDP checks
- Checking e-mail services, such as POP3, IMAP, and SMTP
- Monitoring network services, such as FTP, DHCP, and websites and checking Nagios itself
- Checking database systems
- Monitoring hard drives and network sharing
- Checking system information
- Additional and third-party plugins

Understanding how checks work

Nagios performs checks by running an external command, and uses the return code along with output from the command as information on whether the check worked or not. It is the command's responsibility to verify if a host or service is working at the time the command is invoked.

Nagios itself handles all of the internals, such as scheduling the commands to be run, storing their results, and determining the status of each host and service.

Nagios requires that all plugins follow a specific, easy-to-follow behavior in order for them to work smoothly. These rules are common for both host checks and service checks. It requires that each command returns specific result codes, which are shown in the following table:

Exit code	Status	Description
0	OK	Working correctly
1	WARNING	Working, but needs attention (for example, low resources)
2	CRITICAL	Not working correctly or requires attention
3	UNKNOWN	Plugin was unable to determine the status for the host or service

Standard output from the command is not parsed in any way by Nagios. It is usually formatted in the following way:

```
PLUGIN STATUS - status description
```

Usually, the status description contains human-readable information that is visible using the web interface. Some sample outputs from various plugins and states are as follows:

```
PING OK - Packet loss = 0%, RTA = 0.18 ms
DNS WARNING: 0.015 seconds response time
DISK CRITICAL - free space: /boot 18 MB (8% inode=99%)
```

Nagios plugins use options for their configuration. It is up to the plugin author's host to parse these options. However, most commands that come as part of the Nagios plugins package use standard options and support the`-h` or `--help` options to provide a full description of all the arguments they accept. Standard Nagios plugins usually accept the following parameters:

Option	Description
-h, --help	This provides help
-V, --version	This prints the exact version of the plugin
-v, --verbose	This makes the plugin give a more detailed information on what it is doing
-t, --timeout	This provides the timeout (in seconds); after this time, the plugin will report CRITICAL status
-w, --warning	This provides the plugin-specific limits for the WARNING status
-c, --critical	This provides the plugin-specific limits for the CRITICAL status
-H, --hostname	This provides the hostname, IP address, or Unix socket to communicate with
-4, --use-ipv4	This lets you use IPv4 for network connectivity
-6, --use-ipv6	This lets you use IPv6 for network connectivity

Commands that verify various daemons also have a common set of options. Many of the networking-related plugins use the following options in addition to the preceding standard ones:

Option	Description
-p, --port	This is used to connect to the TCP or UDP port
-w, --warning	This provides the response time that will issue a WARNING status (seconds)
-c, --critical	This provides the response time that will issue a CRITICAL status (seconds)
-s, --send	This provides the string that will be sent to the server
-e, --expect	This provides the string that should be sent back from the server (option might be passed several times; see `--all` for details)

Option	Description
-q, --quit	This provides the string to send to the server to close the connection
-A, --all	In case multiple --expect parameters are passed, this option indicates that all responses need to be received; if this option is not present, at least one matching result indicates a success
-m, --maxbytes	This specifies the maximum number of bytes to read when expecting a string to be sent back from the server; after this number of bytes, a mismatch is assumed
-d, --delay	This provides the delay in seconds between sending a string to server and expecting a response
-r, --refuse	This provides the status that should be indicated in case the connection is refused (ok, warn, crit; defaults to crit)
-M	This provides the status in case the expected answer is not returned by the server (ok, warn, crit; defaults to warn)
-j, --jail	Do not return output from the server in plugin output text
-D, --certificate	The number of days that the SSL certificate must still be valid; requires --ssl
-S, --ssl	Connect using the SSL encryption
-E, --escape	Allows using \n, \r, \t, or \\ to send or quit string; must be passed before the --send or --quit option

The option names are case sensitive. For many plugins, there are options that have their abbreviated name the same, but with different cases. For example, both -e and -E as well as -m and -M are valid options for most of the plugins. It is important to distinguish lowercase and uppercase options.

All of the commands support the --verbose option (or -v for short variant of it) that will print out useful information about the test. It is recommended to add the -v option whenever you run into issues with getting a plugin to work.

This chapter describes the commands provided by a standard distribution Nagios plugin and is based on Version 1.4.16. Before using specific options for a command, it is recommended that you use the --help option and familiarize yourself with the functionality available on your Nagios installation.

All plugins have their nonstandard options, which are described in more detail in this chapter. All commands described in this chapter also have a sample configuration for the Nagios check command. Even though some longer definitions might span multiple lines, please make sure that you put it on a single line in your configuration. Some of the plugins already have their command counterparts configured with the sample Nagios configuration that is installed along with Nagios. Therefore, it is also worth checking if your command's .cfg file contains a definition for a particular command.

Monitoring using the standard network plugins

One of the basic roles of a plugin is to monitor local or remote hosts and verify if they are working correctly. There is a choice of generic plugins to accomplish this task.

Standard networking plugins allow hosts to be monitored using ICMP ECHO (refer to http://en.wikipedia.org/wiki/Ping). This is used to determine whether a computer is responding to IP requests. It is also used to measure the time that a machine takes to respond, and how many packages are lost during the communication. These plugins also try to connect to certain TCP/UDP ports. This is used to communicate with various network-based services to make sure that they are working properly, and respond within a defined amount of time.

Testing the connection to a remote host

Checking if a host is alive is a basic test that should be performed for all remote machines. Nagios offers a command that is commonly used for checking if a host is alive and plugged into the network. The syntax of the plugin is as follows:

```
check_ping -H <host_address> -w <wrta>,<wpl>% -c <crta>,<cpl>%
          [-p packets] [-t timeout] [-4|-6]
```

This command accepts the standard options described previously, as well as the following nonstandard options:

Option	Description
-p, --packets	This provides the number of packets to send; defaults to 5
-w, --warning	This gives WARNING status limit in form of RTA and PKTLOSS percentage
-c, --critical	This gives CRITICAL status limit in form of RTA and PKTLOSS percentage

Round Trip Average (RTA) is the average time taken in milliseconds for the package to return. **Packet Loss (PKTLOSS)** is the maximum percentage of packages that can be lost during communication. For example, for a value of 100, 2 percent means that a ping must return within 0.1 seconds on average and at least 4 out of 5 packages have to come back.

A sample command definition for checking if a host is alive is as follows:

```
define command  {
   command_name  check-host-alive
   command_line  $USER1$/check_ping -H $HOSTADDRESS$
                 -w 3000.0,80% -c 5000.0,100% -p 5
}
```

Testing the connectivity using TCP and UDP

In many cases, Nagios is used to monitor services that work over the network. To check if a service is working properly, it is necessary to make sure that a certain TCP or UDP port is accessible over the network. In such cases, the tests are done by connecting to the service periodically using the plugin, and this may cause entries in the system log regarding connection attempts.

For example, Microsoft SQL Server listens on TCP port 1433. In many cases, it is enough to run generic plugins that check whether a service is available on a specified TCP or UDP port. However, it is recommended that you run specialized plugins for various services such as web or e-mail servers, as these commands also try basic communication with the server and/or measure response time.

Internally, as this command is also handling many other checks, the syntax is almost the same. It is designed so that it behaves slightly differently based on its name. Many other plugins are symbolic links to check_tcp. The check_tcp plugin is mainly intended to test services, that do not have a corresponding Nagios check command. The second command check_udp is also a symbolic link to check_tcp, and the only difference is that it communicates over UDP instead of TCP. Its syntax is as follows:

```
check_tcp|check_udp -H host -p port [-w <warning >] [-c <critcal>]
            [-s <send string>] [-e <expect string>]
            [-q <quit string>] [-A] [-m <maximum bytes>]
            [-d <delay>] [-t <timeout>] [-r <refuse state>]
            [-M <mismatch state>] [-v] [-4|-6]
            [-j] [-D <days to cert expiry>] [-S] [-E]
```

These commands accept several nonstandard options as follows:

Option	Description
-p, --port	To helps connect to the TCP or UDP port
-w, --warning	This provides the response time that will issue a WARNING status (in seconds)
-c, --critical	This provides the response time that will issue a CRITICAL status (in seconds)

An example to verify whether VMware server (1.x and 2.x) is listening to connections is as follows:

```
define command
{
  command_name   check_vmware
  command_line   $USER1$/check_tcp -H $HOSTADDRESS$ -p 902
                 -e "220 VMware"
}
```

For UDP, the following is an example command definition to verify if the OpenVPN server is listening on UDP port 1142:

```
define command
{
  command_name   check_openvpn
  command_line   $USER1$/check_udp -H $HOSTADDRESS$ -p 1142
}
```

Monitoring the e-mail servers

Making sure that all e-mail-related services are working correctly is something that each hosting company and intranet administrator needs to perform on a daily basis. In order to do this, Nagios can watch these servers and make sure things are working as expected. This can be done by a remote machine to make sure that the services are accessible, or can be monitored by the same server that offers these services.

Nagios can make sure that the processes are running and waiting for connections. It is also easy to verify whether a predefined user and password pair is working properly to make sure that a custom authorization system is working properly.

This section describes the commands that check e-mail servers using network connectivity. The plugins that verify specific processes on a server can be used to make sure a particular daemon is up and running as well.

Checking the POP3 and IMAP servers

POP3 is a very popular protocol for retrieving e-mail messages from an e-mail client application. It uses TCP port 110 for unencrypted connections and port 995 for SSL-encrypted connections. Nagios offers means to verify both unencrypted and encrypted POP3 connections that can be made. Even though POP3 is the most popular e-mail retrieving protocol, another protocol is also very common. IMAP is a protocol that is used to access e-mails on remote servers rather than download them to the user's computer. It uses TCP port 143 for standard connections and port 993 for encrypted connections over SSL. The following plugins are based on check_tcp (and are actually symbolic links to check_tcp). The syntax is identical to the original plugin:

```
check_pop|check_imap -H host [-p port] [-w <warning>]
        [-c <critical>]   [-s <send string>]
        [-e <expect string>] [-q <quit string>] [-A]
        [-m <maximum bytes>] [-d <delay>]
        [-t <timeout seconds>] [-r <refuse state>]
        [-M <mismatch state>] [-v] [-4|-6] [-j]
        [-D <days to cert expiry>] [-S] [-E]
```

The only difference between this plugin and the standard command is that the port parameter can be omitted for this plugin, and in this case, a default value for both non-SSL and SSL variants is chosen. In order to enable connection over SSL, either pass the --ssl option, or invoke the command as check_spop instead of check_pop and check_simap instead of check_imap.

The following are sample command definitions that check for a daemon listening on a specified host and verify that a valid POP3 and IMAP welcome message can be retrieved:

```
define command
{
  command_name   check_pop
  command_line   $USER1$/check_pop -H $HOSTADDRESS$
}
define command
{
  command_name   check_imap
  command_line   $USER1$/check_imap -H $HOSTADDRESS$
}
```

However, it seems more useful to verify the actual functionality of the server. It is therefore reasonable also to verify that a predefined username and password is accepted by our POP3 daemon. In order to do that, the example uses -E to escape the newline characters: -s to send commands that authenticate and -e to verify that the user has actually been logged in. Additionally, the -d option is passed to indicate that the command should wait a couple of seconds before analyzing the output. If this option is not passed, the command will return after the first line. The following examples should work with any POP3/IMAP server, but it may be necessary to customize the response for your particular environment:

```
define command
{
   command_name   check_pop3login
   command_line   $USER1$/check_pop -H $HOSTADDRESS$ -E
                  -s "USER $ARG1$\r\nPASS $ARG2$\r\n" -d 5
                  -e "ogged in"
}
define command
{
   command_name   check_imaplogin
   command_line   $USER1$/check_imap -H $HOSTADDRESS$ -E
                  -s "pr01 LOGIN $ARG1 $ARG2$\r\n" -d 5
                  -e "pr01 OK"
}
```

The value that is passed in the -s option is a string with two lines for POP3 and one line for IMAP4. Each line ends with a newline character (\r\n) that are sent as newline characters due to using the -E option.

For POP3, these lines are standard protocol commands to log into an account. The POP3 server should then issue a response stating that the user is authenticated, and this is what the command is expecting to receive because of the -e option. In addition, $ARG1$ and $ARG2$ will be replaced with a username and a password that is supplied in a service check definition, which allows different usernames and passwords to be specified for different checks.

With IMAP4, there is only a slight difference in the protocol dialect. IMAP requires the sending of only a single LOGIN command in order to authenticate. As for POP3, $ARG1$ and $ARG2$ will be replaced with a username and password. In this way, it is possible to set up checks for different users and passwords with a single command definition. The pr01 string can be replaced by any other text without spaces. It is necessary with the IMAP4 protocol to bind requests with answers provided by the server.

Testing the SMTP protocol

Simple Mail Transfer Protocol (SMTP) is a protocol for sending e-mails—both from a client application as well as between e-mail servers. Therefore, monitoring it is also very important from the point of view of availability.

Nagios standard plugins offer a command to check whether an SMTP server is listening. Unlike checks for POP3 and IMAP, the command is available only for this particular protocol; therefore, the options are a bit different:

```
check_smtp -H host [-p port] [-C command] [-R response]
           [-e expect] [-f from addr] [-F hostname]
           [-A authtype -U authuser -P authpass]
           [-w <warning time>] [-c <critical time>]
           [-t timeout] [-S] [-D days] [-n] [-4|-6]
```

The plugin accepts most of the standard options; additional ones are as follows:

Option	Description
-C, --command	This provides the SMTP command to execute on the server (option might be repeated)
-R, --response	This provides the response to expect from the server (option might be repeated)
-f, --from	This attempts to set from where the e-mail is originating
-F, --fqdn	This provides the fully-qualified domain name to send during SMTP greeting (defaults to the local hostname if not specified)
-S, --starttls	This lets you use STARTTLS to initialize connection over SMTP

The port can be omitted and defaults to 25. In this case, the -s option also behaves a bit differently, and it uses the STARTTLS function of SMTP servers instead of connecting directly over SSL. A basic SMTP check command definition looks like the following:

```
define command
{
   command_name   check_smtp
   command_line   $USER1$/check_smtp -H $HOSTADDRESS$
}
```

Most of these options are similar to the standard send/expect parameters in the way they work. Therefore, it is quite easy to create a more complex definition that verifies the sending of e-mails to a specific address:

```
define command
{
   command_name   check_smtpsend
   command_line   $USER1$/check_smtp -H $HOSTADDRESS$
                  -f "$ARG1$" -C "RCPT TO:<$ARG2$>" -R "250"
}
```

This check will attempt to send an e-mail from $ARG1$ to $ARG2$, which will be passed from a check definition. Also, it expects to receive a return code 250, which indicates that no error has occurred.

Monitoring network services

Nagios also offers plugins that monitor different network services. These include commands for checking FTP, DHCP protocol, and WWW servers. It is also possible for Nagios to monitor itself.

Checking the FTP server

Nagios allows you to verify whether an FTP server is listening for connections by using the check_ftp command. This plugin is identical to check_tcp, with the difference that the port is optional. By default, a valid FTP welcome message is expected.

```
check_ftp -H host [-p port] [-w <warning time>]
          [-c <critical time>] [-s <send string>]
```

```
[-e <expect string>] [-q <quit string>]
[-A] [-m <maximum bytes>] [-d <delay>]
[-t <timeout seconds>] [-r <refuse state>]
[-M <mismatch state>] [-v] [-4|-6] [-j]
[-D <days to cert expiry>] [-S] [-E]
```

The port argument can be omitted and defaults to 21, or 990 for SSL-based connections. A sample command definition for checking FTP accepting connections is as follows:

```
define command
{
  command_name  check_ftp
  command_line  $USER1$/check_ftp -H $HOSTADDRESS$
}
```

By using the -s and -e flags, it is also possible to verify if a specified username and password is allowed to log in:

```
define command
{
  command_name  check_ftplogin
  command_line  $USER1$/check_ftp -H $HOSTADDRESS$ -E
                -s "USER $ARG1$\r\nPASS $ARG2$\r\n" -d 5
                -e "230"
}
```

This example is quite similar to POP3 authentication as the commands are the same. The only difference is that the requested response is 230 as this is a code for a successful response to the PASS command.

Verifying the DHCP protocol

If your network has a server or a router that provides the users with IP addresses via DHCP, it would be wise to make sure that this server is also working correctly. Nagios offers a plugin that attempts to request an IP address via a DHCP protocol, which can be used for this purpose. The syntax is a bit different from other plugins:

```
check_dhcp [-v] [-u] [-s serverip] [-r requestedip] [-t timeout]
           [-i interface] [-m mac]
```

This command accepts the options described in the following table:

Option	Description
-s, --serverip	This provides the IP of the server that needs to reply with an IP (option might be repeated)
-r, --requestedip	This indicates that at least one DHCP server needs to offer the specified IP address
-m, --mac	This provides the MAC address that should be used in the DHCP request
-i, --interface	This provides the name of the interface that is to be used for checking (for example eth0)
-u, --unicast	Unicast, for testing a DHCP relay request; this requires -s

Options for DHCP checking are very powerful—they can be used to check if any server is responding to the DHCP requests, for example:

```
define command
{
    command_name   check_dhcp
    command_line   $USER1$/check_dhcp
}
```

This plugin can also be used, as shown in the following command snippet, to verify if specific servers work, if a specified MAC address will receive an IP address, if a specific IP address is returned, or a combination of these checks:

```
define command
{
    command_name   check_dhcp_mac
    command_line   $USER1$/check_dhcp -s $HOSTADDRESS$
                -m $ARG1$ -r $ARG2$
}
```

This check will ensure that a specific machine provides a specific IP for requesting a specific MAC address. This allows checks to be created for specific DHCP rules. This is crucial in the case of networks that need to provide specific devices with IP addresses, which other services depend.

It is also worth noting that such tests are safe from a network's perspective as the IP received from the server is not acknowledged by the Nagios plugin. Therefore, a check for a specific MAC address can be done even if a network card with the same address is currently connected. DHCP works over broadcast IP requests, and therefore, it is not recommended that you set up testing of this service often it might cause excessive traffic for larger networks.

Monitoring the Nagios process

It is possible for Nagios to monitor whether it is running on the local machine. This works by checking the Nagios log file for recent entries, as well as reading the output from the ps system command to ensure that the Nagios daemon is currently running. This plugin is mainly used in combination with NRPE or SSH, which are described in more detail in *Chapter 8, Monitoring Remote Hosts*. However, it can also be deployed to check the same Nagios that is scheduling the command, mainly to make sure that the log files contain recent entries. The syntax and options are as follows:

```
check_nagios -F <status log file> -e <expire_minutes>
             -C <process_string>
```

Option	Description
-F, --filename	This provides the IP address of the server that needs to reply with an IP (option might be repeated)
-e, --expires	This provides the number of minutes after which the log file is assumed to be stale
-C, --command	This provides the command or partial command to search for in the process list

All of the arguments listed previously are required. The check for the --expires option is done by comparing the date and time of the latest entry in the log with the current date and time. The log file is usually called nagios.log and is stored in the directory that was passed in the --localstatedir option during the Nagios compilation. For an installation performed according to the steps given in *Chapter 2, Installing Nagios 4*, the path will be /var/nagios/nagios.log. The Nagios process for such a setup would be /opt/nagios/bin/nagios. An example definition of a command receiving all of the information as arguments is as follows:

```
define command
{
  command_name   check_nagios
  command_line   $USER1$/check_nagios -F $ARG1$ -C $ARG2$
                 -e $ARG3$
}
```

The first argument is the path to the log file, the second is the path to the Nagios daemon binary, and the last one is the maximum acceptable number of minutes since the last log updated.

Testing the websites

Making sure that the websites are up and running 24/7 is vital to many large companies. Verifying that the returned pages contain correct data may be even more important for companies conducting e-commerce. Nagios offers plugins to verify that a web server works. It can also make sure that your SSL certificate is still valid and checks the contents of specific pages to verify that they contain specific text. This command accepts various parameters, which are as follows:

```
check_http -H <vhost> | -I <IP-address> [-u <uri>]
           [-p <port>] [-w <warning time>]
           [-c <critical time>] [-t <timeout>]
           [-L] [-a auth] [-b proxy_auth]
           [-f <ok | warn | critcal | follow>]
           [-e <expect>] [-s string] [-l]
           [-r <regex> | -R <regex>] [-j method]
           [-P string] [-m <min_pg_size>:<max_pg_size>]
           [-4|-6] [-N] [-M <age>] [-A string]
           [-k string] [-S] [--sni]
           [-C <age>] [-T <content-type>]
```

The following table lists the options that differ from their usual behavior, or are not common in other commands:

Option	Description
-H, --hostname	This provides the hostname that should be used for the host HTTP header; the port might be appended, so it is also present in the http header
-I, --IP-address	This provides the IP address to which to connect; if not specified, --hostname is used
-u, --url	This provides the URL to GET or POST (defaults to /)
-j, --method	To use the HTTP method such as GET, HEAD, POST, PUT, DELETE
-P, --post	This will post the encoded HTTP via POST; content is specified as argument
-N, --no-body	Do not wait for the document, only parse the HTTP headers

Option	Description
-M, --max-age	Warn if the document is older than the number of seconds provided; this parameter can also be specified as 15m for minutes, 8h for hours, or 7d for days
-T, --content-type	Specify the http Content-Type header
-e, --expect	The text to expect in the first line of the http response; If specified, the plugin will not handle status code logic (that is, it won't warn about 404)
-s, --string	Search for the specified text in result HTML
-r, --ereg	Search for a specified regular expression in HTML (case sensitive)
-R, --eregi	Search for a specified regular expression in HTML (case insensitive)
-l, --linespan	Allow the regular expression to span across new lines
--invert-regex	Return a state of CRITICAL if the text is found, and OK if it is not found
-a, --authorization	Authorize the page using the basic authentication type; must be passed in the form of <username>:<password>
-b, --proxy-authorization	Authorization for the proxy server; must be passed in the form of <username>:<password>
-A, --useragent	Pass the specified value as the User-Agent http header
-k, --header	Add other parameters to be sent in http header (might be repeated)
-f, --onredirect	How to handle redirects, such as ok, warning, critical, follow
-m, --pagesize	The minimum and maximum HTML page sizes in bytes; as <min>:<max>
-C, --certificate	Specifies how long the certificate has to be valid in days; should be in form of critical_days or critical_days,warning_days
--sni	**Server Name Indication (SNI)** enables SSL/TLS hostname extension support; this allows verification of the SSL-enabled websites with multiple sites on a single IP address

For example, to verify if a main page has at least the specified number of bytes and is returned promptly, the following check can be done:

```
define command
{
   command_name   check_http_basic
   command_line   $USER1$/check_http -H $HOSTADDRESS$ -f follow
                  -m $ARG1$:1000000 -w $ARG2$ -c $ARG3$
}
```

More complex tests of the WWW infrastructure should be carried out frequently. For example, to verify if an SSL-enabled page works correctly and quickly, a more complex test might be required. The following command will verify the SSL certificate and the page size, and it will look for a specific string in the page body:

```
define command
{
   command_name   check_https
   command_line   $USER1$/check_http -H $HOSTADDRESS$ -S -C 14 -u
                  $ARG1$ -f follow -m $ARG1$:$ARG2$ -R $ARG3$
}
```

Checking web pages at a higher level is described in more detail in *Chapter 11, Programming Nagios*, and it uses the custom-written plugins for this purpose.

Monitoring the database systems

Databases allow the storage of information that is used often by entire departments or whole companies. Because most systems usually depend on one or more databases, a failure in these databases can cause all of the underlying systems to go down as well. Imagine a business-critical database failure that went unnoticed over a weekend, making both the company's website as well as e-mail, unavailable. That would be a disaster! A series of scheduled reports that was supposed to be sent out would fail to be generated because of this.

This is why making sure that databases are working correctly and have enough resources to operate might be essential for many companies. Many enterprise-class databases also have table space capacity management that should also be monitored—even though a valid user may be able to log in, this does not necessarily mean that a database is up and running correctly.

Checking MySQL

One of the most commonly used database types is MySQL. It is very often used to provide a basic database for PHP-based web applications. It is also commonly used as a database system for the client-server applications. Nagios offers two plugins to verify if MySQL is working properly. One of the plugins allows checking of connectivity to the database and checking master-slave replication status.
The other one allows the measurement of the time taken to execute an SQL query. The syntax of both the commands, and the definition of their options is as follows:

```
check_mysql [-H host] [-d database] [-P port] [-s socket]
            [-u user] [-p password] [-S]


check_mysql_query -q SQL_query [-w <warn>] [-c <crit>]
                  [-d database] [-H host] [-P port] [-s socket]
                  [-u user] [-p password]
```

Option	Description
-s, --socket	This provides the Unix socket to use for connection, used if -H option was not specified; does not need to be customized in most cases
-P, --port	This provides the port to use for connections (defaults to 3306)
-d, --database	This provides the database to which an attempt to connect is to be made
-u, --username	This provides the username to log in
-p, --password	This provides password to log in
-S, --check-slave	This verifies that the slave thread is running (check_mysql only); this is used for monitoring replicated databases
-w, --warning	This specifies the warning threshold, which is dependent on the plugin used
-c, --critical	This specifies the critical threshold, which is dependent on the plugin used
-q, --query	Query to perform (check_mysql_query only)

For the check_mysql_query command, the -w and -c options specify the limits for the execution time of the specified SQL query. This allows us to make sure that the database performance is within acceptable limits.

The definitions of the check commands for both a simple test and running an SQL query within a specified time are as follows.

```
define command
{
  command_name   check_mysql
  command_line   $USER1$/check_mysql –H $HOSTADDRESS$ –u $ARG1$
                 –p $ARG2$ –d $ARG3$ –S –w 10 –c 30
}
define command
{
  command_name   check_mysql_query
  command_line   $USER1$/check_mysql_query –H $HOSTADDRESS$ –u
                 $ARG1$ –p $ARG2$ –d $ARG3$ –q $ARG4$ –w $ARG5$
                 –c $ARG6$
}
```

Both the examples need username, password, and database name as arguments. The second example also requires an SQL query, warning, and critical time limits.

If the -S option is specified, the plugin will also check whether the replication of MySQL databases is working correctly. This check should be run on the MySQL slave servers to make sure that the replication with the master server is in place. Monitoring the number of seconds by which the slave server is behind the master server can be done using the -w and –c flags. In this case, if the slave server is more than the specified number of seconds behind the master server in the replication process, a `warning` or `critical` status is issued. More information about checking the replication status can be found under the MySQL documentation for the SHOW SLAVE STATUS command (visit http://dev.mysql.com/doc/refman/5.0/en/show-slave-status.html).

Checking PostgreSQL

PostgreSQL is another open source database that is commonly used in hosting companies. It is also used very often for client-server applications. The Nagios plugins package offers a command to check if the PostgreSQL database is working correctly. Its syntax is quite similar to the MySQL command:

```
check_pgsql [-H <host>] [-P <port>] [-w <warn>] [-c <crit>]
            [-t <timeout>] [-d <database>] [-l <logname>]
            [-p <password>]
```

The following table describes the options that this plugin accepts:

Option	Description
-P, --port	This provides the port to use for connections (defaults to 5432)
-d, --database	This is used to connect to the database
-l, --logname	This provides the username to log in
-p, --password	This provides the password to log in

A sample check command that expects username, password, and database name as arguments is as follows:

```
define command
{
  command_name   check_pgsql
  command_line   $USER1$/check_pgsql –H $HOSTADDRESS$ -l $ARG1$
                 -p $ARG2$ -d $ARG3$
}
```

Checking Oracle

Oracle is a popular enterprise-level database server. It is mainly used by medium- and large-sized companies for business-critical applications. Therefore, a failure, or even a lack of disk space, for a single database might cause huge problems for a company. Fortunately, a plugin exists to verify the various aspects of the Oracle database. And it even offers the ability to monitor tablespace storage and cache usage. The syntax is quite different from most Nagios plugins, as the first argument specifies the mode in which the check should be carried out and the remaining parameters are dependent on the first one. The syntax is as follows:

```
check_oracle --tns <SID>
             --db <SID>
             --oranames <Hostname>
             --login <SID>
             --cache <SID> <USER> <PASS> <CRITICAL> <WARNING>
             --tablespace < SID> <USER> <PASS>
                     <TABLESPACE> <CRITICAL> <WARNING>
```

For all checks, Oracle **System Identifier (SID)** can be specified in the form of `<ip>` or `<ip>/<database>`. Because the plugin automatically adds the username and password to the identifier, an SID in the form of `<username>[/<password>]@<ip>[/<database>]` should not be specified, and it will not work in many cases.

The `--tns` option checks if a database is listening for a connection based on the `tnsping` command. This can be used as a basic check of both local and remote databases. Verifying that a local database is running can be done using the `--db` option — in which case, a check is performed by running the Oracle process for a specified database. Verifying a remote Oracle Names server can be done using the `--oranames` mode.

In order to verify if a database is working properly, a `--login` option can be used — this tries to log in using an invalid username and verifies whether the `ORA-01017` error is received; in which case, the database is behaving correctly.

Verifying cache usage can be done using the `--cache` option; in which case, the cache hit ratio is checked. If it is lower than the specified warning or critical limits, the respective status is returned. This allows the monitoring of bottlenecks within the database caching mechanism.

Similarly, for tablespace checking, a `--tablespace` option is provided. A check is carried out against the available storage for the specified tablespace. If it is lower than the specified limits, a warning or critical status is returned (as appropriate).

This plugin requires various Oracle commands to be in the binary path (the `PATH` environment variable). Therefore, it is necessary to have either the entire Oracle installation or the Oracle client installation done on the machine that will perform the checks for the Oracle database. Sample definitions to check the login into the Oracle database and the database cache are as follows:

```
define command
{
   command_name   check_oracle_login
   command_line   $USER1$/check_oracle --login $HOSTADDRESS$
}
define command
{
   command_name   check_oracle_tablespace
   command_line   $USER1$/check_oracle --cache
                  $HOSTADDRESS$/$ARG1$
                  $ARG2$ $ARG3$ $ARG4$ $ARG5$
}
```

The second example requires the passing of the database name, username, password, and critical/warning limits for the cache hit ratio. The critical value should be lower than the warning value.

Checking other databases

Even though Nagios supports verification of some common databases, there are a lot of commonly-used databases for which the standard Nagios plugins package does not provide a plugin. For these databases, the first thing worth checking is the Nagios Exchange (visit `http://exchange.nagios.org/`) as this has a category for database check plugins, with commands for checking various types of databases (such as DB2, Ingres, Firebird, MS SQL, and Sybase).

In some cases, it might be sufficient to use the `check_tcp` plugin to verify whether a database server is up and running. In other cases, it might be possible to use a dynamic language (such as Python, Perl, or Tcl) to write a small script that connects to your database and performs basic tests. See *Chapter 11, Programming Nagios*, for more information on writing the Nagios check plugins.

Monitoring the storage space

Making sure that a system is not running out of space is very important. A lack of disk space for the basic paths such as `/var/spool`, or `/tmp` might cause unexpected results throughout the entire system, such as applications failing due to not being able to write temporary files or local e-mail not being delivered due to lack of disk space. Quotas that are not properly set up for home directories might also cause disk space to run out in a few minutes under certain circumstances.

Nagios can monitor storage space and warn administrators before such problems happen. It is also possible to monitor remote shares on other disks without mounting them. This would be useful for easily monitoring disk space on Windows boxes, without installing the dedicated Windows Nagios tools described in *Chapter 10, Advanced Monitoring*.

Checking the swap space

Making sure that a system is not running out of swap space is essential to the system's correct behavior. Many operating systems have mechanisms that kill the most resource-intensive processes when the system is running out of memory, and this usually leads to many services not functioning properly—many vital processes are not properly respawned in such cases. It is therefore a good idea to monitor swap space usage in order to be able to handle low memory issues on critical systems.

Nagios offers a plugin to monitor each swap device independently, as well as the ability to monitor cumulative values. The syntax and description of these options are as follows:

```
check_swap [-a] [-v] -w limit -c limit
```

Option	Description
-a, --all	This compares all swap partitions one by one; if not specified, only total swap sizes are checked.

Values for the -w and -c options can be supplied in the form of <value>%, in which case the <value> percent must be free in order not to cause an exception to be generated. They can also be supplied in the form <value><unit> (for example, 1000k, 100M, 1G), and in this case, a test fails if less than the specified amount of swap space is available. A sample definition of a check is as follows:

```
define command
{
    command_name   check_swap
    command_line   $USER1$/check_swap -w $ARG1$ -c $ARG2$
}
```

Monitoring the disk status using SMART

Nagios offers a standard plugin that uses **Self-Monitoring, Analysis, and Reporting Technology Syste) (SMART)** technology to monitor and report the failure of disk operations. This plugin operates on top of the SMART mechanism and verifies the status of local hard drives. If supported by the underlying IDE and SCSI hardware. This plugin allows the monitoring of hard disk failures. The syntax is as follows:

```
check_ide_smart [-d <device>] [-i] [-q] [-1] [-O] [-n]
```

The following table provides a description of the accepted options:

Option	Description
-d, --device	The device to verify; if this option is set, no other options are accepted
-i, --immediate	Perform offline tests immediately
-q, --quick-check	Return the number of failed tests
-1, --auto-on	Enable automatic offline tests
-O, --auto-off	Disable automatic offline tests
-n, --nagios	Return output suitable for Nagios

A sample definition of a command to monitor a particular device and report failed tests is as follows:

```
define command
{
  command_name  check_ide_smart
  command_line  $USER1$/check_ide_smart -d $ARG1$ -1 -q -n
}
```

Checking the disk space

One of the most common checks is checking one or more mounted partitions for available space. Nagios offers a plugin for doing this. This plugin offers very powerful functionality and can be set up to monitor one, several, or all partitions mounted on a system. The syntax for the plugin is as follows:

```
check_disk -w limit -c limit [-W limit] [-K limit]
           {-p path | -x device} [-C] [-E] [-e]
           [-g group] [-k] [-l] [-M] [-m] [-R path ]
           [-r path] [-t timeout] [-u unit] [-v] [-X type]
```

The most commonly used options for this plugin are described in the following table:

Option	Description
-w, --warning	This returns a warning status if less than the specified percentage of disk space is free
-c, --critical	Return a critical if less than the specified percentage of disk space is free
-W, --iwarning	Return a warning if less than the specified percentage of inodes are free
-K, --icritical	Return a critical if less than specified percentage of inodes are free
-p, --path	The path or partition to verify (option might be specified multiple times)
-M, --mountpoint	Display the mount point instead of the partition in the result
-l, --local	Check only local file systems
-A, --all	Verify all mount points
-r, --ereg-path	Regular expression to find paths/partitions (case sensitive)
-R, --eregi-path	Regular expression to find paths/partitions (case insensitive)

Values for the -w and -c options can be supplied in the form of <value>%, in which case <value> percent must be free in order not to cause a state to occur. They can also be specified in the form of <value><unit> (for example, 800k, 50M, and 4G); in which case, a test fails if the available space is less than the specified amount. Checks for inode availability (options -W and -K) can only be specified in the form of <value>.

It is possible to check a single partition or specify multiple -p, -r, or -R options, and it is also possible to check if all the matching mount points have sufficient disk space. It is sometimes better to define separate checks for each partition so that if the limits are exceeded on several of these, each one is tracked separately. The sample check commands for a single partition and for all partitions are shown in the following examples:

```
define command
{
  command_name   check_partition
  command_line   $USER1$/check_disk -p $ARG1$ -w $ARG2$ -c $ARG3$
}
define command
{
  command_name   check_local_partitions
  command_line   $USER1$/check_disk -A -l -w $ARG1$ -c $ARG2$
}
```

Both of these commands expect warning and critical levels, but the first example also requires a partition path or device as the first argument. It is possible to build more complex checks either by repeating the -p parameter or by using -r to include several mount points.

Testing the free space for remote shares

Nagios offers plugins that allow the monitoring of remote file systems exported over the SMB/CIFS protocol, the standard protocol for file sharing used by Microsoft Windows. This allows you to check whether a specified user is able to log on to a particular file server and monitor the amount of free disk space on the file server. The syntax of this command is as follows:

```
check_disk_smb -H <host> -s <share> -u <user> -p <password>
               -w <warn> -c <crit> [-W <workgroup>] [-P <port>]
```

Options specific to this plugin are described in the following table:

Option	Description
-s, --share	The SMB share that should be tested
-u, --user	The username to log in to the server (defaults to guest)
-p, --password	The password to use for logging in
-P, --port	The port to be used for connections; defaults to 139

Values for the -w and -c options can be specified in the form <value>%, in which case the <value> percent must be free in order to avoid generating an exception. They can also be specified in the form of <value><unit> (for example, 800k, 50M, and 4G); in which case, the test fails if the available space is less than the specified amount

This command uses the smbclient command to communicate over the SMB protocol. It is therefore necessary to have the Samba client package installed on the machine where the test will be run. Sample command definitions to check connectivity to a share without checking for disk space and also to verify disk space over SMB are as follows:

```
define command
{
   command_name   check_smb_connect
   command_line   $USER1$/check_disk_smb –H $HOSTADDRESS$ -w 100%
                  -c 100% -u $ARG1$ -p $ARG2$ -s $ARG3$
}
define command
{
   command_name   check_smb_space
   command_line   $USER1$/check_disk_smb –H $HOSTADDRESS$
                  -u $ARG1$ -p $ARG2$ -s $ARG3$ -w $ARG4$ -c $ARG5$
}
```

Both of the commands require the passing of a username, password, and share name as arguments. The latter example also requires the passing of warning and critical value limits that should be checked. The first example will only issue a critical state if a partition has no space left. It is also worth noting that Samba 3.x servers report quota as disk space, if this is enabled for the specified user. Therefore, this might not always be an accurate way to measure disk space.

Monitoring the resources

For servers or workstations to be responsive and to be kept from being overloaded, it is also worth monitoring system usage using various additional measures. Nagios offers several plugins to monitor resource usage and to report if the limits set for these checks are exceeded.

Checking the system load

The first thing that should always be monitored is the system load, and it is calculated based on count of processes running or waiting to run. This value reflects the number of processes and the amount of CPU capacity that they are utilizing. This means that if one process is using up to 50 percent of the CPU capacity, the value will be around 0.5. And if four processes try to utilize the maximum CPU capacity, the value will be around 4.0. The system load is measured in three values: the average loads in the last minute, last 5 minutes, and the last 15 minutes. The syntax of the command is as follows:

```
check_load [-r] -w wload1,wload5,wload15 -c cload1,cload5,cload15
```

Option	Description
-r, --percpu	Divide the load averages by the number of CPUs

Values for the -w and -c options should be in the form of three values separated by commas. If any of the load averages exceeds the specified limits, a warning, or critical status will be returned, respectively. Here is a sample command definition that uses warning and critical load limits as arguments:

```
define command
{
  command_name  check_load
  command_line  $USER1$/check_load -w $ARG1$ -c $ARG2$
}
```

Checking the processes

Nagios processes also offer a way to monitor the total number of processes. Nagios can be configured to monitor all processes, only running ones, those consuming CPU, those consuming memory, or a combination of these criteria. The syntax and options are as follows:

```
check_procs -w <range> -c <range> [-m metric] [-s state]
            [-p ppid] [-u user] [-r rss] [-z vsz] [-P %cpu]
            [-a argument-array] [-C command] [-t timeout] [-v]
```

Option	Description
-m, --metric	Select one of the following values for use:
	PROCS: Number of processes (the default)
	VSZ: Virtual memory size of the matching process
	RSS: Resident set memory size of the matching process
	CPU: Percentage CPU time of the matching process
	ELAPSED: Time elapsed in seconds of the matching process
-s, --state	Only check processes that have the specified status; this is the same as the status in the ps command
-p, --ppid	Check the children of the indicated process IDs
-z, --vsz	Check processes with a virtual memory size exceeding value
-r, --rss	Check processes with the resident set memory exceeding value
-P, --pcpu	Check processes with the CPU usage exceeding value
-u, --user	Check processes owned by a specified user
-a, --argument-array	Check processes whose arguments contain a specified value
-C, --command	Check processes with exact matches of the specified value as a command

Values for the -w and -c options can either take a single value or take the form of <min>:<max>. In the first case, a warning or critical state is returned if the value (number of processes by default) exceeds the specified number. In the second case, the appropriate status is returned if the value is lower than <min> or higher than <max>. Sample commands to monitor the total number of processes and to monitor the number of specific processes are as follows. The second code, for example, can be used to check if the specific server is running and has not created too many processes. In this case, warning or critical values should be specified ranging from 1.

```
define command
{
  command_name   check_procs_num
  command_line   $USER1$/check_procs -m PROCS -w $ARG1$ -c $ARG2$
}
define command
{
  command_name   check_procs_cmd
  command_line   $USER1$/check_procs -C $ARG1$ -w $ARG1$ -c $ARG2$
}
```

Monitoring the logged-in users

It is also possible to use Nagios to monitor the number of users currently logged in to a particular machine. The syntax is very simple, and there are no options, except the warning and critical limits.

```
check_users -w limit -c limit
```

A command definition that uses the warning or critical limits specified in the arguments is as follows:

```
define command
{
  command_name   check_users
  command_line   $USER1$/check_users -w $ARG1$ -c $ARG2$
}
```

Monitoring other operations

Nagios also offers plugins for many other operations that are common to daily system monitoring and activities; this section covers only a few of them. It is recommended that you look for remaining commands in both the Nagios plugins package as well as on the Nagios Exchange website.

Checking for updates with APT

Many Linux distributions use **Advanced Packaging Tool** (**APT**) for handling package management (visit `http://en.wikipedia.org/wiki/Advanced_Packaging_Tool`). This tool is used by default on Debian and its derivatives such as Ubuntu. It allows the handling of upgrades and download of packages. It also allows the synchronization of package lists from one or more remote sources.

Nagios provides a plugin that allows you to monitor, if any upgrades are available, and/or perform upgrades automatically. The syntax and options are as follows:

```
check_apt [-d|-u|-U [<opts>]] [-n] [-t timeout]
          [-i <regex>] [-e <regex>] [-c <regex>]
```

Option	Description
`-u, --update`	Perform an apt update operation prior to other operations
`-U, --upgrade`	Perform an apt upgrade operation
`-d, --dist-upgrade`	Perform an apt dist-upgrade operation
`-n, --no-upgrade`	Do not run upgrade or dist-upgrade; useful only with `-u`
`-i, --include`	Include only packages matching a regular expression
`-c, --critical`	If any packages match a regular expression, a critical state is returned.
`-e, --exclude`	Exclude packages matching a regular expression

If the `-u` option is specified, the command first attempts to update apt package information. Otherwise, the package information currently in cache is used. If the `-U` or `-d` option is specified, the specified operation is performed. If `-n` is specified, only an attempt to run the operation is made, without actually upgrading performance monitoring (and not upgrade) activities system. The plugin might also be based on daily updates/upgrades and only monitor.

The following is a command definition for a simple dist-upgrade, as well as for monitoring available packages and issuing a critical state if the Linux images are upgradeable (that is, if newer packages exist). However, this command does not perform the actual upgrades.

```
define command
{
  command_name   check_apt_upgrade
```

```
    command_line    $USER1$/check_apt -u -d
}

define command
{
    command_name    check_apt_upgrade2
    command_line    $USER1$/check_apt -n -u -d
                    -c "^linux-(image|restrict)"
}
```

Monitoring the UPS status

Another useful feature is that Nagios is able to monitor the UPS status over the network. This requires the machine with the UPS to have the Network UPS Tools package (visit http://www.networkupstools.org/) installed and running, so that it is possible to query the UPS parameters. It is also possible to monitor local resources using the same plugin. The syntax and options are as follows:

```
check_ups -H host -u ups [-p port] [-v variable] [-T]
          [-w <warn time>] [-c <crit time>] [-t <timeout>]
```

Option	Description
-u, --ups	The name of the UPS to check
-p, --port	The port to use for TCP/IP connection; defaults to 3493
-T, --temperature	Report the temperature in degrees-celsius
-v, --variable	Variable to output (LINE, TEMP, BATTPCT, or LOADPCT)

The name of the UPS is usually defined in the ups.conf file on the machine to which the command is connecting. The plugin will return an ok state if the UPS is calibrating or running on AC power. A warning state is returned if the UPS claims to be running on batteries, and a critical state is returned in the case of a low battery or if the UPS is off. The following is a sample definition of a check command that gets passed to the UPS name as an argument:

```
define command
{
    command_name    check_ups
    command_line    $USER1$/check_ups -H $HOSTADDRESS$ -u $ARG1$
}
```

Gathering information from the lm-sensors

This is a Linux-specific plugin that uses the lm-sensors package (visit http://www. lm-sensors.org/) to monitor hardware health. The command issues an unknown state if the underlying hardware does not support health monitoring or if the lm-sensors package is not installed, a warning status is shown if a non-zero error is returned by the sensors command, and a critical status if the string ALARM is found within the output from the command. The plugin does not take any arguments and simply reports information based on the sensors command. The command definition is as follows:

```
define command
{
   command_name   check_sensors
   command_line   $USER1$/check_sensors
}
```

Using the dummy check plugin

Nagios also offers a dummy checking plugin. It simply takes an exit code. It is useful for testing dependencies between hosts and/or services and verifying notifications, and can also be used for a service that will be measured using passive checks only. The syntax of this plugin is as follows:

```
check_dummy <exitcode> [<result string>]
```

A sample command to return an ok status as well as critical with a status text supplied as an argument is shown:

```
define command
{
   command_name   check_dummy_ok
   command_line   $USER1$/check_dummy 0
}
define command
{
   command_name   check_dummy_critical
   command_line   $USER1$/check_dummy 2 $ARG1$
}
```

Manipulating other plugins' output

Nagios offers an excellent plugin that simply invokes other checks and converts their status accordingly. This might be useful when a failed check from a plugin is actually an indication that the service is working correctly. This can, for example, be used to make sure that non-authenticated users can't send e-mails while valid users can. The syntax and options are as follows:

```
negate [-t timeout] [-o|-w|-c|-u state] <actual command to run>
```

Option	Description
-o, --ok	This provides a state to which to return, when the actual command returns an ok state
-w, --warning	This provides a state to which to return, when the actual command returns a warning state
-c, --critical	This provides a state to which to return, when the actual command returns a critical state
-u, --unknown	This provides a state to which to return, when the actual command returns an unknown state

The state to return to can either be specified as exit code number or as a string. If no options are specified, only the ok and critical states are swapped. If at least one status change option is specified, only the specified states are mapped. Sample command definitions to check that an SMTP server is not listening and to verify that a user can't log into a POP3 server are as follows:

```
define command
{
    command_name   check_nosmtp
    command_line   $USER1$/negate $USER1$/check_smtp
                   -H $HOSTADDRESS$
}
define command
{
    command_name   check_pop3loginfailure
    command_line   $USER1$/negate -o critical -w ok -c critical
                   $USER1$/check_pop -H $HOSTADDRESS$ -E
                   -s "USER $ARG1$\r\nPASS $ARG2$\r\n" -d 5
                   -e "ogged in"
}
```

The first example does not use state mapping, and the default ok for critical state replacement is done. The second example maps the states, so that if a server is not listening or if the user is actually able to log in, it is considered a critical status for the service.

Additional and third-party plugins

So far, we have used plugins that are part of the standard Nagios Plugins package. It provides plugins for monitoring typical servers. The IT setup often consists of large variety of hardware and software that has to be monitored. There are many devices and services that should be monitored. In many cases, standard plugins are enough to properly monitor them, such as monitoring using PING, SSH, or HTTP.

There are, however, many applications that require more sophisticated checks, such as applications communicating over a custom protocol that can be checked using `check_udp` or `check_tcp` by specifying handshake to perform and expected response. In addition, many services require more sophisticated checks, such as verifying that OpenVPN server performs a proper handshake, which cannot easily be done using `check_udp` or `check_tcp`. A check that it is listening can be done, but it could simply be another service running at the same port.

Monitoring the network software

Monitoring IT resources often requires verifying that the network services are working properly. This can be anything—a web, SSH or FTP server as well as many other protocols. There are also a large number of custom protocols that also require monitoring. Popular network services have a working plugin already that can simply be used. However, often it is up to us to create a check.

In many cases, it is sufficient to just use `check_udp` or `check_tcp` and check for a specific string. It is often enough to just check the result message on the VMware server. With other services, it may also require sending a specific command. For example, the following command definition allows monitoring the Redis service (visit `http://redis.io/` for more details), which has a simple, line-based protocol:

```
define command
{
  command_name  check_redis
  command_line  $USER1$/check_tcp -H $HOSTADDRESS$ -p 6379
                -E -s "PING\r\n" -e "+PONG" -w 1 -c 2
}
```

Redis is a key-value-based store that is often used by server applications to store information and communicate between instances. It is commonly used for large web applications such as cache or temporary data storage.

The preceding example connects to the host on port 6379 (which is the port on which Redis is listening) and sends a PING command followed by newline characters, expecting a +PONG as response. The response time has to be below 1 second for OK status; it is a WARNING if it is below 2 seconds, and a CRITICAL status if it longer than that.

This approach can also be used to also send more complex commands such as authenticating Redis using the AUTH command:

```
define command
{
  command_name   check_redis_auth
  command_line   $USER1$/check_tcp -H $HOSTADDRESS$ -p 6379
                 -E -s "AUTH $ARG1$\r\nSELECT 0\r\n"
                 -e "+OK" -w 1 -c 2
}
```

This check will result in failure if authentication using specified password does not work, as the SELECT command will not return +OK unless the authentication succeeds. Similarly, a check can be made for memcached (visit http://memcached.org/ for more details), which is a cache mechanism often used by web applications as well:

```
define command
{
  command_name   check_memcached
  command_line   $USER1$/check_tcp -H $HOSTADDRESS$ -p 11211
                 -E -s "version\n" -e "VERSION" -w 1 -c 2
}
```

In this case, the only difference is the use of port 11211 (which is the default port for memcached) and sending different commands. The standard check commands can be used for almost all protocols. However, it is a practical solution mainly for text-based protocols, since encoding binary data requires more work and it is often easier to create a custom plugin for this—especially if a library to communicate over the protocol is available. This approach is described in more details in *Chapter 11, Programming Nagios*, of this book.

Using third-party plugins

There are also many cases where a simple monitoring by sending protocol-specific messages is not enough. For instance, monitoring the MySQL replication status requires a dedicated plugin to report delays properly and set warning or critical status if it exceeds the specified threshold.

In such cases, it is best to use the existing plugins if they exist, or write new ones if they don't. The Nagios Exchange at `http://exchange.nagios.org/` is the best place to start looking for plugins as it is historically the first and the largest directory of additions created by the Nagios community.

The website contains a dedicated category for plugins and at the time of writing this book, the directory contains over 3,000 plugins. They are grouped into categories based on the type of checks performed.

The category with largest number of plugins is Network Protocols (visit `http://exchange.nagios.org/directory/Plugins/Network-Protocols`), and it is over 20 percent of all plugins available on the website. It contains ready-to-use plugins to perform various types of checks, such as mail system, VoIP file, and web protocols checks.

Nagios Exchange also has a section for databases with a lot of plugins available. It provides ready-to-use code for monitoring many types of servers such as MySQL, PostgreSQL, Oracle, DB2, and the SQL Server—some of which do not have a dedicated check in the `nagios-plugins` project. For many databases, there are multiple plugins available, ranging from a basic service check to more advanced features, such as monitoring replication status, disk usage, and memory usage. All of the plugins can be found in the Databases section available at `http://exchange.nagios.org/directory/Plugins/Databases`.

The website provides a large number of plugins for monitoring web servers and web applications. This includes checks for common web servers, such as Apache and IIS, but there are also multiple choices for monitoring other web and application servers, such as Nginx, IIS, Tomcat, and JBoss. There are many plugins for monitoring specific solutions, such as Fast-CGI processes, PHP-FPM (a Fast-CGI based solution to run PHP applications with many web servers), and Passenger module (used to serve Ruby on Rails and Python/Django applications on top of Apache and Nginx). Also, there are different plugins aspects of monitoring web servers—number of processes, memory and CPU usage, and many more. The web-related plugins for monitoring can be found on Nagios Exchange under the **Web Servers** category available at `http://exchange.nagios.org/directory/Plugins/Web-Servers`.

Nagios Exchange also provides a lot of ready-to-use plugins to monitor a wide range of devices and services. There are multiple plugins to monitor various operating systems (at `http://exchange.nagios.org/directory/Plugins/ Operating-Systems`), network devices (at `http://exchange.nagios.org/ directory/Plugins/Hardware/Network-Gear`), and network connectivity (at `http://exchange.nagios.org/directory/Plugins/Network- Connections%2C-Stats-and-Bandwidth`).

When using a third-party plugin, either from Nagios Exchange or after downloading from another website directly, it is important to remember about security and licensing issues.

As plugins are run using the same user as Nagios itself, a malicious or erroneous plugin may be able to remove Nagios data files or other important data. It is always best to use a plugin that is in active development, and preferably has its source code available so that in case of problems it is possible to fix them or get support from the author of the plugin.

Some plugins may have licenses that prevent them from being used in certain environments or that require a license in such case. There are also cases where a plugin may depend on libraries or software that requires a license for each server on which it is installed, for instance, a plugin to monitor a proprietary service may require a client library to connect, which may require additional license.

It is also possible to create your own plugins, and as the plugin interface is very easy, it can be done in almost any language — all that is needed is to print the result to standard output and use appropriate exit code to indicate the status. Writing your own plugins is described in more detail in *Chapter 11, Programming Nagios*.

Summary

The Nagios plugins package offers a large variety of checks that can be performed to monitor your infrastructure. Whether you are an administrator of an IT company managing a large network or just want to monitor a small server room, these plugins will allow you to check the majority of the services that you are currently using.

In this chapter, we have learned how the plugins report status to Nagios using standard output and exit codes. We have also learned about the Nagios plugins project and the standard options for all of the plugins within the package.

We have also covered the generic communication plugins for checking remote host connectivity using ping, as well as generic TCP and UDP checking plugins. The chapter also described how to perform checks of standard networking protocols, such as e-mail, FTP, DHCP, website checking as well as Nagios process information.

We have also learned about checking various databases and how it can also be used to monitor the propagation of data to slave databases. The chapter also covers information about monitoring disk and swap space, as well as monitoring system resources and processes.

We have also learned how to monitor additional operations, such as APT package management status, UPS, and lm-sensors. We have also learned how to use third-party plugins in Nagios. The next chapter will cover how to create the Nagios configuration so that it can be used for monitoring both small and large infrastructures. It also covers advanced configuration options such as dependencies, custom variables, inheriting, and flapping.

5
Advanced Configuration

In the previous chapter, we walked through the standard Nagios plugins, which can be used to monitor a large variety of hosts and services. We learned how the plugins can be used to perform specific and generic checking of the IT resources. This chapter describes some guidelines that will help you migrate from small (and increasing) Nagios setups to a flexible model by using templates and grouping effectively. Any experienced administrator knows that there is a huge difference between a working system and a properly configured system. Using this advice will help you and your team survive the switch from monitoring only critical services to checking the health of the majority of your IT infrastructure.

This chapter focuses on how to set up templates, groupings, and the naming structure. However, creating a robust monitoring system involves much more—be sure to read the following chapters that talk about monitoring other servers, setting up multiple hosts that use Nagios to monitor your network and report to a single central machine, as well as how to monitor hosts running the Microsoft Windows operating system.

In this chapter, we will learn the following:

- Setting up and maintaining the configuration files that can grow along with your IT monitoring system
- Configuring the dependencies for easier root cause analysis of IT problems
- Creating the templates for easier management of similar hosts and services
- Using the custom variables for easier customization of objects
- What flapping is and how it works

Creating maintainable configurations

Enormous effort is required to deploy, configure, and maintain a system that monitors your company's IT infrastructure. The configuration for several hundred machines can take months. The effort required will also depend upon the scope of hosts and services that should be tracked — the more precise the checks need to be, the more the time needed to set these up.

If your company plans to monitor a wide range of hosts and services, you should consider setting up a machine dedicated to Nagios that will only take care of this single job. Even though a small Nagios installation consumes little resources, as it grows, Nagios will start using more resources. If you set it to run on the same machine as business-critical applications, it can lead to problems. Therefore, it is always best to set up a dedicated Nagios box, even if this is on a slower machine, right from the beginning.

Very often, a good approach is to start with monitoring only critical parts of your network, such as routers and main servers. You can also start off with only making sure that essential services are working — DHCP, DNS, file sharing, and databases are good examples of what is critical. Of course, if your company does not use file servers or if databases are not critical to the production environment, you can skip these. The next step would be to set up parenting and start adopting more hosts. At some point, you will also need to start planning how to group hosts and services. In the beginning, the configuration might simply be definitions of people, hosts, and services. After several iterations of setting up more hosts and services to be monitored, you should get to a point where all of the things that are critical to the company's business are monitored. This should be an indication that the setting up of the Nagios configuration is complete.

As the number of objects grows, you will need to group them. Contacts need to be defined as groups, because if your team consists of more than one to two people, they will likely rotate over time. So, it's better to maintain a group than change the people responsible for each host individually. Hosts and services should be grouped for many reasons. It makes viewing the status and infrastructure topology on the web interface much easier. Also, after you start defining escalations for your objects, it is much easier to manage these using groups.

You should take some time to plan how group hosts and services should be set up. How will you use the groupings? For escalations? For viewing single host groups via the web interface? Learn how you can take advantage of this functionality, and then plan how you will approach the setup of your groups.

If your network has common services, it is better to define them for particular groups and only once — such as the SSH server for all Linux servers and Telnet for all **AIX (Advanced Interactive eXecutive)** machines, which is an IBM operating system that is mainly used by IBM enterprise-level servers. It is possible to define a service only once, and tell Nagios to which hosts or host groups the service should be bound. By specifying that all Linux servers offer SSH, and all AIX servers offer telnet, it will automatically add such services to all of the machines in these groups. This is often more convenient than specifying services for each of the hosts separately.

In such cases, you should either set up a new host group or use an existing one to keep track of the hosts that offer a particular service. Combined with keeping a list of host groups inside each host definition, this makes things much easier to manage — disabling a particular host also takes care of the corresponding service definitions.

It is also worth mentioning that Nagios performs and schedules service checks in a much better way than it does host checks — the service checks are scheduled in a much better way. That is why it is recommended that you do not schedule host checks at all. You can set up a separate service for your hosts that will send a ping to them and report how many packets have returned and the approximate time taken for them to return.

Nagios can be set up to schedule host checks only if one of the hosts is failing (that is, it is not responding to the pings). A host will be periodically checked until it recovers. In this way, problems with hosts will still be detected, but host checks will only be scheduled on demand. This will cause Nagios to perform much better than it would if regular checks of all hosts on your network are made. To disable regular host checks, simply don't specify the check interval for the hosts that you want checked only on demand.

Configuring the file structure

A very important issue is how to store all our configuration files. We can put every object definition in a single file, but this will not make it easy to manage. As mentioned in *Chapter 2, Installing Nagios 4*, it is recommended to store different types of objects in separate folders.

Assuming your Nagios configuration is in /etc/nagios, it is recommended that you create folders for all types of objects in the following manner:

```
/etc/nagios/commands
/etc/nagios/timeperiods
/etc/nagios/contacts
/etc/nagios/hosts
/etc/nagios/services
```

Of course, these files will need to be added to the `nagios.cfg` file. After having followed the instructions in *Chapter 2, Installing Nagios 4*, these directories should already be added to our main Nagios configuration file.

It would also be worthwhile to use a version control mechanism such as **Git** (visit `http://www.git-scm.com/`), **Hg (Mercurial**, visit `http://mercurial.selenic.com/)` or **SVN (Subversion**, visit `http://subversion.tigris.org/`) to store your Nagios configuration. While this will add overhead to the process of applying configuration changes, it will also prevent someone from overwriting a file accidentally. It will also keep track of who changed which parts of the configuration, so you will always know whom to blame if things break down.

You might consider writing a simple script that will perform an export from the source code repository into a temporary directory, verify that Nagios works fine by using the `nagios -v` command and. Only if that did not fail, we will copy the new configuration in place of the older one and restart Nagios. This will make deployment of configuration changes much easier, especially in cases where multiple people are managing it.

As for naming the files themselves — for time periods, contacts, and commands, it is recommended that you keep single definitions per file, as in `contacts/nagiosadmin.cfg`. This greatly reduces naming collisions and also makes it much easier to find particular object definitions.

Storing hosts and services might be done in a slightly different way — host definitions should go to the `hosts` subdirectory, and the file should be named the same as the hostname, for example, `hosts/localhost.cfg`. Services can be split into two different types and stored, depending on how they are defined and used.

Services that are associated with more than one host should be stored in the services subdirectory. A good example is the SSH service, which is present on the majority of systems. In this case, it should go to `services/ssh.cfg`, and use host groups to associate it with the hosts that actually offer connection over this protocol.

Services that are specific to a host should be handled differently. It's best to store them in the same file as the host definition. A good example might be checking the disk space on partitions that might be specific to a particular machine, such as checking the `/oracle` partition on a host that's dedicated to Oracle databases.

For handling groups, it is recommended to create files called `groups.cfg`, and define all groups in it, without any members. Then, while defining a contact, host, or group, you can define to which groups it belongs by using the `contactgroups`, `hostgroups`, or `servicegroups` directives accordingly. This way, if you disable a particular object by deleting or commenting out its definition, the definition of the group itself will still work.

If you plan on having a large number of both check command and notify command definitions, you may want to split this into two separate directories — `checkcommands` and `notifycommands`. You can also use a single commands subdirectory, prefix the file names, and store the files in a single directory, for example, `commands/check_ssh.cfg` and `commands/notify_jabber.cfg`.

Defining the dependencies

It is a very common scenario that computers, or the applications they offer, depend on other objects to function properly. A typical example is a database on which an e-mail or web server will depend. Another one is a host behind a private network that depends on an OpenVPN service to work. As a system administrator, your job is to know these relations — if you plan to reinstall a database cluster, you need to let people know there will be downtime for almost all applications. Nagios should also be aware of such relations.

In such cases, it is very useful for system monitoring software to consider these dependencies. When analyzing which hosts and services are not working properly, it is good to analyze such dependencies and discard things that are not working because of other failures. This way, it will be easier for you to focus on the real problems. Therefore, it allows you to get to the root cause of any malfunction much faster.

Nagios allows you to define how hosts and services depend on each other. This allows very flexible configurations and checks, and distinguishes it from many other less advanced system monitoring applications. Nagios provides very flexible mechanisms for checking hosts and services — it will take all dependencies into account. This means that if a service relies on another one to function properly, Nagios will perform checks to make sure that all dependent services are working properly. In case a dependent service is not working properly, Nagios may or may not perform checks and may or may not send out any notifications, depending on how the dependency is defined. This is logical, because the service will most probably not work properly if a dependent object is not working.

Nagios also offers the ability to specify parents for hosts. This is, in a way, similar to dependencies, as both specify that one object depends on another object. The main difference is that parents are used to define the infrastructure hierarchy. Parent definitions are also used by Nagios to skip checks for hosts that will obviously be down. Dependencies, on the other hand, can be used to suppress notifications about the problems that are occurring due to dependent services being down, but they do not necessarily cause Nagios to skip checking a particular host or service. Another difference is that parents can only be specified for hosts, whereas dependencies can be set up between hosts and services.

Dependencies also offer more flexibility in terms of how they are configured. It is possible to specify which states of the dependent host or service will cause Nagios to stop sending out notifications. You can also tell Nagios when it should skip performing checks, based on the status of the dependent object.

Dependencies might also be valid only at certain times, for example, a back-up service that needs to monitor your system all of the time, but that needs to have access to networked storage only between 11 PM and 4 AM.

To aid in describing how objects depend on each other, Nagios documentation uses two terms—*master* and *dependent* objects. When defining dependency, a master object is the object that needs to be working correctly in order for the other object to function. Similarly, the dependent object is the one that needs another object in order to work. This terminology will be used throughout this section, to avoid confusion.

Creating the host dependencies

Let's start with host dependency definitions. These are objects that have several attributes, and each dependency can actually describe one or more dependencies, for example, it is possible to tell Nagios that 20 machines rely on a particular host in a single dependency definition.

Here is an example of a dependency specifying that during maintenance, a Windows backup storage server in another branch depends upon a VPN server.

```
define hostdependency
{
    dependent_host_name            backupstorage-branch2
    host_name                      vpnserver-branch1
    dependency_period              maintenancewindows
}
```

The following table describes all of the available directives for defining a host dependency. Items in bold are required when specifying a dependency:

Option	Description
dependent_host_name	Defines hostnames that are dependent on the master hosts, separated by commas
dependent_hostgroup_name	Defines the host group names whose members are dependent on the master hosts, separated by commas
host_name	Defines the master hosts, separated by commas

Option	Description
hostgroup_name	Defines the host groups whose members are to be the master hosts, separated by commas
inherits_parent	Defines whether a dependency should inherit dependencies of the master hosts
execution_failure_criteria	Specifies which master host states should prevent Nagios from checking the dependent hosts, separated by commas; it can be one or more of the following:
	n: none, checks should always be executed
	p: pending state (no check has yet been done)
	o: host UP state
	d: host DOWN state
	u: host UNREACHABLE state
notification_failure_criteria	Specifies which master host states should be prevented from generating notifications about the dependent host's status changes, separated by commas; it can be one or more of the following:
	n: none, notification should always take place
	p: pending state (no check has yet been done)
	o: host UP state
	d: host DOWN state
	u: host UNREACHABLE state
dependency_period	Specifies the time periods during which the dependency will be valid; if not specified, the dependency is always valid

The question is where to store such dependency files. As for service definitions, it is recommended that you store dependencies specific to a particular host in the file containing the definition of the dependent host. For the previous example, we would put it in the `hosts/backupstorage-branch2.cfg` file.

When defining a dependency that will describe a relationship between more than one master or dependent host, it's best to put these into a generic file for dependencies—for example, we can put it in `hosts/dependencies.cfg`. Another good option is to put the dependency definitions that only affect a single master host in the master host's definition.

If you are defining a dependency that covers more than one master or dependent host, it is best to use host groups to manage the list of hosts that should be included in the dependency's definition. This can be one or more host group names, and very often, these groups will also be the same as for the service definitions.

Creating the service dependencies

Service dependencies work in a similar way as host dependencies. For hosts, you need to specify one or more master hosts and one or more dependent hosts; for services, you need to define a master service and a dependent service.

Service dependencies can be defined only for a single service, but on multiple hosts. For example, you can tell Nagios that POP3 services on the `emailservers` host group depend on the LDAP service on the `ldapserver` host.

Here is an example of how to define such a service dependency:

```
define servicedependency
{
   host_name                        ldapserver
   service_description              LDAP
   dependent_hostgroup_name         emailservers
   dependent_service_description    POP3
   execution_failure_criteria       c,u
   notification_failure_criteria    c,u,w
}
```

The following table describes all available directives for defining a service dependency. Items in bold are required when specifying a dependency:

Option	Description
dependent_host_name	Defines the hostnames whose services should be taken into account for this dependency, separated by commas
dependent_hostgroup_name	Defines the host group names whose members' services should be taken into account for this dependency, separated by commas
dependent_service_description	Defines the service that should be the dependent service for all the specified dependent hosts
host_name	Defines the master hosts whose services should be taken into account by this dependency, separated by commas
hostgroup_name	Defines the master host groups whose members' services should be taken into account by this dependency, separated by commas

Option	Description
service_description	Defines the service that should be the master service for all the provided master hosts
inherits_parent	Specifies whether this dependency should inherit the dependencies of the master hosts
execution_failure_criteria	Specifies which master service states should prevent Nagios from checking the dependent services, separated by commas; it can be one or more of the following:
	n: none, checks should always be executed
	p: pending state (no check has yet been done)
	o: service OK state
	w: service WARNING state
	c: service CRITICAL state
	u: service UNKNOWN state
notification_failure_criteria	Specifies which master service states should be prevented from generating notifications for the dependent service status changes, separated by commas; it can be one or more of the following:
	n: none, checks should always be executed
	p: pending state (no check has yet been done)
	o: service OK state
	w: service WARNING state
	c: service CRITICAL state
	u: service UNKNOWN state
dependency_period	Specifies the time periods during which the dependency will be valid; if not specified, the dependency is always valid

As in the case of host dependencies, there is a question of where to store the service dependency definitions. A good answer to this is that store dependencies in the same files where the dependent service definitions are kept. If you are following the previous suggestions regarding how to keep services in the file structure, then for a service bound to a single host, both service and the related dependencies should be kept in the same file as the host definition itself. If a service is used by more than one host, it is kept in a separate file. In this case, dependencies related to that service should also be kept in the same file as the service.

Using the templates

The templates in Nagios allow you to create a set of parameters that can then be used in the definitions of multiple hosts, services, and contacts. The main purpose of the templates is to keep parameters that are generic to all objects, or a group of objects, in one place. This way, you can avoid putting the same directives in hundreds of objects, and your configuration is more maintainable.

> Nagios allows an object to inherit from single or multiple templates. The templates can also inherit from other templates. This allows the creation of very simple templates, where objects inherit from a single template as well as complex templating system, where actual objects (such as services or hosts) inherit from multiple templates. It is recommended to start with a simple template. Multiple templates are more useful when monitoring larger number of hosts and services across multiple sites.

It is also good to start using templates for hosts and services, and decide how they should be used. Sometimes, it is better to have one template, inherit another, and create a hierarchical structure. In many cases, it is more reasonable to create hosts so that they use multiple templates. This functionality allows the inheritance of some options from one template and some parameters from another template. The following is an illustration of how the templates can be structured using both techniques:

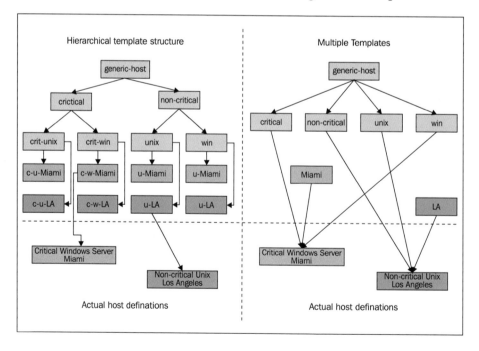

This example illustrates how the templates can be structured using both hierarchy and multiple templates inheritance. The preceding diagram shows how to use templates for host definitions. Similar rules apply for services as well, but the inheritance structure might be quite different.

In both of the methods shown in the preceding diagram, there is a distinction between `critical` and `non-critical` servers. Hosts are also split into ones that are Unix-based and ones that are Windows-based. There is also a distinction between the two branches that are configured—`Miami` and `LA` (Los Angeles). Furthermore, there is also a `generic-host` template that is used by every other template.

Usually, such distinctions make sense, because Windows and Unix boxes might be checked differently. Based on the operating system and the location of the machine, different people should be assigned as contacts in case of problems. There may also be different time periods during which these hosts should be checked.

The example on the left shows the inheritance of one type of parameter at a time. First, a distinction is made between critical and non-critical machines. Usually, both types have different values for the notification and check intervals, as well as the number of checks to perform before generating a notification for a problem. The next step is to differentiate between Windows- and Unix- based servers—this might involve the `check` command to verify that a server is up. The last step is to define templates for each system in both of the branches (`Miami` and `LA`). The actual host definition inherits from one template in the final set of templates.

The example on the right uses a slightly different approach. It first defines different templates for Unix and Windows systems. Next, a pair of templates for critical and noncritical machines is also defined. Finally, a set of templates defines the branches `Miami` and `LA`. The actual host definition inherits templates for the operating system, for the level of criticality and for the branch to which it belongs. It inherits parameters partially from each of the templates.

In both cases, attributes that are passed at different levels are the same, even though the approach is different. Usually, the templates that define the operating system also define how a host check should be done. They might also indicate the time period over which a host should be checked.

Templates for critical and noncritical machines usually specify how notifications should be carried out. If a host is crucial to infrastructure, its owners should be notified in a more aggressive way. Similarly, machines that are not affecting business directly do not need that much attention.

Templates for locations usually define the owners of the machines. The locations are not always branches, as in this example; they can be branches, floors, or even network connection types. Locations can also point machines to their parent hosts— usually computers located in the same place that are connected to the same router.

Creating the templates

Defining the templates in Nagios is very similar to defining actual objects. You simply define the template as the required object type. The only difference is that you need to specify the `register` directive and specify a value of 0 for it. This will tell Nagios that it should not treat this as an actual object, but as a template. You will also need to use the `name` directive for defining template names. You do not need to specify other directives for naming objects, such as `host_name`, `contact_name`, or `service_description`.

When defining an object, simply include the `use` directive and specify all of the templates to be used as its value. If you want to inherit from multiple templates, separate all of them by commas.

The following is an example of defining a template for a Linux server and then using this in an actual host definition:

```
define host   {
    register                0
    name                    generic-servers
    check_period            24x7
    retry_interval          1
    check_interval          15
    max_retry_attempts      5
    notification_period     24x7
    notification_interval   60
    notification_options    d,r
}
define host
{
    register                0
    use                     generic-servers
    name                    linux-servers
    check_command           check-host-alive
    contact_groups          linux-admins
}
define host
{
    use                     linux-servers
    host_name               ubuntu1
    address                 192.168.2.1
}
```

As mentioned earlier, templates use `name` for defining the template, and the actual host uses the `host_name` directive.

Inheriting from multiple templates

Nagios allows us to inherit from multiple templates and the templates using other (nested) templates. It's good to know how Nagios determines the order in which every directive is looked for in each of the templates. When inheriting attributes from more than one template, Nagios tries to find the directive in each of the templates, starting from the first one. If it is found in the first template, that value is used; if not, Nagios checks for a value in the second one. This cycle continues until the last template in the list. If any of the templates is also inheriting from another template, then a check for the second level of templates is done recursively. This means that checking for a directive will perform a recursive check of all of the templates that are inherited from the currently checked one.

The following illustration shows an example of this situation. The actual host definition inherits three templates—B, F, and G. Template B inherits A, F inherits D and E, and finally, D inherits attributes from template C.

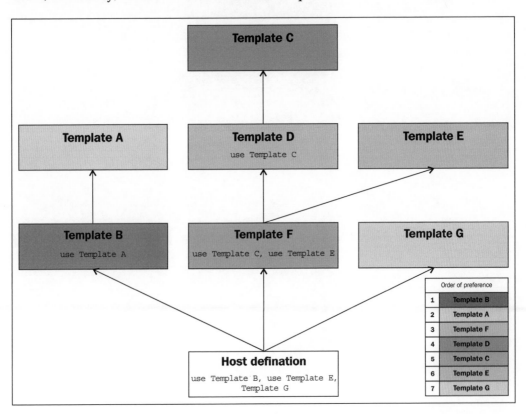

If Nagios tries to find any directive related to this host, the first thing that will be checked is the actual host definition. If the host does not include the directive, Nagios will first look under B, as this is the first template that should be used. If it is not found in B, Nagios will recursively try to find the attribute in A, as it is used by template B. The next step is to look in F along with all of the templates it is using. F inherits D and E. The first one to check is B along with all parent templates—this dictates that D, C, and the next E should now be checked. If the attribute is still not found, then template G is used. Let's assume that the following directives (among others) are defined for the previous illustration:

```
define host
{
    register            0
    name                A
    check_period        workinghours
    retry_interval      1
    check_interval      15
}
define host
{
    register            0
    use                 A
    name                B
    check_period        24x7
}
define host
{
    register            0
    name                D
    use                 C
    max_retry_attempts  4
}
define host
{
    register            0
    name                E
    max_retry_attempts  3
}
define host
{
```

```
    register              0
    use                   D,E
    name                  F
    notification_interval 30
}
define host
{
    use                   B,F,G
    host_name             ubuntu1
    address               192.168.2.1
    notification_interval 20
}
```

For this particular example, the values for the `address` and `notification_ interval` directives are taken directly from the host `ubuntu1` definition. Even though `notification_interval` is also defined in F, it is overwritten by the actual host definition.

The value for `max_retry_attempts` is taken from the template D, regardless of whether it is also defined in C. Even though the template E also defines a value for it, as D is put before E, the values defined in both of them are taken from D.

The value for `check_period` is taken from B, which overwrites the value defined for the template A. Values for `retry_interval` and `check_interval` are taken from A.

Even though the preceding examples mention host configurations, templates for other types of objects work in the same way. Templates are often used extensively for service definitions. They usually use a similar approach as the one for hosts. It is a good idea to define templates for branches depending on the priority or type of service, such as a template common for all services in a specific branch, another template for all services for web / mail / other applications and for critical / non-critical / backup servers. This increases the maintainability of the configurations, especially for the larger setups. It is much easier to change contact address or notification settings for all the critical applications if that info is defined in the template used by all services. In this case, our configuration may have several templates, and most of the service definitions will just re-use existing templates, perhaps only specifying how checks for those services should be made.

Contacts, on the other hand, usually use only a couple of templates. They depend on the working hours and the notification preferences. The remaining parameters can be kept in an individual contact's definition. Very often, users may have their own preferences on how they should be notified, so it's better not to try and design templates for that.

Using the custom variables

The custom variables allow you to include your own directives when defining objects. These can then be used in commands. This allows you to define objects in a more concise way, and define service checks in a more general fashion.

The idea is that you define directives that are not standard Nagios parameters in host, service, or contact objects, and they can be accessed from all commands, such as check commands, notifications, and event handlers. This is very useful for complex Nagios configurations where you might want commands to perform nontrivial tasks for which they will require additional information.

Let's assume we want Nagios to check that the hosts have correct MAC addresses. We can then define a service once and use that custom variable for the check command. When defining an object, a custom variable needs to be prefixed with an underscore and written in uppercase.

The custom variables are accessible as the following macros:

- `$_HOST<variable>$`: This is used for directives defined within a host object
- `$_SERVICE<variable>$`: This is used for directives defined within a service object
- `$_CONTACT<variable>$`: This is for directives defined within a contact object

For the preceding example, a macro definition would be `$_HOSTMAC$`.

These variables can be used for command definitions, notifications, or time periods. The following is an example of a contact and notification command that uses a custom variable for the Jabber address:

```
define contact
{
  contact_name                  jdoe
  alias                         John Doe
  host_notification_commands host-notify-by-jabber
  _JABBERID                     jdoe@jabber.yourcompany.com
}
define command
{
  command_name         host-notify-by-jabber
  command_line         $USER1$/notify_via_jabber $_CONTACTJABBERID$
                       "Host $HOSTDISPLAYNAME$ changed state to
                       $HOSTSTATE$"
}
```

Of course, you will also need a plugin to send notifications over Jabber. This can be downloaded from the Nagios project on SourceForge (visit `http://nagios.sf.net/download/contrib/notifications/notify_via_jabber`). The previous example will work with any other protocol you might be using. All that's needed is a plugin that will send commands over such a protocol.

A very useful client called EKG2 (visit `http://www.ekg2.org/`) allows you to send messages over various protocols, including Jabber, and has a pipe that can be used to send messages over these protocols. A sample command to do this can be as follows:

```
define command
{
    command_name        host-notify-by-ekg2
    command_line        /usr/bin/printf "%b" "msg $_CONTACTEKGALIAS$
                        Host $HOSTDISPLAYNAME$ changed state to
                        $HOSTSTATE$\n" >>~/.ekg2/.pipe
}
```

A major benefit of custom variables is that they can also be changed on the fly over an external command pipe. This way, the custom variables functionality can be used in more complex configurations. Event handlers may trigger changes in the attributes of other checks.

An example might be that a ping check with 50 ms and 20 percent packet loss limits are made to ensure that the network connectivity is working correctly. However, if the main router is down and a failover connection is used, the check is set to a more relaxed limit of 400 ms and 50 percent packet loss.

An example configuration might be as follows:

```
define service
{
    host_name           router2
    service_description PING
    check_command       check_ping_limits
    _LIMITS             50.0,20%
}
define command
{
    command_name        check_ping_limits
    command_line        $USER1$/check_ping -H $HOSTADDRESS$
                        -w $_SERVICELIMITS$ -c $_SERVICELIMITS$
}
```

When a service that checks if the main router is up (that is, it is in a critical state) an event handler will invoke a change in the limits by sending a CHANGE_CUSTOM_SVC_ VAR command (http://www.nagios.org/developerinfo/externalcommands/ commandinfo.php?command_id=140) over the external commands pipe to set the _LIMITS custom variable.

Chapter 6, Notifications and Events, covers event handlers and external commands pipe in more detail. So, it is recommended that you read this chapter in order to understand this approach better.

Understanding flapping

Flapping is a situation where a host or service changes states very rapidly — constantly switching between working correctly and not working at all. This can happen due to various reasons — a service might crash after a short period of operating correctly or due to some maintenance work being done by system administrators.

Nagios can detect that a host or service is flapping, if Nagios is configured to do so. It does so by analyzing previous results in terms of how many state changes have taken place within a specific period of time. Nagios keeps a history of the 21 most recent checks and analyzes changes within that history.

The following is an screenshot illustrating the 21 most recent check results, which means that Nagios can detect up to 20 state changes in the recent history of an object. It also shows how Nagios detects state transitions:

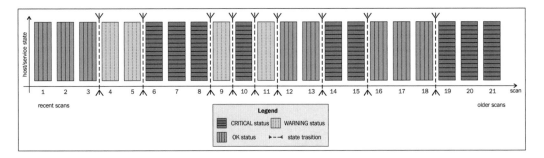

Nagios then finds all of the changes between different states, and uses them to determine if a host or service is flapping. It checks to see if a state is the same as the result from the previous check, and if it has changed, a state transition is counted at this place. In the preceding example, we have nine transitions.

Nagios calculates a flapping threshold based on this information. The value reflects how many of the state changes have occurred recently. If there are no changes in the last 21 state checks, the value would be 0 percent. If all checks have different states, the flapping threshold would be 100 percent.

Nagios also differentiates older results from newer ones. This means that a state transition that took place during the previous 18th check will cause the flapping threshold to be much lower than a transition that took place during the previous third check.

In our case, if Nagios would only take the number of transitions into account, the flapping threshold would be 45 percent. The weighted algorithm used in Nagios would calculate the flapping threshold as more than 45 percent, because there have been many changes in the more recent checks.

Nagios takes threshold values into consideration when estimating whether a host or service has started or stopped flapping. The configuration for each object allows the definition of low and high flapping thresholds.

If an object was not flapping previously, and the current flapping threshold is equal to or greater than the high flap threshold, Nagios assumes that the object has just started flapping. If an object was flapping previously and the current threshold is lower than the low flap threshold, Nagios assumes the object has just stopped flapping.

The following chart shows how the flapping threshold for an object has changed over time, and when Nagios assumed it started and stopped flapping. In this case, the high flap threshold is set to 40 percent and the low flap threshold is set to 25 percent. Red vertical lines indicate when Nagios assumed the flapping to have started and stopped, and the grey area shows where the service was assumed to be flapping.

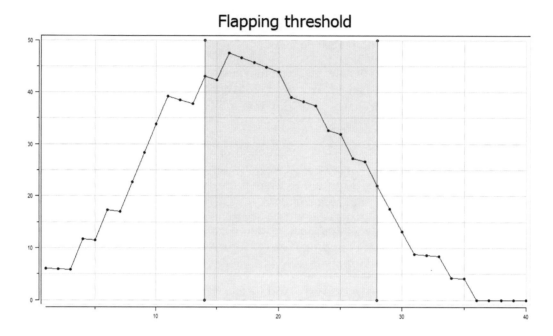

It is worth noting that the low flap threshold should be lower than the high flap threshold. This prevents the situation where after one state transition, flapping would be detected and the next check would tell Nagios that the object has stopped flapping. If both the attributes are set to the same value, an object might be identified as having started and stopped flapping often. This can happen when the flapping threshold changes from below threshold to above threshold or vice versa. This might cause Nagios to send out large number of notifications and cause its performance to degrade.

Summary

When creating or extending Nagios configurations to monitor large number of resources, spend some time planning the layout of your configuration. Some people recommend one file for each single definition, while others recommend storing things in a single file per host. We recommend keeping similar things in the same file and maintaining a directory-based set of files.

In this chapter, we have learned about setting up a directory and file naming structure for configurations. Using proper guidelines for naming and creating the files will help make the configuration maintainable when managing tens and thousands of hosts and services.

We have also defined dependencies, and covered how it can be used to make Nagios automatically notice when a problem is related to other host or when the service is not working properly. We have also learned how to use templates to help define a large number of objects, and how multiple inheritance can be used to automate the defined objects.

This chapter also describes how to use custom variables to access specific information about a host, service, or contact from another object, such as specifying limits for check commands or protocol-specific identification for sending notifications. We have also learned what flapping is and how Nagios uses it to prevent sending notifications about hosts or services that keep changing their state.

The next chapter describes notifications and events in more details. It will help us set up an efficient way to let the IT department know about errors, and when things are back to normal. It will also show how event handlers can be used to proactively fix problems before anyone is notified.

6
Notifications and Events

We already know how notifications work in Nagios. The previous chapters described how Nagios sends information to the users when a problem occurs and how it decides to notify people. Previously, our examples were limited to sending an e-mail 24 hours a day or only during working days.

In this chapter, we will cover the following topics:

- Setting up notifications effectively—when they should be sent; how they should be sent; and how to use multiple methods of notifying users, such as setting up Nagios to send a text message to your mobile during the day or to send you a message on Jabber or HipChat only when you are online

- Using escalations that allow sending information about the host or service status when it is failing for a long period of time—for example, notifying a manager when a critical service has been down for over four hours

- Sending commands via the Nagios external commands, such as adding comments on hosts and services, modifying notification settings

- Using event handlers that can be set up to be run whenever a service status changes

Creating effective notifications

This section covers notifications in more depth and details how Nagios can tell other people about what is happening. We will discuss a simple approach, as well as a more complex one on how notifications can make your life easier.

In many cases, a plain e-mail notification about a problem may not always be the right thing to do. As people's inboxes get cluttered with e-mails, the usual approach is to create rules to move certain messages that they don't even read to separate folders. There's a pretty good chance that if people start getting a lot of notifications to which they won't need to react, they'll simply ask their favorite mailing program to move these messages into a *do not look in here unless you have plenty of time* folder. Moreover, in such cases, if there is an issue they should be handling at the time, they will most probably miss the notification e-mail.

This section talks about what can be implemented in your company to make notifications more convenient for the IT staff. Limiting the amount of irrelevant information sent to various people tends to decrease their response time, because they will have much less information to filter out.

Using multiple notifications

The first feature that many Nagios administrators overlook is the ability to create more than one notification command: Nagios can notify you on both instant messaging (such as Jabber or HipChat) and e-mail. It can also send you an SMS. A disadvantage is that at some point you might end up receiving text messages at 2 A.M. about an outage of a machine that may be down for the next three days, which is not critical.

At this point, it's worth mentioning that there's another easy solution. The approach is to create multiple contacts for a single person. For example, you can set up different contacts when you're at work and when you're offline, and define a profile that ensures that you are not disturbed too much during the night.

For example, to handle various times of the day in a different fashion, you can set up the following contacts:

- `jdoe-workhours`: This is a contact that will only receive notifications during working hours; notifications will be carried out using both the corporate IM system and e-mails

- `jdoe-daytime`: This is a contact that will only receive notifications between 7 A.M. and 10 P.M., excluding working hours; notifications will be sent as a text or a pager message and an e-mail

- `jdoe-night`: This would be a contact that will only receive notifications between 10 P.M. and 7 A.M.; notifications will only be sent out as an e-mail

All entries would also contain `contactgroups` pointing to the same groups that the single `jdoe` contact entry used to contain. In this way, the other objects, such as hosts, services, or contact groups related to this user would not be affected. All entries would also reside in the same file, for example, `contacts/jdoe.cfg`.

The main drawback of this approach is that logging on to the web interface would require using one of the previous users or keeping the `jdoe` contact without any notifications, just to be able to log on to the interface.

The preceding example combined the creation of multiple contacts and the use of multiple notification commands to achieve a convenient way of getting notified about a problem. Using only multiple contacts also works fine. Another approach to the problem is to define different contacts for different ways to be notified—for example, `jdoe-email`, `jdoe-sms`, and `jdoe-jabber`. This way, you can define different contact methods for various time periods—instant messages during working hours, text messages while on duty, and an e-mail when not at work.

Another important issue is to make sure that as few people as possible are notified of the problem. Imagine there is a host without an explicit administrator assigned to it. A notification about a problem is sent out to 20 different people. In such a case, either each of them will assume that someone else will resolve the problem, or people will run into a communication problem over discussing who will actually handle it.

Teams that closely cooperate with each other usually solve these issues with ease—knowledgeable people start discussing an issue and a natural solution to solve the issue comes out of the discussion. However, the teams that are distributed across various locations or that have inefficient communication within their team will run into problems in such cases.

That is why it is a good idea to either nominate a coordinator who will assign tasks as they arise, or try to maintain a short list of people responsible for each machine. If you need to make sure that other people will investigate the problem if the person responsible for the machine cannot do it immediately, then it is a good idea to resort to escalations for this purpose. These are described later in this chapter.

Previously, we mentioned that notifications only via e-mail may not always be the best thing to do. For example, they don't work well for situations that require quick response times. There are various reasons behind this. First, e-mails are slow—even though the e-mail lands on your mail server in a few seconds, people usually only poll their e-mails every few minutes. Second, people tend to filter e-mails and skip those in which they are not interested.

Another good reason why e-mails should not always be used is that they stay in your e-mail account until you actually fetch and read them. If you have been on a two-week vacation and a problem has occurred, should you still be worried when you read it after you get back? Has the issue been resolved already?

If your team needs to react to problems promptly, using e-mails as the basic notification method is definitely not the best choice. Let's consider what other possibilities exist to notify users of a problem effectively.

As already mentioned, a very good choice is to use instant messaging or **Short Message Service (SMS)** as the basic means of notification, and only use e-mail as the last resort. Some companies might also use the client-server approach to notify the users of the problems, perhaps integrated with showing Nagios' status only for particular hosts and services. **NagiosExchange** has plenty of available solutions you can use to handle notifications effectively. Visit http://exchange.nagios.org/ for more details.

Sending instant messages via Jabber

The first and the most powerful option for notifications is to use **Jabber** (http://www.jabber.org/). There is an existing script for this that is available in the contributions repository on the Nagios project website (visit http://nagios. sf.net/download/contrib/notifications/notify_via_jabber). This is a small Perl script that sends messages over Jabber. You may need to install additional system packages to handle Jabber connectivity from Perl. On Ubuntu, this requires running the following command:

```
root@ubuntu1:~# apt-get install libnet-jabber-perl
```

If you are using **Central Perl Archive Network (CPAN)**, which is the source for Perl modules and documentation (visit http://www.cpan.org/), to install Perl packages, then simply run the following command:

```
root@ubuntu1:~# cpan install Net::Jabber
```

In order to use the notification plugin, you will need to customize the script—change the SERVER, PORT, USER, and PASSWORD parameters to those of an existing account. Our recommendation is to create a separate account for Nagios notifications—you will need to set up authorizations for each user to which you want to send notifications.

After modifying the script, it can be used for notifications as follows:

```
define command{
        command_name      notify-host-by-jabber
        command_line      /path/to/notify_via_jabber $_CONTACTJABBERID$
"Nagios Host Notification Type: $NOTIFICATIONTYPE$ Host: $HOSTNAME$\
nState: $HOSTSTATE$ Address: $HOSTADDRESS$ Info: $HOSTOUTPUT$ "
        }


define command{
        command_name      notify-service-by-jabber
        command_line      /path/to/notify_via_jabber $_CONTACTJABBERID$
"Nagios Service Notification Type: $NOTIFICATIONTYPE$ Service:
$SERVICEDESC$ Host: $HOSTALIAS$ Address: $HOSTADDRESS$ State:
$SERVICESTATE$ Additional Info: $SERVICEOUTPUT$"
        }
```

The preceding commands can be used for host and service notifications, and will send a descriptive message using Jabber to the specified user. The $_ CONTACTJABBERID$ text will be replaced with the current contact's _JABBERID custom variable.

Please note that due to the way Jabber works, the best approach for the notify_ via_jabber script would be to use the same Jabber server as that used by clients to receive notifications.

As you plan to monitor servers and, potentially, even outgoing Internet connectivity, it would not be wise to use public Jabber servers to report errors. Therefore, it is a good idea to set up a private Jabber server, probably on the same host on which the Nagios monitoring system is running.

There are multiple desktop clients for the Jabber protocol that can be used to receive Nagios notifications in a convenient way. Pidgin, available at http://www.pidgin. im/, is a cross-platform instant messaging client with multiple protocol support and includes support for Jabber.

Notifying users with text messages

There are extremely useful packages to send SMS (text messages sent from mobile phones) and multiple interfaces to send SMS information via the Internet—such as http://www.twilio.com/, which offers a service to send SMS to phones across a large number of countries.

Using Twilio to send notifications from Nagios is straightforward. Download the twilio-sms command line from https://www.twilio.com/labs/bash/sms. It also requires creating a configuration file that specifies account information for Twilio. For an installation performed according to the steps given in *Chapter 2, Installing Nagios 4*, the location for the file is /opt/nagios/.twiliorc.

Next, create a Nagios command that uses the twilio-sms command directly, as follows:

```
define command{
        command_name        notify-host-by-twilio
        command_line        echo "Nagios $NOTIFICATIONTYPE$ Host: $HOSTNAME$
State: $HOSTSTATE$" | /path/to/twilio-sms $_CONTACTSMSNUMBER$
        }
define command{
        command_name        notify-service-by-twilio
        command_line        echo "Nagios $NOTIFICATIONTYPE$ Svc:
$SERVICEDESC$ Host: $HOSTALIAS$ State: $SERVICESTATE$" | /path/to/twilio-
sms $_CONTACTSMSNUMBER$
        }
```

The downside of using Internet-based notification services is that if Internet connectivity is down, it is not possible for Nagios to send notifications. This may be a problem for Internet providers who need to be sure that their customers are online all the time.

Another possibility to send notifications is to use GSM terminals or USB modems that offer a convenient way to send SMS notifications. Both GSM terminals and USB modems can be used to send text messages via regular SIM cards, which only require GSM coverage and not Internet access. These devices are usually connected via USB or a serial port.

There are multiple tools that allow managing GSM terminals/modems, such as Gammu (http://wammu.eu/gammu/) and Gnokii (http://www.gnokii.org/).

Both are very common applications, and when setting up a GSM terminal, it is best to check both for how well a specific hardware is supported and choose the program that supports this specific GSM terminal better. Depending on the exact hardware used, additional steps to set up drivers and/or configure Gammu/Gnokii may be needed. It is recommended to refer to the documentation for both Gammu/Gnokii, as well as the GSM terminal's documentation.

After setting up, both Gammu and Gnokii provide command-line tools to send SMS messages. The following example shows how to send messages using Gammu:

```
define command{
        command_name        notify-host-by-gammu
        command_line        echo "Nagios $NOTIFICATIONTYPE$ Host: $HOSTNAME$
State: $HOSTSTATE$" | /path/to/gammu --sendsms TEXT $_CONTACTSMSNUMBER$
        }
define command{
        command_name        notify-service-by-gammu
        command_line        echo "Nagios $NOTIFICATIONTYPE$ Svc:
$SERVICEDESC$ Host: $HOSTALIAS$ State: $SERVICESTATE$" | /path/to/gammu
--sendsms TEXT $_CONTACTSMSNUMBER$
        }
```

Current mobile phones also offer cheap Internet connectivity, and smart devices offer the possibility to write custom applications in Java, .NET, Ruby, Python, and Tcl, among many other languages. Therefore, you can also create a client-server application that queries the server for the status of selected hosts and services. It can even be unified with a notification command that pushes the changes down to the application immediately.

Integrating with HipChat

There are also multiple specialized tools for communication within organizations — such as HipChat, a service available at http://www.hipchat.com/. It is a popular online service for group and direct communication within a company. The service has extensive APIs is commonly used to send notifications in addition to regular messaging.

HipChat offers rooms for group communications that are often used to receive notifications as well, for example, a room for Nagios notifications, where the IT staff resides and receives notifications instantly. The chat can then also be used quickly and informally to assign tasks to individuals.

There is a ready-to-use, freely available solution to integrate Nagios with HipChat named *hipsaint*, which is available at `https://github.com/hannseman/hipsaint`.

To use it, simply download the source code and run the installation script as follows:

```
$ python setup.py install
```

Next, create new commands to send notification to specific rooms as follows:

```
define command {
    command_name    notify-host-by-hipchat
    command_line    hipsaint --token=tokenid --room=roomid --type=host
--inputs="$HOSTNAME$|$LONGDATETIME$|$NOTIFICATIONTYPE$|$HOSTADDRESS$|$HOS
TSTATE$|$HOSTOUTPUT$" -n
}


define command {
    command_name    notify-service-by-hipchat
    command_line    hipsaint --token=tokenid --room=roomid --type=service
--inputs="$SERVICEDESC$|$HOSTALIAS$|$LONGDATETIME$|$NOTIFICATIONTYPE$|$HO
STADDRESS$|$SERVICESTATE$|$SERVICEOUTPUT$" -n
}
```

All of the above are ways to send notifications about host/service statuses, which are more convenient than regular e-mails. Letting the IT staff know about problems (and once they are resolved) and being able to communicate to other people in your team/company is essential. Using e-mails may be a good solution in many cases; however, it is a good idea to spend some time on researching for a convenient and non-intrusive approach to use for Nagios notifications.

Apart from the examples previously mentioned, there are many more ready-to-use solutions available online. Many of them are listed on Nagios Exchange at `http://exchange.nagios.org/directory/Addons/Notifications`.

Understanding escalations

A common problem with resolving problems is that a host or a service may have unclear ownership. Often, there is no single person responsible for a host or service, which makes resolution of the problem difficult. It is also typical to have a service with subtle dependencies on other things, which by themselves are small enough not to be monitored by Nagios. In such a case, it is good to include lower management in the escalations, so that they are able to focus on problems that haven't been resolved in a timely manner.

Here is a good example: a database server might fail because a small Perl script, which is run prior to actual start and cleans things up, has entered an infinite loop. The owner of this machine is notified. But the question is, who should be fixing it? The script owner? Or perhaps the database administrator? Often, this ends up in different teams assuming someone else should resolve it—programmers waiting on database administrators and vice versa.

In such cases, escalations are a great way to solve such complex problems. In the previous example, if the problem has not been resolved for two hours, the IT team coordinator or manager would be notified. Another hour later, he/she would get another e-mail. At that point, an urgent meeting would be scheduled with the developer who owns the script and the database admin to discuss how this could be solved.

Of course, in real-world scenarios, escalations to the management alone does not solve all problems. However, often situations need a coordinator who will take care of communicating issues between teams and trying to find a company-wide solution. Business-critical services also require much higher attention. In such cases, following an escalation ladder for all major problems can really benefit the company.

Setting up escalations

Nagios offers many ways to set up escalations depending on your needs. Escalations should not be sent out just after a problem occurs because that would create confusion and prevent smaller problems from being solved. Usually, escalations are set up so that additional people are informed only if a problem has not been resolved after a certain amount of time.

From a configuration point of view, all escalations, are defined as separate objects. There are two types of objects—`hostescalation` and `serviceescalation`. Escalations are configured so that they start and stop being active along with the normal host or service notifications. In this way, if you change the `notification_interval` directive in a host or service definition, the times at which escalations start and stop will also change.

A sample escalation for a company's main router is as follows:

```
define hostescalation
{
    host_name              mainrouter
    contactgroups          it-management
    first_notification     2
```

```
    last_notification        0
    notification_interval 60
    escalation_options       d,u,r
}
```

This will define an escalation for the mainrouter host. With this escalation, the it-management contact group will also get notifications, starting with the second notification. In addition, it will cause the notifications about the host to be in a DOWN and UP state even when it recovers. How Nagios handles notifications and escalations is described in more detail in the next section of the chapter.

The following table describes all available directives to define a host escalation. Items in bold are required when specifying an escalation.

Option	Description
host_name	This specifies a list of all hosts for which the escalation should be defined, and is separated by commas.
hostgroup_name	This specifies a list of all host groups for which the escalation should be defined. All hosts inside the said host groups will have the escalation defined for them. It is separated by commas.
contacts	This is a list of all contacts that should receive notifications related to this escalation, and is separated by commas. At least one contact or contact group needs to be specified for each escalation.
contactgroups	This is a list of all contacts groups that should receive notifications related to this escalation, and is separated by commas. At least one contact or contact group needs to be specified for each escalation.
first_ notification	This is the number of notifications after which this escalation becomes active. Setting this to 0 causes notifications to be sent until the host recovers from the problem.
last_notification	This is the number of notifications after which this escalation stops being active.
notification_ interval	This specifies the interval (the number of minutes) between sending notifications related to this escalation.
escalation_period	This specifies the time period during which an escalation is valid. If it is not specified, this defaults to 24 hours a day, 7 days a week.

Option	Description
`escalation_ options`	This specifies the host states for which notification types should be sent and is separated by commas. This can be one or more of the following:

- d: host DOWN state

- u: host UNREACHABLE state

- r: host recovery (UP state)

Service escalations are defined in a way that is very similar to host escalations. You can specify one or more hosts or host groups, as well as a single service description. A service escalation will be associated with this service on all hosts mentioned in the host_name and hostgroup_name attributes.

The following is an example of a service escalation for an OpenVPN check on the company's main router:

```
define serviceescalation
{
    host_name               mainrouter
    service_description     OpenVPN
    contactgroups           it-management
    first_notification      2
    last_notification       0
    notification_interval 60
    escalation_options      w,c,r
}
```

This will define an escalation for the OpenVPN service running on the mainrouter host. With this escalation, the it-management contact group will also get notifications, starting with the second notification. The escalation will cause notifications about the service to be in WARNING and CRITICAL states even when it recovers.

The following table describes all the available directives to define a service escalation. Items in bold are required when specifying an escalation.

Option	Description
host_name	This specifies a list of all the hosts for which the escalation should be defined, and is separated by commas.
hostgroup_name	This specifies a list of all host groups that the escalation should be defined for. All hosts inside the said host groups will have the escalation defined for them. It is separated by commas.
service_ description	This is the service for which the escalation is being defined.
contacts	This is a list of all contacts that should receive notifications related to this escalation, and is separated by commas. At least one contact or contact group needs to be specified for each escalation.
contactgroups	This is a list of all contact groups that should receive notifications related to this escalation, and is separated by commas. At least one contact or contact group needs to be specified for each escalation.
first_ notification	This is the number of notifications after which this escalation becomes active.
last_ notification	This is the number of notifications after which this escalation stops being active. Setting this to 0 causes notifications to be sent until the service recovers from the problem.
notification_ interval	This specifies the interval (the number of minutes) between sending notifications related to this escalation.
escalation_ period	This specifies the time period during which an escalation is valid. If it is not specified, this defaults to 24 hours a day, 7 days a week.
escalation_ options	This specifies the service states for which notification types should be sent, and is separated by commas. This can be one or more of the following: • r: service recovers (OK state) • w: service WARNING state • c: service CRITICAL state • u: service UNKNOWN state

Understanding how escalations work

Let's consider the following configuration—a service along with two escalations:

```
define service
{
  use                    generic-service
  host_name              mainrouter
  service_description    OpenVPN
  check_command          check_openvpn_remote
  check_interval         15
  max_check_attempts     3
  notification_interval 30
  notification_period    24x7
}
# Escalation 1
define serviceescalation
{
  host_name              mainrouter
  service_description    OpenVPN
  first_notification     4
  last_notification      8
  contactgroups          it-escalation1
  escalation_options     w,c
  notification_period    24x7
  notification_interval 15
}
# Escalation 2
define serviceescalation
{
  host_name              mainrouter
  service_description    OpenVPN
  first_notification     8
  last_notification      0
  contactgroups          it-escalation2
  escalation_options     w,c,r
  notification_period    24x7
  notification_interval 120
}
```

In order to show how the escalations work, let's take an example—a failing service. A service fails for a total of 16 hours and then recovers; for the clarity of the example, we'll skip the `soft` and `hard` states and the time required for `hard` state transitions.

Service notifications are set up so that the first notification is sent out 30 minutes after failure, which is then repeated every 60 minutes. The next notification is sent 1.5 hours after the actual failure, and so on. The service also has two escalations defined for it:

- `Escalation 1`: It is first triggered along with the fourth service notification that is sent out. The escalation stops being active after the eighth service notification about the failure. It only sends out reports about problems, not recovery. The `escalation_options` is set to `w, c`, which is the `WARNING` and `CRITICAL` states. The interval for this escalation is 15 minutes.

- `Escalation 2`: It is first triggered along with the eighth service notification and never stops. The `last_notification` directive is set to `0`. It sends out reports about problems and recovery. The `escalation_options` is set to `w, c, r`, which is the `WARNING`, `CRITICAL`, and `RECOVERY` states. The interval for this escalation is two hours.

The following diagram shows when both the escalations are sent out:

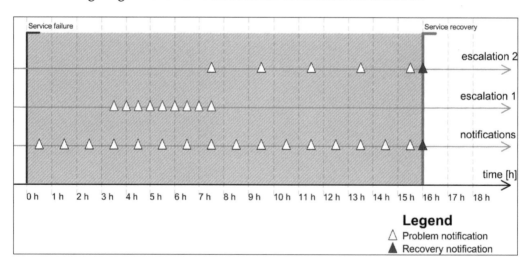

The notifications for the service are sent out 0.5, 1.5, 2.5, 3.5 … hours after the occurrence of the initial service failure.

`Escalation 1` becomes active after 3.5 hours, which is when the fourth service notification is sent out. The last notification related to `escalation 1` is sent out 7.5 hours after the initial failure. This is when the eighth service notification is sent out. It is sent every 30 minutes, so a total of nine notifications related to `escalation 1` are sent out.

`Escalation 2` becomes active after 7.5 hours, which is when the eighth service notification is sent out. The last notification related to `escalation 2` is sent out when the problem is resolved and concerns the actual problem resolution. It is sent every two hours, so a total of four notifications related to `escalation 2` are sent out.

Escalations can be defined to be independent of each other. There is no reason why `Escalation 2` cannot start after the sixth service notification is sent out. There are also no limits on the number of escalations that can be set up for a single host or service.

The main point is that escalations should be defined reasonably so that they don't overload the management or other teams with problems that can be solved without their interference.

Escalations can also be used to contact different people for a certain set of objects based on time periods. If an escalation has the `first_notification` option set to 1 and the `last_notification` option set to 0, then all notifications related to this escalation will be sent out exactly in the same way as notifications for the service itself. For example, on working days, regular IT staff may handle problems; however, during holidays, if notifications about problems should also go to the CritSit team, then you can simply define an escalation saying that during the `holidays` time period, the CritSit group should also be notified when the first notification is sent out. The following is an example that is based on the OpenVPN service defined earlier:

```
define serviceescalation
{
    host_name               mainrouter
    service_description     OpenVPN
    first_notification      1
    last_notification       0
    contactgroups           CritSit
    notification_period     holidays
    notification_interval 30
    escalation_options      w,c,r
}
```

The preceding definitions specify both the service and its escalation. Please note that the `notification_interval` option is set to the same value in both the object and the escalation.

Sending commands to Nagios

Nagios offers a very powerful mechanism to receive events and commands from external applications—the external commands pipe. This is a pipe file created on a filesystem that Nagios uses to receive incoming messages. The filename is `rw/nagios.cmd`, and it is located in the directory passed as the `localstatedir` option during compilation. If you have followed the compilation and installation instructions given in *Chapter 2, Installing Nagios 4*, the filename will be `/var/nagios/rw/nagios.cmd`.

The communication does not use any authentication or authorization. The only requirement is to have write access to the pipe file. An external command file is usually writable by the owner and the group; usually, the group used is `nagioscmd`. If you want a user to be able to send commands to the Nagios daemon, simply add that user to this group.

A small limitation of the command pipe is that there is no way to get any results, and so, it is not possible to send query commands to Nagios. Therefore, by just using the command pipe, you have no confirmation that the command you have just passed to Nagios has actually been processed or will be processed soon. It is, however, possible to read the Nagios logfile and check if it indicates that the command has been parsed correctly, if necessary.

An external command pipe is used by the web interface to control how Nagios works. The web interface does not use any other means to send commands or apply changes to Nagios. This gives us a good understanding of what can be done with the external command pipe interface.

From the Nagios daemon perspective, there is no clear distinction as to who can perform what operations. Therefore, if you plan to use the external command pipe to allow users to submit commands remotely, you need to make sure that the authorization is in place so that unauthorized users cannot send potentially dangerous commands to Nagios.

The syntax to format commands is easy. Each command must be placed on a single line and end with a newline character. The syntax is as follows:

```
[TIMESTAMP] COMMAND_NAME;argument1;argument2;...;argumentN
```

TIMESTAMP is written as UNIX time; that is, the number of seconds since 1970-01-01 00:00:00. This can be created using the date +%s system command. Most programming languages also offer the means to get the current UNIX time. Commands are written in upper case. This can be one of the commands that Nagios should execute, and the arguments depend on the actual command.

All of the commands that can be sent to Nagios using the external command pipe are defined in the documentation available at http://www.nagios.org/ developerinfo/externalcommands/commandinfo.php.

Adding comments to hosts and services

One of the commands that can be sent to Nagios via the external pipe are commands to add a comment for a host or service. This can be used by automated processes to add comments regarding

For example, to add a comment to a host stating that it has passed a security audit, one can use the following shell command:

```
echo "['date +%s'] ADD_HOST_COMMENT;somehost;1;Security Audit;
  This host has passed security audit on 'date +%Y-%m-%d'"
  >/var/nagios/rw/nagios.cmd
```

This will send an ADD_HOST_COMMENT command to Nagios over the external command pipe. Nagios will then add a comment to the host, somehost, stating that the comment originated from Security Audit. The first argument specifies the hostname to add the comment to; the second tells Nagios if this comment should be persistent. The next argument describes the author of the comment, and the last argument specifies the actual comment text.

Similarly, adding a comment to a service requires the use of the ADD_SVC_COMMENT command. The command's syntax is very similar to the ADD_HOST_COMMENT command, except that the command requires the specification of the hostname and the service name.

For example, to add a comment to a service stating that it has been restarted, use the following code:

```
echo "['date +%s'] ADD_SVC_COMMENT;router;OpenVPN;1;nagiosadmin;
Restarting the OpenVPN service" >/var/nagios/rw/nagios.cmd
```

The first argument specifies the hostname to which to add the comment; the second is the description of the service to which Nagios should add the comment. The next argument tells Nagios if this comment should be persistent. The fourth argument describes the author of the comment, and the last argument specifies the actual comment text.

You can also delete a single comment or all comments using the DEL_HOST_ COMMENT, DEL_ALL_HOST_COMMENTS, DEL_SVC_COMMENT, or DEL_ALL_SVC_COMMENTS commands.

Scheduling host and service checks

Other commands worth mentioning are related to scheduling checks on demand. Very often, it is necessary to request that a check must be carried out as soon as possible; for example, when testing a solution.

This time, let's create a script that schedules a check of a host, all services on that host, and a service on a different host, as follows:

```sh
#!/bin/sh

NOW='date +%s'

echo "[$NOW] SCHEDULE_HOST_CHECK;somehost;$NOW" \
    >/var/nagios/rw/nagios.cmd
echo "[$NOW] SCHEDULE_HOST_SVC_CHECKS;somehost;$NOW" \
    >/var/nagios/rw/nagios.cmd
echo "[$NOW] SCHEDULE_SVC_CHECK;otherhost;Service Name;$NOW" \
    >/var/nagios/rw/nagios.cmd

exit 0
```

The commands SCHEDULE_HOST_ and SCHEDULE_HOST_SVC_CHECKS accept a hostname and the time at which the check should be scheduled. The SCHEDULE_SVC_ CHECK command requires the specification of a service description as well as the name of the host on which to schedule the check.

Normal scheduled checks, such as the ones previously scheduled , might not actually take place at the time that you scheduled them. Nagios also needs to take allowed time periods into account, as well as verify whether the checks were disabled for a particular object or for Nagios entirely.

There are cases when you'll need to force Nagios to preform a check. In such cases, you should use the SCHEDULE_FORCED_HOST_ , SCHEDULE_FORCED_HOST_SVC_CHECKS, and SCHEDULE_FORCED_SVC_CHECK commands. They work in exactly the same way as previously described, but make Nagios skip the checking of time periods and ensure that the checks are disabled for a particular object. In this way, a check will always be performed regardless of other Nagios parameters.

Modifying custom variables

Other commands worth using are related to the custom variables feature, which is detailed in *Chapter 5, Advanced Configuration*. When you define a custom variable for a host, service, or contact, you can change its value on the fly with the external command pipe.

Because these variables can then be directly used by check or notification commands and event handlers, it is possible to make other applications or event handlers change these attributes directly without modifications to the configuration files.

A good example would be the IT staff using an application that allows receiving notifications, for example, Growl, a notification system for OS X and Windows (visit http://growl.info/ and http://www.growlforwindows.com/ for more details).

It is then possible for a helper application also to periodically send information about the last known IP address, and that information is then passed to Nagios, assuming that the person is in the office. This can then be passed to a notification command to use that specific IP address while sending a message to the user.

Assuming that the username is jdoe and the custom variable name is DESKTOPIP, the message that would be sent to the Nagios external command pipe would be as follows:

```
[1206096000] CHANGE_CUSTOM_CONTACT_VAR;jdoe;DESKTOPIP;12.34.56.78
```

This would cause a later use of $_CONTACTDESKTOPIP$ to return a value of 12.34.56.78.

Nagios offers the `CHANGE_CUSTOM_CONTACT_`, `CHANGE_CUSTOM_HOST_VAR`, and `CHANGE_CUSTOM_SVC_VAR` commands to modify custom variables in contacts, hosts, and services, respectively.

The commands previously explained are just a small subset of the full capabilities of the Nagios external command pipe. For a complete list of commands, visit `http://www.nagios.org/developerinfo/externalcommands/commandlist.php`, where the **External Command List** can be seen.

External commands are usually sent from event handlers or from the Nagios web interface. You will find external commands most useful when writing event handlers for your system, or when writing an external application that interacts with Nagios.

Creating event handlers

Event handlers are commands that are triggered whenever the state of a host or service changes. They offer functionalities similar to those of notifications. The main difference is that the event handlers are called for each type of change and even for each `soft` state change. This provides the ability to react to a problem before Nagios notifies it as a `hard` state and sends out notifications about it. Another difference is what the event handlers do: instead of notifying users that there is a problem, event handlers carry out actions automatically.

For example, if a service is defined with `max_check_attempts` set to 4, the `retry_interval` set to 1, and `check_interval` set to 5, then the following example illustrates when event handlers will be triggered and with what values for $SERVICESTATE$, $SERVICESTATETYPE$, and $SERVICEATTEMP$ macro definitions:

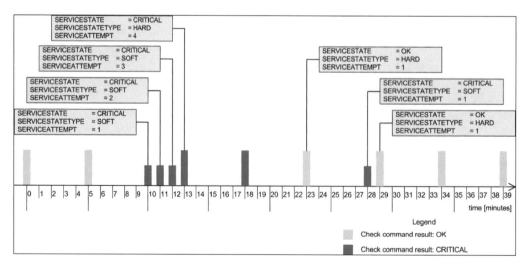

Event handlers are triggered for each state change, for example, in minutes, 10, 23, 28, and 29. When writing an event handler, it is necessary to check whether an event handler should perform an action at that particular time. See the example in the following section for more details.

Event handlers are also triggered for each soft check attempt. It is also triggered when the host status becomes hard (when `max_check_attempts` attempts of checks have been made and the service has not recovered). In this example, these occur at minutes 11, 12, and 13. It's important to know that the events will run if no state change has occurred and the object is in a `hard` state; for example, no events are triggered in minutes 5, 18, 34, and 39.

Restarting services automatically

A typical example might be that your web server process tends to crash once a month. Because this is rare, it is very difficult to debug and resolve it. Therefore, the best way to proceed is to restart the server automatically until a solution to the problem is found.

If your configuration has `max_check_attempts` set to 4, as in the preceding example, then a good place to try to restart the web server is after the third soft failure check; in the previous example, this would be minute 12.

Assuming that the restart has been successful, the previous figure would look like what is shown in the following figure:

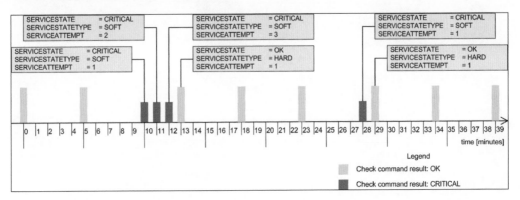

Please note that no hard critical state has occurred since the event handler resolved the problem. If a restart cannot resolve the issue, Nagios will only try it once as the attempt is done only in the third soft check.

Event handlers are defined as commands, similar to check commands. The main difference is that the event handlers only use macro definitions to pass information to the actual event handling script. This implies that the $ARGn$ macro definitions cannot be used, and arguments cannot be passed in the host or service definition by using the ! separator.

In the previous example, we would define the following command:

```
define command
{
  command_name restart-apache2
  command_line $USER1$/events/restart_apache2
          $SERVICESTATE$ $SERVICESTATETYPE$ $SERVICEATTEMPT$
}
```

The command would need to be added to the service. For both hosts and services, this requires adding an event_handler directive that specifies the command to be run for each event that is fired. In addition, it is good to set event_handler_enabled to 1 to make sure that event handlers are enabled for this object.

The following is an example of a service definition:

```
define service
{
  host_name              localhost
  service_description    Webserver
  use                    apache
  event_handler          restart-apache2
  event_handler_enabled  1
}
```

Finally, a short version of the script is as follows:

```
#!/bin/sh

# use variables for arguments
SERVICESTATE=$1
SERVICESTATETYPE=$2
SERVICEATTEMPT=$3
```

```
# we don't want to restart if current status is OK
if [ "$SERVICESTATE" != "OK" ] ; then

    # proceed only if we're in soft transition state
    if [ "$SERVICESTATETYPE" == "SOFT" ] ; then

        # proceed only if this is 3rd attempt, restart
        if [ "$SERVICESTATEATTEMPT" == "3" ] ; then

            # restarts Apache as system administrator
            sudo service apache2 restart
        fi

    fi

fi

exit 0
```

Because we're using sudo here, obviously the script needs an entry in the sudoers file to allow the nagios user to run the command without a password prompt. An example entry for the sudoers file is as follows:

```
nagios ALL=NOPASSWD: /usr/sbin/service
```

This will tell sudo that the /usr/sbin/service command can be run by the nagios user and passwords will not be requested before running the command.

According to our script, the restart is only done after the third check fails. Assuming that the restart was successful, the next Nagios check will notify that Apache is running again. As this is considered a soft state, Nagios has not yet sent out any notifications about the problem.

If the service does not restart correctly, the next check will cause Nagios to set this failure as a hard state. At this point, notifications will be sent out to the object owners.

You can also try performing a restart in the second check. If that does not help, then during the third attempt, the script can forcefully terminate all Apache2 processes using the `killall` or `pkill` command. After this has been done, it can try to restart the service, as seen in the following example:

```
# proceed only if this is 3rd attempt, restart
if [ "$SERVICESTATEATTEMPT" == "2" ] ; then

  # restart Apache as system administrator
  sudo service apache2 restart
fi


# proceed only if this is 3rd attempt, restart
if [ "$SERVICESTATEATTEMPT" == "3" ] ; then
  # try to terminate apache2 process as system administrator
  sudo pkill apache2

  # starts Apache as system administrator
  sudo service apache2 start
fi
```

Similar to the previous example, it requires adding an entry in the `sudoers` file. It also requires the adding of the `pkill` command, as seen in the following code. The whole path to the command is `/usr/bin/pkill`:

```
nagios ALL=NOPASSWD: /usr/bin/pkill
nagios ALL=NOPASSWD: /usr/sbin/service
```

Another common scenario is to restart one service if another one has just recovered—for example, you might want to restart the e-mail servers that use a database for authentication if the database has just recovered from a failure state. The reason is that some applications may not manage disconnected database handles correctly. This can lead to the service working correctly from the Nagios perspective, but not allowing some of the users in due to internal problems.

If you have set this up for hosts or services, it is recommended that you keep flapping enabled for these services. It often happens that due to incorrectly planned scripts and the relations between them, some services might be stopped and restarted.

In such cases, Nagios will detect these problems and stop running event handlers for these services, which will cause fewer malfunctions to occur. It is also recommended that you keep notifications set up so that people also get information on when flapping starts and stops.

Modifying notifications

Nagios also offers the ability to change various parameters related to notifications. These parameters are modified via an external command pipe, similar to a few of the commands shown in the previous section.

A good example would be when Nagios contact persons have their workstations connected to the local network only when they are actually at work (which is usually the case if they are using notebooks), and turn their computers off when they leave work. In such a case, a ping check for a person's computer could trigger an event handler to toggle that person's attributes.

Let's assume that our `jdoe` user has two actual contacts — `jdoe-email` and `jdoe-jabber` — each for different types of notifications. We can set up a host corresponding to the `jdoe` workstation. We will also set it up to be monitored every five minutes and create an event handler. The handler will change the host and service notification time period of `jdoe-jabber` to `none` on a hard host down state. On a host up state change, the time period for `jdoe-jabber` will be set to `24x7`. In this way, the user will only get Jabber notifications if he or she is at work.

Nagios offers commands to change the time periods during which a user wants to receive notifications. The commands for this purpose are CHANGE_CONTACT_HOST_NOTIFICATION_TIMEPERIOD and CHANGE_CONTACT_SVC_NOTIFICATION_TIMEPERIOD. Both commands take the contact name and the time period as their arguments.

An event handler script that modifies the user's contact time period based on the state is as follows:

```
#!/bin/sh

NOW='date +%s'
CONTACT=$1-jabber
if [ "$2,$3" = "DOWN,HARD" ] ; then
    TP=none
else
    TP=24x7
fi
echo "[$NOW] CHANGE_CONTACT_HOST_NOTIFICATION_TIMEPERIOD;
    $CONTACT;$TP" \
    >/var/nagios/rw/nagios.cmd
echo "[$NOW] CHANGE_CONTACT_SVC_NOTIFICATION_TIMEPERIOD;
    $CONTACT;$TP" \
    >/var/nagios/rw/nagios.cmd
exit 0
```

The command should pass $CONTACTNAME$, $SERVICESTATE$, and $SERVICESTATETYPE$ as parameters to the script.

In case you need a notification about a problem that has been re-sent, use the SEND_CUSTOM_HOST_NOTIFICATION or SEND_CUSTOM_SVC_NOTIFICATION command. These commands take host names or host and service names, additional options, author name, and comments that should be added to the notification.

The additional options allow us to specify if the notification should also include all escalation levels (a value of 1), if Nagios should skip time periods for specific users (a value of 2), and if Nagios should increment notifications counters (a value of 4). Options are stored bitwise, so a value of 7 (1 + 2 + 4) would enable all of these options. The notification including escalations would be sent to all. It will be forced and the escalation counters will be increased. The option value of 3 means that the notification should be broadcasted to all escalations as well, and the time periods should be skipped.

To send a custom notification, including escalations, about the main router to all users, send the following command to Nagios:

```
[1206096000] SEND_CUSTOM_HOST_NOTIFICATION;router1;3;jdoe;RESPOND ASAP
```

Using adaptive monitoring

Nagios provides a very powerful feature named adaptive monitoring that allows the modification of various check-related parameters on the fly. This is done by sending a command to the Nagios external command pipe.

The first thing that can be changed on the fly is the command to be executed by Nagios, along with the attributes that will be passed to it—an equivalent of the check_command directive in the object definition. In order to do that, we can use the CHANGE_HOST_CHECK_COMMAND or CHANGE_SVC_CHECK_COMMAND command. These require the hostname or the hostname and service description, and the check command as arguments.

This can be used to change how hosts or services are checked, or to only modify parameters that are passed to the check commands; for example, a check for ping latency can be modified based on whether a primary or a backup connection is used. An example to change a check command of a service, which changes the command and its specified parameters, is as follows:

```
[1206096000]
  CHANGE_SVC_CHECK_COMMAND;linux1;PING;check_ping!500.0,50%
```

A similar possibility is to change the custom variables that are used later in a check command. An example where the following command and service are used is as follows:

```
define command
{
    command_name            check-ping
    command_line            $USER1$/check_ping -H $HOSTADDRESS$
                            -p $_SERVICEPACKETS$

                            -w $_SERVICEWARNING$
                            -c $_SERVICECRITICAL$


}
define service
{
    host_name               linux2
    service_description      PING
    use                      ping
    check_command            check-ping
    _PACKETS                 5
    _WARNING                 100.0,40%
    _CRITICAL                300.0,60%
}
```

This example is very similar to the one we saw earlier. The main benefit is that parameters can be set independently; for example, one event handler might modify the number of packets to send, while another can modify the warning and/or critical state limits.

The following is an example to modify the warning level for the ping service on a linux1 host:

```
[1206096000] CHANGE_CUSTOM_SVC_VAR;linux1;PING;_WARNING;500.0,50%
```

It is also possible to modify event handlers on the fly. This can be used to enable or disable scripts that try to resolve a problem. To do this, you need to use the CHANGE_HOST_EVENT_HANDLER and CHANGE_SVC_EVENT_HANDLER commands.

In order to set an event handler command for the Apache2 service mentioned previously in this section, send the following command:

```
[1206096000] CHANGE_SVC_EVENT_HANDLER;localhost;webserver;
restart-apache2
```

Please note that setting an empty event handler disables any previous event handlers for this host or service. The same comment also applies when modifying the check command definition. In case you are modifying commands or event handlers, please make sure that the corresponding command definitions actually exist; otherwise, Nagios might reject your modifications.

Another feature that you can use to fine-tune the execution of checks is the ability to modify the time period during which a check should be performed. This is done with the `CHANGE_HOST_CHECK_TIMEPERIOD` and `CHANGE_SVC_CHECK_TIMEPERIOD` commands. Similar to the previous commands, these accept the hostname or the host and service names, and the new time period to be set. Consider the following example:

```
[1206096000] CHANGE_SVC_CHECK_TIMEPERIOD;localhost;webserver;
  workinghours
```

As is the case with command names, you need to make sure that the time period you are requesting to be set exists in the Nagios configuration. Otherwise, Nagios will ignore this command and leave out the current check time period.

Nagios also allows modifying intervals between checks—both for the normal checks, and retrying during `soft` states. This is done through the `CHANGE_NORMAL_HOST_CHECK_`, `CHANGE_RETRY_HOST_CHECK_INTERVAL`, `CHANGE_NORMAL_SVC_CHECK_INTERVAL`, and `CHANGE_RETRY_SVC_CHECK_INTERVAL` commands. All of these commands require passing the hostname or the host and service names, as well as the intervals that should be set.

A typical example of when intervals are modified on the fly is when the priority of a host or service relies on other parameters in your network. An example might be a failover server that will only be run if the primary server is down.

It is very important to make sure that the host and all of the services on it are working properly before actually performing scheduled backups. During idle time, its priority might be much lower. Another issue might be that monitoring the failover server should be performed more often in case the primary server fails.

An example to modify the normal interval for a host to every 15 minutes is as follows:

```
[1206096000] CHANGE_NORMAL_HOST_CHECK_INTERVAL;backupserver;15
```

There is also the possibility to modify how many checks need to be performed before a state is considered to be hard. The commands for this are `CHANGE_MAX_HOST_CHECK_ATTEMPTS` and `CHANGE_MAX_SVC_CHECK_ATTEMPTS`.

The following is an example command to set the maximum retries for a host to 5:

```
[1206096000] CHANGE_MAX_HOST_CHECK_ATTEMPTS;linux1;5
```

There are many more commands that allow the fine-tuning of monitoring and check settings on the fly. It is recommended that you get acquainted with all of the external commands that your version of Nagios supports, as mentioned in the section introducing the external commands pipe.

Summary

In this chapter, we have learned how to use the notification mechanism more effectively by sending information about the host and service status using multiple protocols such as SMS or instant messaging. This can be used to reduce the number of e-mails sent and reduce the chances of failure information getting caught by spam or e-mail filters.

We have also learned about escalations, and how those can be used automatically to inform additional people when a problem has not been resolved in a timely manner. This can be especially important in large organizations or when there is no clear ownership of one or more resources.

The chapter also covered sending commands to Nagios and how that can be used to add information about hosts and services, scheduling checks, and changing custom variables.

We have also learned how to create event handlers and how those can be used automatically to attempt to restart a service and/or change notification settings.

The chapter also covered adaptive notifications and how events or external applications can fine-tune the check settings for hosts and services.

The next chapter will cover passive checks and **Nagios Service Check Acceptor** (**NSCA**). These can be used to notify Nagios about the host and service status from external applications or other Nagios instances, including sending the information across networks.

7
Passive Checks and NSCA

Nagios is a very powerful platform because it is easy to extend. The previous chapters talked about the check command plugins and how they can be used to check any host or service that your company might be using. Another great feature that Nagios offers is the ability for third-party software or other Nagios instances to report information on the status of services or hosts. This way, Nagios does not need to schedule and run checks by itself; other applications can report information as it is available to them. In this chapter we will cover the following topics:

- Understanding the difference between active and passive checks
- Setting up passive checks in Nagios as well as enabling them for specific hosts and services
- Troubleshooting common errors related to passive checks
- An overview of what NSCA is
- Setting up the NSCA server to allow receiving check results
- Submitting host and service check results using the NSCA client binary
- Configuring NSCA for secure communication

Understanding passive checks

The previous parts of this book often mentioned Nagios performing checks on various software and machines. In such cases, Nagios decides when a check is to be performed, runs the check, and stores the result. These types of checks are called **active checks**.

Nagios also offers another way to work with the statuses of hosts and services. It is possible to configure Nagios so that it will receive status information sent over a command pipe. In such cases, checks are done by other programs and their results are sent to Nagios. Nagios will still handle all notifications, event handlers, and dependencies between hosts and services.

Active checks are most common in the Nagios world. They have a lot of advantages and some disadvantages. One of the problems is that such checks can take only a few seconds to complete; a typical timeout for an active check to complete is 10 or 30 seconds. In many cases, the time taken is not enough as some checks need to be performed over a longer period of time to have satisfactory results. A good example might be running a check that takes several hours to complete; in this case, it does not make sense to raise the global `service_check_timeout` option. Instead, schedule these checks outside of Nagios and only report the results back after the checks are complete.

There are also different types of checks including external applications or devices that want to report information directly to Nagios. This can be done to gather all critical errors in a single, central place. These types of checks are called **passive checks**.

For example, when a web application cannot connect to the database, it will let Nagios know about it immediately. It can also send reports after a database recovery, or periodically, even if connectivity to the database has consistently been available, so that Nagios has an up-to-date status. This can be done in addition to active checks to identify critical problems earlier.

Another example is where an application already processes information such as network bandwidth utilization. In this case, adding a module that reports current utilization along with the `OK`/`WARNING`/`CRITICAL` state to Nagios seems much easier than using active checks for the same job.

Often, there are situations where active checks obviously fit better. In other cases, passive checks are the way to go. In general, if a check can be done quickly and does not require long-running processes, it should definitely be done as an active service. If the situation involves reporting problems that will be sent independently by Nagios from other applications or machines, it is definitely a use case for a passive check. In cases where the checks require the deployment of long-running processes or monitoring information constantly, this should be done as a passive service.

Another difference is that active checks require much less effort to be set up when compared to passive checks. In the first case, Nagios takes care of the scheduling, and the command only needs to perform the actual checks and mark the results as `OK`/`WARNING`/`CRITICAL` based on how a check command is configured. Passive checks require all the logic related to what should be reported and when it should be checked to be put in an external application. This usually calls for some effort.

The following diagram shows how both active and passive checks are performed by Nagios. It shows what is performed by Nagios in both cases and what needs to be done by the check command or an external application for passive checks.

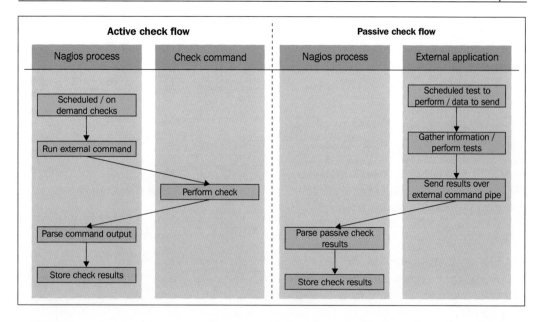

Nagios also offers a way of combining the benefits of both active and passive checks. Often, you have situations where other applications can report whether a certain service is working properly or not. However, if the monitoring application is not running or some other issue prevents it from reporting, Nagios can use active checks to keep the service status up-to-date.

A good example would be a server that is a part of an application processing job queues using a database. It can report each problem when accessing the database. We want Nagios to monitor this database, and as the application is already using it, we can add a module that reports this to Nagios.

The application can also periodically let Nagios know if it succeeded in using the database without problems. However, if there are no jobs to process and the application is not using it, Nagios will not have up-to-date information about the database.

Configuring passive checks

The first thing that needs to be done in order to use passive checks for your Nagios setup is to make sure that you have the following options in your main Nagios configuration file, such as `/etc/nagios/nagios.cfg`, if Nagios was set up according to instructions from *Chapter 2, Installing Nagios 4*:

```
accept_passive_service_checks=1
accept_passive_host_checks=1
```

It would also be good to enable the logging of incoming passive checks; this makes determining the problem of not processing a passive check much easier. The following directive allows it:

```
log_passive_checks=1
```

Setting up hosts or services for passive checking requires an object to have the `passive_checks_enabled` option set to 1 for Nagios to accept passive check results over the command pipe. If only passive checks will be sent to Nagios, it is also advised that you disable active checks by setting the `active_checks_enabled` option to 0. The following is an example of the required configuration for a host that accepts passive checks and has active checks disabled:

```
define host
{
  use                       generic-host
  host_name                 linuxbox01
  address                   10.0.2.1
  active_checks_enabled     0
  passive_checks_enabled    1
}
```

Configuring services is exactly the same as with hosts. For example, to set up a very similar service, all we need to do is to use the same parameters as those for the hosts:

```
define service
{
  use                    ping-template
  host_name              linuxbox01
  service_description    PING
  active_checks_enabled  0
  passive_checks_enabled 1
}
```

In this case, Nagios will never perform any active checks on its own and will only rely on the results that are passed to it. We can also configure Nagios so that if no new information has been provided within a certain period of time, it will use active checks to get the current status of the host or service. If up-to-date information has been provided by a passive check during this period, then it will not perform active checks.

In order to do this, we need to enable active checks by setting the `active_checks_enabled` option to 1 without specifying the `normal_check_interval` directive. For Nagios to perform active checks when there is no up-to-date result from passive checks, you need to set the `check_freshness` directive to 1 and set `freshness_threshold` to the duration after which a check should be performed. The time specified in the `freshness_threshold` option is specified in seconds.

The first parameter tells Nagios that it should check whether the results from the checks are up-to-date. The next parameter specifies the number of seconds after which Nagios should consider the results to be out of date. Attributes can be used for both hosts and services. A sample definition for a host that runs an active check if there has been no result provided within the last two hours is as follows:

```
define host
{
  use                    generic-host
  host_name              linuxbox02
  address                10.0.2.2
  check_command          check-host-alive
  check_freshness        1
  freshness_threshold    7200
  active_checks_enabled  1
  passive_checks_enabled 1
}
```

The following is an illustration showing when Nagios will invoke active checks:

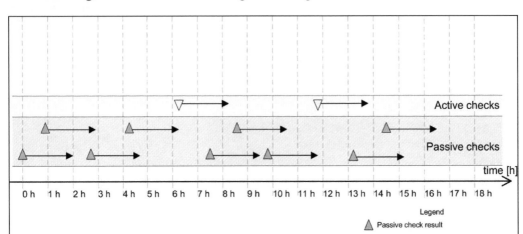

Each time there is at least one passive check result that is still valid (in other words, that was received within the past two hours), Nagios will not perform any active checks. However, two hours after the last passive or active check result is received, Nagios will perform an active check to keep the results up-to-date.

Sending passive check results for hosts

Nagios allows applications and event handlers to send out passive check results for host objects. In order to use them, the host needs to be configured to accept passive check results. In order to be able to submit passive check results, we need to configure Nagios to allow the sending of passive check results and set the host objects to accept them.

Submitting passive host check results to Nagios requires sending a command to the Nagios external command pipe. This way, the other applications on your Nagios server can report the status of the hosts.

The command to submit passive checks is PROCESS_HOST_CHECK_RESULT (visit
http://www.nagios.org/developerinfo/externalcommands/commandinfo.php?
command_id=115). This command accepts the hostname, status code, and the textual
output from a check. The host status code should be 0 for an UP state, 1 for DOWN,
and 2 for an UNREACHABLE state. The following is a sample script that will accept the
hostname, status code, and output from a check and will submit these to Nagios:

```
#!/bin/sh

NOW=`date +%s`
HOST=$1
STATUS=$2
OUTPUT=$3

echo "[$NOW] PROCESS_HOST_CHECK_RESULT;$HOST;$STATUS;$OUTPUT" \
    >/var/nagios/rw/nagios.cmd

exit 0
```

As an example of the use of this script, the command sent to Nagios for host01,
status code 2 (UNREACHABLE), and output router 192.168.1.2 down would be as
follows:

```
[1206096000] PROCESS_HOST_CHECK_RESULT;host01;2;router
192.168.1.2 down
```

While submitting results, it is worth noting that Nagios might take some time to
process them, depending on the intervals between checks of the external command
pipe in Nagios. Unlike active checks, Nagios will not take network topology into
consideration by default. This is very important in situations where a host behind a
router is reported to be down because the router is actually down.

By default, Nagios handles results from active and passive checks differently. When
Nagios plans and receives results from active checks, it takes the actual network
topology into consideration and performs a translation of the states based on these
results. This means that if Nagios receives a result indicating that a host is down, it
assumes that all child hosts are in an UNREACHABLE state.

When a passive result check comes in to Nagios, Nagios expects that the result
already has a network topology included. When a host is reported to be DOWN
as a passive check result, Nagios does not perform a translation from DOWN to
UNREACHABLE. Even if its parent host is currently DOWN, the child host state is also
stored as DOWN.

How Nagios handles passive check results can be defined in the main Nagios configuration file. In order to make Nagios treat passive host check results in the same way as active check results, we need to enable the following option:

```
translate_passive_host_checks=1
```

By default, Nagios treats host results from passive checks as hard results. This is because, very often, passive checks are used to report host and service statuses from other Nagios instances. In such cases, only reports regarding hard state changes are propagated across Nagios servers. If you want Nagios to treat all passive check results for hosts as if they were soft results, you need to enable the following option in the main Nagios configuration file:

```
passive_host_checks_are_soft=1
```

Sending passive check results for services

Passive service checks are very similar to passive host checks. In both the cases, the idea is that Nagios receives information about host statuses over the external command pipe. As with passive checks of hosts, all that is needed is to enable the global Nagios option to accept passive check results and to also enable this option for each service that should allow the passing of passive check results.

The results are passed to Nagios in the same way as they are passed for hosts. The command to submit passive checks is PROCESS_SERVICE_CHECK_RESULT (visit http://www.nagios.org/developerinfo/externalcommands/commandinfo.php? command_id=114 for more details). This command accepts the hostname, service description, status code, and the textual output from a check. Service status codes are the same as those for active checks — 0 for OK, 1 for WARNING, 2 for CRITICAL, and 3 for an UNKNOWN state. The following is a sample script that will accept the hostname, status code, and output from a check and submit these to Nagios:

```
#!/bin/sh

CLOCK=`date +%s`
HOST=$1
SVC=$2
STATUS=$3
OUTPUT=$4

echo "[$CLOCK] PROCESS_SERVICE_CHECK_RESULT;$HOST;$SVC;$STATUS;
    $OUTPUT">/var/nagios/rw/nagios.cmd

exit 0
```

As a result of running the script, the command that is sent to Nagios for `host01`, service `PING`, status code `0` (`OK`), and output `RTT=57 ms` is as follows:

```
[1206096000] PROCESS_SERVICE_CHECK_RESULT;host01;PING;0;RTT=57 ms
```

A very common scenario for using passive checks is a check that takes a very long time to complete. When submitting results, it is worth noting that Nagios might take some time to process them, depending on the intervals between checks of the external command pipe in Nagios.

A major difference between hosts and services is that service checks differentiate between soft and hard states. When new information regarding a service gets passed to Nagios via the external command pipe, Nagios treats it in the same way as if it had been received by an active check. If a service is set up with a `max_check_attempts` directive of `5`, then the same number of passive check results would be needed in order for Nagios to treat the new status as a hard state change.

The passive service checks are often used to report the results of long lasting tests that were run asynchronously. A good example of such a test is checking whether there are bad blocks on a disk. This requires trying to read the entire disk directly from the block device (such as `/dev/sda1`) and checking if the attempt has failed. This can't be done as an active check as reading the device takes a lot of time and larger disks might require several hours to complete. For this reason, the only way to perform such a check is to schedule it from the system, for example, by using the cron daemon (visit `http://man.linuxquestions.org/index.php?query=cron`). The script should then post results to the Nagios daemon.

The following is a script that runs the `dd` system command (visit `http://man.linuxquestions.org/index.php?query=dd`) to read an entire block device. Based on whether the read was successful or not, the appropriate status code along with the plugin output is sent out.

```
#!/bin/sh

SVC=$1
DEVICE=$2
TMPFILE=`mktemp`
NOW=`date +%s`
PREFIX="[$NOW] PROCESS_SERVICE_CHECK_RESULT;localhost;$SVC"

# try to read the device
dd bs=1M if=$DEVICE of=/dev/null >$TMPFILE 2>&1
CODE=$?
```

```
RESULT=`grep copied <$TMPFILE`
rm $TMPFILE

if [ $CODE == 0 ] ; then
    echo "$PREFIX;0;$RESULT"
else
    echo "$PREFIX;2;Error while checking device $DEVICE"
fi

exit 0
```

If the check fails, then a `critical` status, along with text stating that there was a problem checking the specific device, is sent out to Nagios. If the check was successful, an output mentioning number of bytes and the speed of transfer is sent out to Nagios. A typical output would be something like this:

```
254951424 bytes (255 MB) copied, 9.72677 seconds, 26.2 MB/s
```

The hostname is hardcoded to `localhost`. Using this script requires configuring a service to have active checks disabled and passive checks enabled. As the checks will be done quite rarely, it's recommended that you set `max_check_attempts` to 1. It is also possible to use the `badblocks` (please visit `http://linux.die.net/man/8/badblocks` for more details) command to check for bad blocks on a hard drive.

Troubleshooting errors

It's not always possible to set up passive checks correctly the first time. In such cases, it is a good thing to try to debug the issue one step at a time in order to find any potential problems. Sometimes, the problem could be a configuration issue, while in other cases, it could be an issue such as the mistyping of the host or service name.

One thing worth checking is whether the Web UI shows changes after you have sent the passive result check. If it doesn't, then at some point, things are not working correctly. The first thing you should start with is enabling the logging of external commands and passive checks. To do this, make sure that the following values are enabled in the main Nagios configuration file:

```
log_external_commands=1
log_passive_checks=1
```

In order for the changes to take effect, a restart of the Nagios process is needed. After this has been done, Nagios will log all commands passed via the command pipe and log all of the passive check results it receives.

A very common problem is that the application or script cannot write data to the Nagios command pipe. In order to test this, simply try to write to the Nagios external command pipe in the same manner that the application/script's user is running. For example, if the script is running as the user daemon, try the following as root:

```
root@ubuntuserver:# su -s/bin/sh daemon
$ echo TEST >/var/nagios/rw/nagios.cmd
```

The su command will switch the user to the specified user. The next line is run as the user daemon and an attempt to write to the Nagios external command pipe is made. The -s flag for the su command forces /bin/sh as the shell to use. It is useful in cases where the user's default shell is not a proper shell, that is, it is set to /bin/false for security reasons to prevent the account from interactive shell access.

If the preceding command runs fine and no errors are reported, then your permissions are set up correctly. If an error shows up, you should add the user to the nagioscmd group as described in *Chapter 2, Installing Nagios 4*. The following command will add the user daemon to the nagioscmd group:

```
root@ubuntuserver:# adduser daemon nagioscmd
```

The next thing to do is to manually send a passive check result to the Nagios command pipe and check whether the Nagios log file was received and parsed correctly. To do this, run the following command as the same user that the application or script is running as:

```
root@ubuntuserver:# su -s/bin/sh daemon
$ echo "[`date +%s`] PROCESS_HOST_CHECK_RESULT;host1;2;test" \
  >/var/nagios/rw/nagios.cmd
```

The name host1 needs to be replaced with an actual hostname from your configuration. A few seconds after running this command, the Nagios log file should reflect the command that we have just sent. You should see the following lines in your log:

```
EXTERNAL COMMAND: PROCESS_HOST_CHECK_RESULT;host1;2;test
[1220257561] PASSIVE HOST CHECK: host1;2;test
```

If both of these lines are in your log file, then we can conclude that Nagios has received and parsed the command correctly. If only the first line is present, then it means either that the option to receive passive host check results is disabled globally or that it is disabled for this particular object. The first thing you should do is to make sure that your main Nagios configuration file contains the following line:

```
accept_passive_host_checks=1
```

Next, you should check your configuration to see whether the host definition has passive checks enabled as well. If not, simply add the following directive to the object definition:

```
passive_checks_enabled  1
```

If you have misspelled the name of the host object, then the following will be logged:

```
Warning:  Passive check result was received for host 'host01',
but the host could not be found!
```

In this case, make sure that your hostname is correct. Similar checks can also be done for services. You can run the following command to check if a passive service check is being handled correctly by Nagios:

```
root@ubuntuserver:# su -s/bin/sh daemon
$ echo "[`date +%s`] PROCESS_SERVICE_CHECK_RESULT;host1;APT;0;test" \
  >/var/nagios/rw/nagios.cmd
```

Again, `host1` should be replaced by the actual hostname, and APT needs to be an existing service for that host. After a few seconds, the following entries in the Nagios log file (`/var/nagios/nagios.log`) will indicate that the result has been successfully parsed:

```
EXTERNAL COMMAND: PROCESS_SERVICE_CHECK_RESULT;host1;APT;0;test
```

```
PASSIVE SERVICE CHECK: host1;APT;0;test
```

If the second line is not in the log file, there are two possible causes. One is that the global option to accept service passive checks by Nagios is disabled. You should start by making sure that your main Nagios configuration file (`/etc/nagios/nagios.cfg`) contains the following line:

```
accept_passive_service_checks=1
```

The other possibility is that the host does not have passive checks enabled. You should make sure that the service definition has passive checks enabled as well, and if not, add the following directive to the object definition:

```
  define host
  {
    host_name                   host1
    passive_checks_enabled      1
  }
```

If you have misspelled the name of the host or service, then the following information will be logged in the Nagios log file:

```
Warning:  Passive check result was received for service 'APT' on host
'host1', but the service could not be found!
```

Using NSCA

Passive checks are sent to Nagios via the external command pipe. As it is a named pipe on a specific machine, the main problem is that all passive check results need to be sent from this machine.

Very often, checks need to be carried out on one or more remote hosts. This requires a mechanism to pass results from the machines that perform the tests to the computers running the Nagios daemon, which will process the results. This is why NSCA was developed. It is a client-server application that allows the passing of service and host check results over the network. This protocol allows the use of encryption, so the results are sent securely.

NSCA allows the sending of results directly to the Nagios external command pipe. It consists of two parts: the server and the client. The part responsible for receiving check results and passing them to Nagios is the server. The server listens on a specific TCP port for NSCA clients passing information. It accepts and authenticates incoming connections and passes these results to the Nagios external command pipe. All information is encrypted using the MCrypt library (visit http://mcrypt. sourceforge.net/).

The client part accepts one or more host or service check results on a standard input and sends them to the NSCA server using the specified IP address and port. Each line received on the standard input is a single check result that should be sent to the NSCA server. An NSCA client can be used to transmit more than one result over a period of time. Therefore, it is not necessary to launch a new NSCA client instance for each new result.

Authentication is done using the MCrypt libraries for encryption, and NSCA uses a password to verify that the status message is valid. You should either generate a random password or choose a password that is not dictionary based and use uppercase and lowercase letters as well as one or more digits. It is necessary to specify the same encryption method along with exactly the same password for both the client and the server in order for it to work properly. The following illustration shows how passive checks are done on the same host as well as when sent over the network using NSCA:

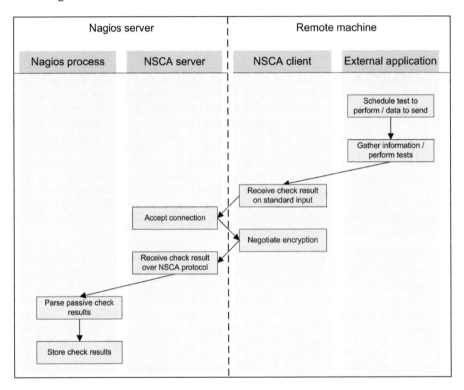

This example shows how the results are passed down directly from an external application to the Nagios daemon. Most complex operations are performed directly by NSCA. The application only needs to gather results from the check or checks, spawn the send_nsca binary, and make sure that the results are sent out properly.

NSCA is also commonly used in conjunction with distributed Nagios monitoring. This means that more than one computer runs a Nagios server and the results are distributed between Nagios servers running on different machines. In such cases, NSCA is often used to pass information from one machine to another (this is known as distributed monitoring and is described in detail in *Chapter 10, Advanced Monitoring*).

Downloading NSCA

NSCA is a part of the main Nagios project, and its source code can be downloaded from the same Nagios download page as the rest of Nagios. Many Linux distributions already contain prebuilt NSCA binaries. If you are not an experienced user and just want to test NSCA out, you might want to try the prebuilt binaries.

For Ubuntu Linux, the package name is `nsca`. So all that you need to do is to run the following command:

```
apt-get install nsca
```

For systems that offer `yum` for downloading packages, the command is as follows:

```
yum install nsca
```

NSCA binaries for various operating systems can also be found on Nagios Exchange, at `http://exchange.nagios org/`. There is also a binary for Microsoft Windows operating systems. This allows the creation of applications that monitor desktop computers and report the results directly to Nagios.

In order to build NSCA from sources, we will need to download the source code. This can be downloaded from the Nagios project page and can be found in the **addons** section (visit `http://www.nagios.org/download/addons/` for more details). The file is named in the format `nsca-2.9.1.tar.gz`, where `2.9.1` is the version of NSCA. It is always recommended that you download the latest version.

Compiling NSCA

 If you do not plan to compile NSCA from the source and intend to use a prebuilt set of binaries, you should continue to the next section.

NSCA requires a small set of prerequisites to be installed on the system which include a standard set of tools, required for compilation, to be present on the system. For encryption, the `libmcrypt` package, along with the development files, needs to be installed as well. On an Ubuntu Linux system, this requires the installation of the packages by executing the following command:

```
apt-get install gcc make binutils cpp pkg-config libmcrypt-dev libc6-dev
```

For RedHat Enterprise Linux and CentOS, the command is as follows:

```
yum install gcc make binutils cpp pkgconfig mcrypt-devel glibc-devel
```

For other Linux distributions, the commands to run and install the packages and package names might be slightly different, but the package names should be similar to that of either Ubuntu or RedHat/CentOS packages. Please make sure that you install the standard compilation utilities as you might often be building NSCA for machines that you did not compile Nagios on. This means that they might not have the basic development libraries and compiler installed.

The next step is to run the configuration script to set up parameters for the compilation process. Assuming that we want NSCA to be installed in the same way as the Nagios setup (detailed in *Chapter 2, Installing Nagios 4*), the following `configure` script should be run:

```
sh configure \
    --sysconfdir=/etc/nagios \
    --prefix=/opt/nagios \
    --localstatedir=/var/nagios \
    --libexecdir=/opt/nagios/plugins \
    --with-nsca-user=nagios \
    --with-nsca-grp=nagioscmd
```

In case any of the tools or files are missing, the configuration script will abort indicating what the missing part is. If this happens, you should install the missing binaries or libraries. How you should do this depends on the exact operating system and distribution used. For Ubuntu systems, it should be by using the same command as the one used for building Nagios:

```
apt-get install gcc make binutils cpp libpq-dev libmysqlclient15-dev\
                libssl0.9.8 libssl-dev pkg-config apache2 \
                libgd2-xpm libgd2-xpm-dev libgd-tools \
                libpng12-dev libjpeg62-dev \
                perl libperl-dev libperl5.8 libnet-snmp-perl
```

After a successful run of the configuration script, you should see a message stating that you can now build NSCA binaries. The next step is to run the following `make` command to build the NSCA client and server:

```
make all
```

If you plan to build only the client or server part, use the `make send_nsca` or `make nsca` commands, respectively. If the compilation of NSCA has failed with `src/nsca.c line 480` or similar, it may be because of a bug present in the latest NSCA version at the time of writing this book. The bug is documented at `http://tracker.nagios.org/view.php?id=379` and the fix is to change `line 480` of `src/nsca.c` to:

```
checkresult_test_fd=open(checkresult_test,O_WRONLY|O_CREAT,0644);
```

The binaries are built as `src/send_nsca` and `src/nsca`. The first one is the NSCA client, and the other one is the server. You can install the binaries by running the following command manually:

```
install src/nsca /opt/nagios/bin/nsca
install src/send_nsca /opt/nagios/bin/send_nsca
```

You can also copy the binaries manually: copy the `send_nsca` client to the machines that will send the results to Nagios, and send `nsca` to the machine where Nagios is running. However, this may cause library incompatibilities and is only recommended when both the target machine and machine where the binaries were built are using same operating system, version, and are both either 32-bit or 64-bit machines, that is, it is not recommended that you copy binaries from a 32-bit Ubuntu Linux system to a 64-bit CentOS system.

Configuring the NSCA server

Now that we have working binaries for the NSCA server, either compiled from sources or installed from packages, we can proceed with configuring the NSCA server to listen for incoming connections. There are a couple of ways in which it can be set up: as a standalone process that handles incoming connections, as part of `inetd` (visit `http://en.wikipedia.org/wiki/inetd`), or as the `xinetd` setup (visit `http://www.xinetd.org/`). In either case, we will need a configuration file that will tell it which encryption algorithm to use and the password that will be used to authenticate NSCA client connections. NSCA also needs to know the path of the Nagios external command pipe.

The main difference between these two installation types is that the standalone version requires fewer resources to handle a larger number of incoming connections. On the other hand, `inetd`- or `xinetd`-based NSCA is much easier to set up. An `inetd`-based setup is easier to maintain. Several `inetd` implementations also allow the configuration of connections only from specific IP addresses or the acceptance of connections only from specific users for Unix systems. There is no ideal way in which NSCA should be set up.

The configuration file is similar to that of the main Nagios configuration file: each parameter is written in the format `<name>=<value>`. If you compiled NSCA from the source, a default configuration can be found in the `sample-config/nsca.cfg` file.

The first parameter that should be set is `password`. This should be set to the same value for the NSCA server and all NSCA clients. It's best to set it to a random string. Using a dictionary-based password might leave your Nagios setup susceptible to attacks; malicious users might send fake results that cause event triggers to perform specific actions.

Another option that needs to be set is `decryption_method`, which specifies the algorithm to be used for encryption. This is an integer value. A list of possible values and what they mean can be found in the sample configuration file. Both `decryption_method` and `password` need to be set to the same value on the server side and the client side. A sample configuration is as follows:

```
server_address=192.168.1.1

server_port=5667

nsca_user=nagios

nsca_group=nagioscmd

command_file=/var/nagios/rw/nagios.cmd

password=ok1ij2uh3yg

decryption_method=1
```

The `server_address` option is optional and specifies the IP address that NSCA should listen for. If omitted, NSCA will listen on all available IP addresses for incoming connections. When it is specified, NSCA will only accept connections from the specified IP address. The specified `decryption_method` value of 1 means XOR, which provides no encryption and should not be used in production. Security and proper configuration of encryption is described in detail later in this chapter.

The remainder of this section will assume that the NSCA server configuration file is located at `/etc/nagios/nsca.cfg`. At this point, it is good to create an NSCA configuration based on the preceding example or the sample NSCA configuration file, `nsca.cfg`.

The fastest way to start NSCA is to start it manually in standalone mode. In this mode, NSCA handles listening on the specified TCP port and changing the user/group by itself. To do this, simply run the NSCA binary with the following parameters:

```
/opt/nagios/bin/nsca -c /etc/nagios/nsca.cfg --daemon
```

If you plan to have NSCA start up along with Nagios, it is a good idea to add a line to your `/etc/init.d/nagios` script that runs Nagios at system boot. Running NSCA should go in the `start` section, and stopping NSCA (via the `killall` command—see http://en.wikipedia.org/wiki/killall—or by using the `pid` file) should be put in the `stop` section of the `init` script. The NSCA source distribution also comes with a script that can be placed as `/etc/init.d/nsca` to start and stop the NSCA server.

Another possibility is to configure NSCA to run from the `inetd` or `xinetd` super-server daemons. This requires adding the definition of the NSCA server to the proper configuration files, and those daemons will handle accepting connections and spawning actual NSCA processes when needed. In order to add the NSCA definition to `inetd` or `xinetd`, we first need to add a service definition of the TCP port used. In order to do that, we need to add the following line to the `/etc/services` file:

```
nsca 5667/tcp
```

This will indicate that TCP port 5677 maps to the service name `nsca`. This information is used later by the super-server daemons to map port numbers to names in the configuration. For `inetd`, we also need to add the service configuration to the `/etc/inetd.conf` file. A sample definition is as follows:

```
nsca stream tcp nowait nagios /opt/nagios/bin/nsca -c /etc/nagios/nsca.
cfg --inetd
```

The following entry should be written to the `inetd.conf` file as a single line. We should reload `inetd` by running the following script:

```
/etc/init.d/inetd reload
```

This will cause it to reload the service definitions. NSCA should be run whenever a connection on port 5667 comes in. Setting up NSCA using `xinetd` is very similar. All that's needed is to create a `/etc/xinetd.d/nsca` file with the following contents:

```
service nsca
{
        flags           = REUSE
        socket_type     = stream
        wait            = no
        user            = nagios
        group           = nagioscmd
        server          = /opt/nagios/bin/nsca
        server_args     = -c /etc/nagios/nsca.cfg --inetd
        log_on_failure  += USERID
        disable         = no
}
```

Next, we need to reload `xinetd` by running the following command:

```
/etc/init.d/xinetd reload
```

And after that the NSCA should also be run when a connection on port 5667 comes in. You might add the `only_from` statement in the `xinetd` service definition to limit IP addresses from which a connection can come in. It works differently from `server_address` in the NSCA configuration. The `only_from` option specifies the addresses of the remote machines that will be allowed to connect. On the other hand, the `server_address` option is used to specify the IP addresses that NSCA will listen on.

When running under `inetd` or `xinetd`, the NSCA server ignores the `server_address`, `server_port`, `nsca_user`, and `nsca_group` parameters from the configuration files. These attributes are configured at the `inetd/xinetd` level. These attributes are only meaningful when running NSCA in standalone mode.

Sending results over NSCA

Now that our NSCA server is up and running, we can continue with actually submitting results over the network. We will need the `send_nsca` client binary on all of the machines that will report passive check results to Nagios.

There are various prebuilt binaries available at Nagios Exchange, including a native Win32 binary, which allows the sending of results from any check using NSCA. As it is a prebuilt version, there is no need to compile or install it. Simply copy the binary to a Windows machine, and it can be used with any valid NSCA client configuration.

As with the NSCA server, the client uses a configuration file. This requires the specification of the `password` and `encryption_method` parameters. Here is a sample configuration that can be used in conjunction with the configuration for a server created earlier:

```
password=ok1ij2uh3yg
encryption_method=1
```

The NSCA client accepts the status results that should be sent out to the server on standard input. Each line indicates a single result from a check. The syntax of the host check result that should be passed to `send_nsca` is as follows:

```
<hostname>[TAB]<return code>[TAB]<plugin output>
```

The return code is the same as the one for sending passive checks: 0 for UP, 1 for DOWN, and 2 for UNREACHABLE. Sending a passive service check result requires the specification of the service name as well:

```
<hostname>[TAB]<service name>[TAB]<return code>[TAB]<plugin output>
```

In this case, the return codes are the same as the exit codes for checks: 0 for OK, 1 for WARNING, 2 for CRITICAL, and 3 for UNKNOWN. Exit codes have been explained in detail in *Chapter 4, Using the Nagios Plugins*. The command differentiates the host and service checks by the number of fields that are passed in a line.

 As the tab character is the separator for the NSCA protocol, the plugin output should not contain any additional tab characters as this may cause NSCA not to work properly.

The NSCA client command has the following syntax:

```
send_nsca -H <host_address> [-c config_file]
          [-p port] [-to to_sec] [-d delim]
```

The -H option specifies the name of the NSCA server to which messages should be transmitted. The -p option specifies the port to send messages on; the port defaults to 5667 if nothing is specified. The timeout in seconds is specified using the -to flag. A field delimiter can also be specified using the -d option; if this is omitted, it defaults to tab-delimited. The easiest way to test whether you can send data to NSCA correctly is to try to send a host status for a valid computer. As send_nsca accepts information on standard input, it is enough to run an echo command and send its output to the NSCA client. A sample script is provided as follows:

```
#!/bin/sh

HOST=localhost
NSCAHOST=127.0.0.1

echo -e "$HOST\t1\tHost temporarily down" | \
    /opt/nagios/bin/send_nsca -H $NSCAHOST
    -c /etc/nagios/send_nsca.cfg

exit 0
```

The script will send a report that the host, localhost, is currently down with the status description, Host temporarily down. The NSCAHOST variable is used to specify the destination to which the NSCA server should send messages. While the preceding example is set to 127.0.0.1, it should be replaced with the actual IP address of your Nagios server. A similar script can be written for sending service-related reports to Nagios. The only difference is that the return codes mean something different and that the service name is sent along with the hostname. The following is an example that sends a warning state:

```
#!/bin/sh

HOST=localhost
SERVICE="NSCA test"
NSCAHOST=127.0.0.1

echo -e "$HOST\t$SERVICE\t1\tService in warning state" | \
    /opt/nagios/bin/send_nsca -H $NSCAHOST
    -c /etc/nagios/send_nsca.cfg

exit 0
```

This example sends out a warning status to Nagios over NSCA. The parameters are very similar, and the main difference is in the return codes. Moreover, a service description also needs to be passed; in this case, it is NSCA test. If the service has max_check_attempts set to anything other than 1, the script needs to send out multiple status messages to Nagios. This can be done by piping multiple echo commands into a single send_nsca binary.

Applications that pass multiple results over a short period of time might pass multiple status results without having to rerun send_nsca for each result. Instead, you can simply send multiple lines to the same send_nsca process, and it will send information on all of the statuses to Nagios. This approach reduces the overhead of spawning multiple new processes.

Configuring NSCA for secure communication

Both passive checks and NSCA allow the sending of statuses for machines and applications to Nagios. This produces several types of security concerns. If a malicious user is able to send reports to Nagios, he or she can force a change to the status of one or more objects by frequently sending its status. He or she can also flood Nagios or NSCA with a large number of invalid requests that might cause performance problems. This might stop Nagios from receiving actual passive check results. For example, SNMP traps may not be passed to Nagios; if the trap is not received, it will prevent the running of an event handler that may fix the problem.

Therefore, being able to send results to Nagios should be made as secure as possible so that only authorized applications can communicate with it. Securing passive checks that are sent directly over external command pipe is relatively easy. It only requires the external command pipe to be accessible to Nagios and to the applications that are allowed to send data to it.

Securing NSCA is a more complex issue and requires ensuring that every step of the communication is secure. The first step is to make sure that the NSCA configuration files have adequate access rights. They should be set so that the NSCA daemon and clients are able to read them but other users cannot. In the client case, the issue is that all users who invoke send_nsca should be able to read its configuration file. This will ensure that your NSCA password and encryption methods cannot be read by unauthorized users.

Another thing that affects your setup security is whether the password used for communications is strong. It is recommended that you use a random password composed of lowercase and uppercase letters as well as digits. It is also recommended that you use one of the algorithms based on MCrypt, not the simple XOR algorithm. The recommended values are 16, which is RIJNDAEL-256 or 9, which is Twofish. Both are very secure encryption algorithms.

The next step is to make sure that only authorized IP addresses are allowed to send information to the NSCA server. This can be done either through xinetd configuration or by using a system firewall such as netfilter/iptables (http://www.netfilter.org/) for Linux. In both cases, it is best to define a list of allowed IPs and automatically reject connections from unknown hosts.

Summary

Nagios allows both the monitoring of services on its own and the receipt of information about computer and service statuses from other applications. Being able to send results directly to Nagios creates a lot of opportunities for extending how Nagios can be used.

In this chapter, we learned about passive checks—the difference between active and passive checks and how to enable receiving passive check results. The chapter also covered how to submit passive check results to Nagios for both hosts and services.

We also learned how to troubleshoot not being able to send passive check results to Nagios properly. We have learned about NSCA, which is a tool for sending passive check results over a network. We also talked through how to set up NSCA server and client both by using binary distributions and by compiling NSCA from sources. We also set up an NSCA server that will receive passive check results.

We learned how to send passive check results to Nagios remotely using the send_nsca binary and how to set up NSCA securely.

The next chapter will cover how to monitor remote hosts and how SSH protocol can be used to run checks remotely in a secure way. It will also cover **Nagios Remote Plugin Executor** (**NRPE**), which is a client-server protocol that allows running checks remotely.

8
Monitoring Remote Hosts

Nagios offers various ways of monitoring the computers and services. The previous chapter talked about passive checks and how they can be used to submit results to Nagios. It also discussed NSCA, which can be used to send check results from other machines to the Nagios server.

This chapter talks about another approach to check the service status. It uses Nagios active checks that run the actual check commands on different hosts. This approach is most useful in cases where resources local to a particular machine are to be checked. A typical example is monitoring disk or memory usage. Checking if your operating system is up-to-date is also an example of such a test. This type of data cannot be checked without running commands on the target computer.

Remote checks are usually used in combination with the Nagios plugins package that use either **SSH** or **Nagios Remote Plugin Executor (NRPE)** to run the plugins on the remote machine. This makes monitoring remote systems very similar to monitoring a local computer, with a difference only in the actual running of the commands on the remote machine. In this chapter, we will cover the following topics:

- Using SSH for monitoring the remote hosts and services and setting up the public key authentication for performing checks
- Running multiple checks at once over SSH
- Troubleshooting the SSH-based checks
- Using NRPE for performing remote checks and setting up NRPE as a system service
- Configuring NRPE-based checks in Nagios
- Passing command arguments using NRPE
- Troubleshooting NRPE-based connections

Monitoring over SSH

Very often, Nagios is used to monitor computer resources such as CPU utilization, memory, and disk space. One way in which this can be done is to connect over SSH and run a Nagios check plugin.

This requires setting up SSH to authenticate using public keys. This works because the Nagios server has an SSH private key, and the target machine is configured to allow users with that particular key to connect without prompting them for password.

Nagios offers a `check_by_ssh` plugin that takes the hostname and the actual command to run on the remote server. It then connects using SSH, runs the plugin, and returns both output and exit code from the actual check performed on the remote machine to Nagios running on the local server. Internally, it runs the SSH client to connect to the server, and runs the actual command to run along with its attributes on the target machine. After the check has been performed, the output along with the check command's exit code is returned to Nagios.

Thanks to this, regular plugins can be run from the same machine as the Nagios daemon, as well as remotely over SSH without any changes to the plugins. Using the SSH protocol also means that the authorization process can be automated using the key-based authentication so that each check is done without any user activity. This way, Nagios is able to log in to remote machines automatically without using any passwords. The following is an illustration of how such a check is performed:

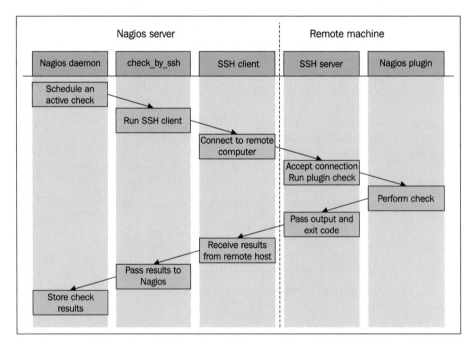

Once Nagios schedules an active check to be performed, the `check_by_ssh` plugin runs the `ssh` command to connect to the remote host's SSH server. It then runs the actual plugin, which is located on the remote host, waits for the result, and returns it to the SSH protocol. The SSH client passes this information down to the `check_by_ssh` plugin that, in the end, returns to the Nagios daemon.

Even though the scenario might seem a bit complicated, it works quite efficiently and requires little setup to work properly. It also works with various flavors of Unix systems as the SSH protocol, clients, and the shell syntax for commands used by the `check_by_ssh` plugin is the same on all the systems.

Configuring the SSH connection

SSH provides multiple ways for a user to authenticate. One of them is the password-based authentication, which means that user specifies a password, the SSH client sends it to remote machine, and the remote machine checks if the password is correct.

Another form of verifying whether a user or program can access the remote machine is the public key-based authentication. It uses asymmetric cryptography (visit http:// en.wikipedia.org/wiki/Public-key_cryptography for more details) to perform the authentication and provides a secure way to authenticate without specifying any credentials. It requires the user to generate an authentication key, which consists of a public and private key. By default, the file name is ~/.ssh/id_rsa for the private key and ~/.ssh/id_rsa.pub for the public key. The public key is then put on the remote machines, and it allows them to verify the user. The SSH protocol then takes care of the authentication—it only requires the client machine to have the private key and the remote machine to be configured to accept it by adding the public key to remote user's SSH authorized keys file (~/.ssh/authorized_keys in most cases).

Setting up remote checks over SSH requires a few steps. The first step is to create a dedicated user for performing checks on the machine on which the remote checks will be run. We will also need to set up directories for the user. The steps to create directory structure on the remote machine is very similar to the steps performed for the entire Nagios installation.

The first thing that needs to be performed on the Nagios server is the creation of a private and public key pair that will be used to log in to all the remote machines without using passwords. We will need to execute the `ssh-keygen` command to generate it. A sample session is shown in the following command snippet:

```
root@nagiosserver:~# su -s /bin/bash nagios
nagios@nagiosserver:~$ ssh-keygen
Generating public/private rsa key pair.
```

```
File in which to save the key (/opt/nagios/.ssh/id_rsa): <enter>
Created directory '/opt/nagios/.ssh'.
Enter passphrase (empty for no passphrase): <enter>
Enter same passphrase again: <enter>
Your identification has been saved in /opt/nagios/.ssh/id_rsa.
Your public key has been saved in /opt/nagios/.ssh/id_rsa.pub.
The key fingerprint is:
c9:68:47:bd:cd:6e:12:d3:9b:e8:0d:cf:93:bd:33:98 nagios@nagiosserver
nagios@nagiosserver:/root$
```

As in most cases, it was not possible to log in as the user nagios directly on which. We used the su command to switch users along with the -s flag to force the shell to be /bin/bash. The <enter> text means that the question was answered with the default reply. The private key is saved as /opt/nagios/.ssh/id_rsa, and the public key has been saved in the /opt/nagios/.ssh/id_rsa.pub file.

Next, we need to set up the remote machines that we will monitor. All the following commands should be executed on the remote machine that is to be monitored, unless explicitly mentioned. First, let's create a user and group named nagios:

```
root@remotehost:~# groupadd nagios
root@remotehost:~# useradd -g nagios -d /opt/nagios nagios
```

We do not need the nagioscmd group as we will need only the account to log in to the machine. The computer that only performs checks does not have a full Nagios installation along with the external command pipe that needs a separate group.

The next thing that needs to be done is the compiling of the Nagios plugins. You will probably also need to install the prerequisites that are needed for Nagios. Detailed instructions on how to do this can be found in *Chapter 2, Installing Nagios 4*. For the rest of the section, we will assume that the Nagios plugins are installed in the /opt/nagios/plugins directory, similar to how they were installed on the Nagios server.

It is best to install plugins in the same directory on all the machines they will be running. In this case, we can use the $USER1$ macro definition when creating the actual check commands in the main Nagios configuration. The USER1 macro points to the location where Nagios plugins are installed in the default Nagios installations. This is described in more detail in *Chapter 2, Installing Nagios 4*. Next, we will need to create the /opt/nagios directory and set its permissions:

```
root@remotehost:~# mkdir /opt/nagios
root@remotehost:~# chown nagios:nagios /opt/nagios
root@remotehost:~# chmod 0700 /opt/nagios
```

You can make the `/opt/nagios` directory permissions less restrictive by setting the mode to `0755`. However, it is recommended not to make the users' home directories readable for all users. We will now need to add the public key from the `nagios` user on the remote machine that is running the Nagios daemon, as shown in the following command snippet:

```
root@remotehost:~# mkdir /opt/nagios/.ssh

root@remotehost:~# echo 'ssh-rsa … nagios@nagiosserver' \
    >>/opt/nagios/.ssh/authorized_keys

root@remotehost:~# chown nagios.nagios \
    /opt/nagios/.ssh /opt/nagios/.ssh/authorized_keys
root@remotehost:~# chmod 0700 \
    /opt/nagios/.ssh /opt/nagios/.ssh/authorized_keys
```

When running the command, you should replace the entire text `ssh-rsa … nagios@nagiosserver` with the actual contents of the `/opt/nagios/.ssh/id_rsa.pub` file on the computer running the Nagios daemon. If your machine is maintained by more than one person, you might replace the `nagios@nagiosserver` string to a more readable comment such as `Nagios on nagiosserver SSH check public key`.

Make sure that you change the permissions for both the `.ssh` directory and the `authorized_keys` file, as many SSH server implementations ignore public key-based authorization if the files can be read or written to by other users on the system.

In order to configure multiple remote machines to be accessible over `ssh` without a password, you will need to perform all the steps mentioned earlier, except the key generation at the computer running the Nagios server, as a single private key will be used to access multiple machines. Assuming everything was done successfully, we can now move on to testing if the public key-based authorization actually works. To do that, we will try to run the `ssh` client in verbose mode and see whether using the previously generated key works fine. In order to check that our connection can now be successfully established, we need to try to connect to the remote machine from the computer that has the Nagios daemon running. We will use the `ssh` client with the verbose flag to make sure that our connection works properly:

```
nagios@nagiosserver:~$ ssh -v nagios@192.168.2.1
OpenSSH_4.6p1 Debian-5ubuntu0.2, OpenSSL 0.9.8e 23 Feb 2007
debug1: Reading configuration data /etc/ssh/ssh_config
debug1: Applying options for *
debug1: Connecting to 192.168.2.1 [192.168.2.1] port 22.
```

```
debug1: Connection established.
debug1: identity file /opt/nagios/.ssh/id_rsa type 1
(...)
debug1: SSH2_MSG_KEXINIT sent
debug1: SSH2_MSG_KEXINIT received
debug1: kex: server->client aes128-cbc hmac-md5 none
debug1: kex: client->server aes128-cbc hmac-md5 none
debug1: SSH2_MSG_KEX_DH_GEX_REQUEST(1024<1024<8192) sent
debug1: expecting SSH2_MSG_KEX_DH_GEX_GROUP
debug1: SSH2_MSG_KEX_DH_GEX_INIT sent
debug1: expecting SSH2_MSG_KEX_DH_GEX_REPLY
The authenticity of host '192.168.2.1 (192.168.2.1)' can't be
established.
RSA key fingerprint is cf:72:1e:40:03:a4:e0:9b:6c:84:4e:e1:2d:ea:56:fc.
Are you sure you want to continue connecting (yes/no)? yes
Warning: Permanently added '192.168.2.1' (RSA) to the list of known
hosts.
debug1: ssh_rsa_verify: signature correct
debug1: SSH2_MSG_NEWKEYS sent
debug1: expecting SSH2_MSG_NEWKEYS
debug1: SSH2_MSG_NEWKEYS received
debug1: SSH2_MSG_SERVICE_REQUEST sent
debug1: SSH2_MSG_SERVICE_ACCEPT received
debug1: Authentications that can continue: publickey,password
debug1: Next authentication method: publickey
debug1: Offering public key: /opt/nagios/.ssh/id_rsa
debug1: Server accepts key: pkalg ssh-rsa blen 277
debug1: read PEM private key done: type RSA
debug1: Authentication succeeded (publickey).
debug1: channel 0: new [client-session]
debug1: Entering interactive session.
debug1: Sending environment.
debug1: Sending env LANG = en_US.UTF-8
$
```

As we were connecting to the remote machine for the first time, ssh prompted us to
check whether we had accepted the remote machine's key to a list of known hosts.
This needs to be done only once for a specific host.

Also, note that we need to test the connection from the Nagios account so that the keys that are used for authentication as well as the list of known hosts are the same ones that will be used by the Nagios daemon later.

Assuming that we have the Nagios plugins installed on the remote machine in the `/opt/nagios/plugins` directory, we can try to use the `check_by_ssh` plugin from the computer running Nagios to the remote machine by running the following command:

```
nagios@nagiosserver:~$ /opt/nagios/plugins/check_by_ssh \
    -H 192.168.2.1 -C "/opt/nagios/plugins/check_apt"
APT OK: 0 packages available for upgrade (0 critical updates).
```

We are now sure that the checking itself works fine, and we can move on to how `check_by_ssh` can be used and what its syntax is.

Using the check_by_ssh plugin

As mentioned earlier, Nagios uses a separate check command that connects to a remote machine over SSH and runs the actual check command on it. The command has very powerful features and can be used to query a single service status by using active checks. It can also be used to perform and report multiple checks at once as passive checks. The following is the syntax of the command:

```
check_by_ssh -H <host> -C <command> [-fqv]  [-1|-2]  [-4|-6]
              [-S [lines]]  [-E [lines]]  [-t timeout]  [-i identity]
              [-l user]  [-n name]  [-s servicelist]  [-O outputfile]
              [-p port]  [-o ssh-option]
```

The following table describes all the options accepted by the plugin. Items required are marked in bold:

Option	Description
-H, --hostname	This provides the hostname or IP address of the machine to connect to; this option must be specified
-C, --command	This provides the full path of the command to be executed on the remote host along with any additional arguments; this option must be specified
-l, --logname	This lets you log in as a specific user; if omitted, it defaults to the current user (usually nagios) or any other user specified in the per-user SSH client configuration file

Option	Description
`-I, --identity`	This specifies the path to the SSH private key to be used for authorization; if omitted, then `~/.ssh/id_rsa` is used by default
`-o, --ssh-option`	This allows passing SSH-specific options that will be passed as the `-o` option to the `ssh` command
`-q, --quiet`	This stops SSH from printing warning and information messages
`-w, --warning`	This specifies the time in seconds after which the connection should be terminated and a warning should be issued to Nagios
`-c, --critical`	This specifies the time in seconds after which the connection should be terminated and a critical should be issued to Nagios
`-t, --timeout`	This specifies the time in seconds after which the connection should be terminated and checks should be stopped; defaults to 10 seconds
`-p, --port`	This specifies the port to connect over SSH; defaults to 22
`-1, --proto1`	This will let you use the SSH protocol Version 1
`-2, --proto2`	This will let you use the SSH protocol Version 2; this is the default
`-4`	This will let you use IPv4 protocol for SSH connectivity
`-6`	This will let you use IPv6 protocol for SSH connectivity
`-S, --skip-stdout`	This will let you ignore all or the provided number of lines from the standard output
`-E, --skip-stderr`	This will let you use ignore all or the provided number of lines from the standard error
`-f`	This tells SSH to work in the background just after connecting, instead of using a terminal

The only required flags are `-H` to specify the IP address or hostname to connect as well as `-C` to specify the command to be used. The remaining parameters are optional. If they are not passed, SSH defaults and the timeout of 10 seconds will be used.

The `-S` and `-E` options are used to skip messages that are written by the SSH client or the remote machine, regardless of the commands executed. For example, to properly check machines printing MOTD, even for noninteractive sessions, it is required to skip it by using one of the options.

When specifying commands, they usually need to be enclosed in single or double quotation marks. This is because the entire command that should be run needs to be passed to `check_by_ssh` as a single argument. If one or more arguments contain spaces, single quote characters will have to be used.

For example, when checking for disk usage remotely, we need to quote the entire command as well; this is because it's safer to quote the path to the drive we're checking, as shown here:

```
nagios@nagios1:~$ /opt/nagios/plugins/check_by_ssh -H 192.168.2.1 -C \
    "/opt/nagios/plugins/check_disk -w 15% -c 10% -p '/'"
DISK OK - free space: / 243 MB (17% inode=72%)
```

The preceding example is a typical usage of the check_by_ssh plugin as an active check. It performs a single check and returns the status directly using the standard output and exit code. This is how it is used as an active check from within Nagios.

If you want to use check_by_ssh to deploy checks locally on the same machine as the one on which Nagios is running, you will need to add the SSH key from id_rsa. pub to the authorized_keys file on that machine as well. In order to verify that it works correctly, try logging in to the local machine over SSH. Now that the plugin works when invoked manually, we need to configure Nagios to make use of it.

Usually, for commands that will be performed both locally and remotely, the approach is to create a duplicate entry for each command with a prefix, for example, _by_ssh. Assuming that we have the command that checks swap usage locally, the definition is as follows:

```
define command
{
  command_name   check_swap
  command_line   $USER1$/check_swap -w $ARG1$ -c $ARG2$
}
```

Then, assuming that we will also check the swap usage on remote machines, we need to define the following remote counterpart:

```
define command
{
  command_name   check_swap_by_ssh
  command_line   $USER1$/check_by_ssh -H $HOSTADDRESS$ -C
                 "$USER1$/check_swap -w $ARG1$ -c $ARG2$"
}
```

Usually, services are defined for groups for example, a service should be defined to check swap space usage on all the Linux servers. In such cases, you can use the `check_swap_by_ssh` command even for checking the local machine – the overhead for such a check is larger than the one for calling the plugin directly. However, in many cases, it makes managing the configuration much easier. You can also set up two sets of services similar to the following example:

```
define service
{
  use                   generic-service
  host_name             localhost
  service_description   SWAP
  check_command         check_swap
}
define service
{
  use                   generic-service
  host_name             !localhost
  hostgroup_name        linux-servers
  service_description   SWAP
  check_command         check_swap_by_ssh
}
```

This way, `localhost` will use the `check_swap` command and all the remaining machines that are part of the `linux-servers` host group will use the `check_swap_by_ssh` check command. This way, you can slightly reduce the overhead related to monitoring the machine on which Nagios is running.

Performing multiple checks

A completely different approach is to make `check_by_ssh` perform multiple tests and report them directly to Nagios over the external command pipe. This way, the results are sent to Nagios as passive check results. So, specified services need to accept passive check results.

The reason for this approach is that the SSH protocol negotiations introduce a lot of overhead related to the protocol itself. For hosts with heavy load, it is more efficient to log in once and run all the checks instead of performing a complete login for each check.

A drawback of doing multiple checks is that it is not trivial to schedule these directly from Nagios. The typical approach to passive checks is to schedule checks from an external application such as cron (`http://man.linuxquestions.org/index.php?query=cron`).

An alternate approach is to create a dummy service that will launch passive checks in the background. The actual result for this service would also be to check whether running the tests was successful or not. Another benefit of this approach is that the checks will be performed even if the `cron` daemon is currently disabled, as Nagios will still take care of scheduling the checks done by it.

When using `check_by_ssh` to report multiple results as passive checks, the following options need to be specified:

Option	Description
-n, --name	This provides the short name of the host that the tests refer; this is the name of the host that will be used when sending the results over the external command pipe
-s, --services	These are the names of the services that the tests refer, separated by colon; these are the names of services that will be used when sending results over the external pipe
-O, --output	This is the path to the external command pipe to which the results of all the checks should be sent

The preceding options are specific to performing multiple checks only. The remaining options described earlier must also be specified—especially the -H and -C options. The second one needs to be specified multiple times, each for one check. The number of -C parameters must match the number of entries in the -s parameter so that each result can be mapped to a service name. The following example reports disk check results for three partitions:

```
/opt/nagios/plugins/check_by_ssh -H 192.168.2.1 -O /tmp/out1 -n ubuntu1 \
    -s "DISK /:DISK /usr:DISK /opt" \
    -C "/opt/nagios/plugins/check_disk -w 15% -c 10% -p /" \
    -C "/opt/nagios/plugins/check_disk -w 15% -c 10% -p /usr" \
    -C "/opt/nagios/plugins/check_disk -w 15% -c 10% -p /opt"
```

This command will put the output into `/tmp/out1`, similar to the following example:

```
[1206096000] PROCESS_SERVICE_CHECK_RESULT;ubuntu1;DISK /:DISK CRITICAL...
[1206096000] PROCESS_SERVICE_CHECK_RESULT;ubuntu1;DISK /usr:DISK OK   ...
[1206096000] PROCESS_SERVICE_CHECK_RESULT;ubuntu1;DISK /opt:DISK OK   ...
```

As mentioned previously, it is very common to write a script that is run as an active check. This script is set up as a service that is only responsible for running multiple checks for other services. Results from those services are passed as passive check results.

The following is a sample script that runs several tests and reports their results back to Nagios:

```sh
#!/bin/sh

COMMANDFILE=$1
HOSTNAME=$2
HOSTADDRESS=$3
PLUGINPATH=$4

$PLUGINPATH/check_by_ssh -H $HOSTADDRESS -t 30 \
    -o $COMMANDFILE -n $HOSTNAME \
    -s "SWAP:Root Partition:Processes:System Load" \
    -C "$PLUGINPATH/check_swap -w 20% -c 10%" \
    -C "$PLUGINPATH/check_disk -w 20% -c 10% -p /" \
    -C "$PLUGINPATH/check_procs -w 100 -c 200" \
    -C "$PLUGINPATH/check_load -w 5,3,2 -c 10,8,7" \
      (
        echo "BYSSH CRITICAL problem while running SSH"
        exit 2
      )

echo "BYSSH OK checks launched"
exit 0
```

For the remaining part of the section, let's assume that the script is in the `/opt/nagios/plugins` directory and is called `check_linux_services_by_ssh`. The script will perform several checks, and if any of them fail, it will return a critical result as well. Otherwise, it will return an `OK` status and the remaining results will be passed as passive check results. We will also need to configure Nagios, both services that will receive their results as passive checks, and the service that will actually schedule the checks properly.

All the services that are checked via the `check_by_ssh` command itself have a very similar definition. They only need to accept passive checks and don't have any active checks scheduled. The following is a sample definition for the SWAP service:

```
define service
{
  use                   generic-service
  host_name             !localhost
```

```
    hostgroup_name          linux-servers
    service_description     SWAP
    active_checks_enabled   0
    passive_checks_enabled  1
}
```

All other services will also need to have a very similar definition. We might also define a template for such services and only create services that use it. This will make the configuration more readable. Now, we need to define a command definition that will launch the passive check script written earlier:

```
define command
{
  command_name     check_linux_services_by_ssh
  command_line     $USER1$/check_linux_services_by_ssh
  "$COMMANDFILE$"  "$HOSTNAME$" "$HOSTADDRESS$" "$USER1$"
}
```

All the parameters that are used by the script are passed directly from the Nagios configuration. This makes reconfiguring various paths easier. The next step is to define an actual service that will run these checks:

```
define service
{
  use                     generic-service
  host_name               !localhost
  hostgroup_name          linux-servers
  service_description     Check Services By SSH
  active_checks_enabled   1
  passive_checks_enabled  0
  check_command           check_linux_services_by_ssh
  check_interval          30
  check_period            24x7
  max_check_attempts      1
  notification_interval   30
  notification_period     24x7
  notification_options    c,u,r
  contact_groups          linux-admins
}
```

This will cause the checks to be scheduled every 30 minutes. It will also notify the Linux administrators if any problem occurs with the scheduling of the checks. An alternative approach is to use the `cron` daemon to schedule the launch of the previous script. In such a case, the `Check Services By SSH` service is not needed. In this case, scheduling of the checks is not done in Nagios, but we will still need to have the services for which the status will be reported.

In such a case, we need to make sure that `cron` is running to have up-to-date results for the checks. Such verification can be done by monitoring the daemon using Nagios and the `check_procs` plugin. The first thing that needs to be done is to adapt the script to not print out the results in case everything worked fine and hardcode paths to the Nagios files:

```sh
#!/bin/sh

COMMANDFILE=/vat/nagios/rw/nagios.cmd
PLUGINPATH=/opt/nagios/plugins
HOSTNAME=$1
HOSTADDRESS=$2

$PLUGINPATH/check_by_ssh -H $HOSTADDRESS -t 30 \
    -o $COMMANDFILE -n $HOSTNAME \
    -s "SWAP:Root Partition:Processes:System Load" \
    -C "$PLUGINPATH/check_swap -w 20% -c 10%" \
    -C "$PLUGINPATH/check_disk -w 20% -c 10% -p /" \
    -C "$PLUGINPATH/check_procs -w 100 -c 200" \
    -C "$PLUGINPATH/check_load -w 5,3,2 -c 10,8,7" \
    || (
        echo "BYSSH CRITICAL problem while running SSH"
        exit 2
    )

#echo "BYSSH OK checks launched"
exit 0
```

Actual changes have been highlighted. The next step is to add entry to the Nagios user, `crontab`. This can be done by running the `crontab -e` command as the `nagios` user or the `crontab -u nagios -e` command as the administrator. Assuming that the check should be performed every 30 minutes, the `crontab` entry should be as follows:

```
*/30 * * * * /opt/nagios/plugins/check_linux_services_by_ssh
```

For more details on how an entry in `crontab` should look, please consult the manual page (http://linux.die.net/man/5/crontab).

Troubleshooting the SSH-based checks

If you have followed the steps from the previous sections carefully, then most probably, everything should be working smoothly. However, in some cases, your setup might not be working properly, and you will need to find the root cause of the problem.

The first thing that you should start with is using the check_ssh plugin to make sure that SSH is accepting connections on the host that we are checking. For example, we can run the following command:

```
root@ubuntu1:~# /opt/nagios/plugins/check_ssh -H 192.168.2.51

SSH OK - OpenSSH_4.7p1 Debian-8ubuntu1.2 (protocol 2.0)
```

Where, 192.168.2.51 is the name of the IP address of the remote machine we want to monitor. If no SSH server is set up on the remote host, the plugin will return Connection refused status, and if it failed to connect, the result will state No route to host. In these cases, you need to make sure that the SSH server is working and all routers and firewalls do not filter out connections for SSH, which is TCP port 22.

Assuming that the SSH server is accepting connections, the next thing that can be checked is whether the SSH key-based authorization works correctly. To do this, switch to the user the Nagios process is running as. Next, try to connect to the remote machine. The following are sample commands to perform this check:

```
root@ubuntu1:~# su nagios -

$ ssh -v 192.168.2.51
```

This way, you will check the connectivity as the same user at which Nagios is running checks. You can also analyze the logs that will be printed to the standard output, as described earlier in this chapter. If the SSH client will prompt you for a password, then your keys are not set up properly. It is a common mistake to set up keys on the root account instead of setting them up on the nagios account. If this is the case, then create a new set of keys as the correct user and verify whether these keys are working correctly now. Assuming this step worked fine, the next thing to be done is checking whether invoking an actual check command produces correct results. For example:

```
root@ubuntu1:~# su nagios -

$ ssh 192.168.2.51 /opt/nagios/plugins/check_procs

PROCS OK: 51 processes
```

This way, you will check the connectivity as the same user at which Nagios is running checks. The last check is to make sure that the check_by_ssh plugin also returns correct information. An example of this is given as follows:

```
root@ubuntu1:~# su nagios -
$ /opt/nagios/plugins/check_by_ssh -H 192.168.2.1 \
    /opt/nagios/plugins/check_procs
PROCS OK: 52 processes
```

If the last step also worked correctly, it means that all check commands are working correctly. If you still have issues with the running of the checks, then the next thing you should investigate is if Nagios has been properly configured and whether all commands, hosts, and services are set up in the correct way.

Monitoring using NRPE

Nagios Remote Plugin Executor (**NRPE**) is a daemon for running check commands on remote computers. It is designed explicitly to allow the central Nagios server to trigger checks on other machines in a secure manner.

NRPE offers a very good security mechanism along with encryption mechanisms. It is possible to specify a list of machines that can run checks via NRPE and which plugins can be run along with aliases that should be used by the central Nagios server.

The main difference is that the communication overhead is much smaller than for the SSH checks. This means that both the central Nagios server and the remote machine need less CPU time to perform a check. This is mainly important for Nagios servers that deal with a lot of checks that are performed remotely on machines. If the SSH overhead compared to NRPE is only 1 second, then for performing 20,000 checks, we can save 5.5 hours that would be spent on negotiations.

It also offers a better level of security than SSH mechanisms in terms of the remote machine's safety. It does not provide complete access to the destination machines from the Nagios central server and forbids running any commands outside the predefined check commands. This is very important in situations where Nagios is monitoring machines that might store sensitive information. In such a case, SSH-based solution might not be acceptable due to security policies.

NRPE checks work in the same way as SSH checks in many aspects. In both the cases, the Nagios check command connects to the remote machine and sends a request to run a plugin installed on that machine. NRPE uses a custom protocol. It offers more flexibility in terms of which checks can be executed (and which checks not) as well as which hosts can connect to the NRPE daemon running on the remote machine. It also requires much less overhead to send the command to NRPE and receive output from it as compared to performing checks using the SSH protocol.

Another difference between NRPE and the SSH-based checks is that NRPE allows running only a single command and can be used so that the results are passed back as active checks. However, the ability to perform multiple checks that the check_by_ssh plugin offers is not possible using NRPE.

NRPE uses the TCP protocol with SSL encryption on top of it. Enabling encryption is optional, but it is recommended for companies that require security to be at a high level. By default, NRPE communicates on port 5666. The connection is always made from the machine running the Nagios daemon to the remote machine. If your company has firewalls set up for local connectivity, make sure that you allow communications from port 5666 of your Nagios server. The following is an illustration of how such a check is performed:

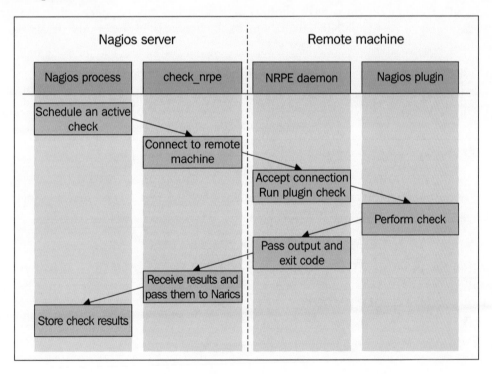

Nagios determines that an active check should be performed. It runs the `check_nrpe` plugin that connects to the remote host's NRPE daemon. After the NRPE daemon accepts this as a valid host to send commands to, `check_nrpe` sends the command to be run along with any parameter to the remote machine.

Next, the NRPE daemon translates these into the actual system command to be run. In case the specified command is not configured to be run, the NRPE daemon will reject this request. Otherwise, it will run the command and pass the results back to `check_nrpe` on the machine hosting the Nagios daemon. This information is then passed back to the Nagios daemon and stored in the data files and/or databases.

The NRPE package consists of two parts: the NRPE daemon and the NRPE check command. The first one needs to be running on all remote machines that are to be monitored using this method. The NRPE check command (`check_nrpe`) is a Nagios plugin to perform active checks and needs to be installed on the machine on which the Nagios daemon is running.

Obtaining NRPE

NRPE is a core add-on for Nagios, and it is maintained by the Nagios development team. NRPE can be downloaded as both source code and binary packages. In the first case, you can compile NRPE from sources by yourself. In the binary packages, you have a ready-to-use set of binaries.

The NRPE source package can be downloaded from the Nagios download page (`http://www.nagios.org/download/addons`). NRPE can be found in the **Addons** section of the page. The file is named in the form of `nrpe-2.15.tar.gz`.

Many Linux distributions already contain prebuilt NRPE binaries. If you want to use precompiled packages instead of building them yourself, then this is the way to go.

For Ubuntu Linux, the package names are `nagios-nrpe-server` and `nagios-nrpe-plugin` for the daemon and client, respectively. For Ubuntu, the command to install the client and the server is as follows:

```
apt-get install nagios-nrpe-server nagios-nrpe-plugin
```

For **Red Hat Enterprise Linux (RHEL)**, CentOS, and Fedora systems that have `yum` installed, the package names are `nagios-nrpe` and `nagios-plugins-nrpe` for the daemon and the client respectively. The command to install both client and server is as follows:

```
yum install nagios-nrpe nagios-plugins-nrpe
```

Microsoft Windows version of the NRPE daemon can be found in the **NRPE_NT** project on SourceForge (http://sourceforge.net/projects/nrpent/). It offers the same functionality as its Unix version and is configured in the same way.

The Nagios plugins do not provide the Windows version, so you will need to compile Nagios plugins using the Cygwin package (visit http://www.cygwin.com/). You can also provide only your own check commands and set up NRPE_NT to use those. In the case of Microsoft Windows, it is important to remember that your plugins need to be command-line tools and cannot be created as GUI–based tools.

Monitoring Microsoft Windows-based machines and using the NRPE protocol for performing the checks is described in more detail in *Chapter 10, Advanced Monitoring*.

Compiling NRPE

If you are using NRPE from prebuilt packages, you can skip this section and resume with the NRPE configuration information. Compiling NRPE requires a standard compiler, linker, and similar tools to be present on your system. It also needs the OpenSSL package along with the actual openssl command line, which is used to generate the Diffie-Hellman key for each instance.

On an Ubuntu Linux system, installing the prerequisite packages can be done by performing the following command:

```
apt-get install gcc make binutils cpp pkg-config libc6-dev \
        libssl-dev openssl
```

For other systems, the commands and package names might differ a bit, but should be very similar. It is also recommended to install the same prerequisites as those for compiling Nagios and the Nagios plugins. These packages should already be there from when the actual plugins were built. However, in case the compilation fails, it would be a good idea to install all packages that were also used for the Nagios build. For Ubuntu Linux, this would require running the following command:

```
apt-get install gcc make binutils cpp libpq-dev libmysqlclient15-dev \
                libssl0.9.8 libssl-dev pkg-config apache2 \
                libgd2-xpm libgd2-xpm-dev libgd-tools \
                libpng12-dev libjpeg62-dev \
                perl libperl-dev libperl5.8 libnet-snmp-perl
```

More information on what packages should be installed on other operating systems and how to do this can be found in *Chapter 2, Installing Nagios 4*.

Now that our packages are set up, the next step is to run the `configure` script that will set up the NRPE parameters and create the Diffie-Hellman key.

For standard paths and users that were used in *Chapter 2, Installing Nagios 4,* the command is as follows:

```
sh configure \
    --sysconfdir=/etc/nagios \
    --libexecdir=/opt/nagios/plugins \
    --prefix=/opt/nagios \
    --localstatedir=/var/nagios \
    --with-nrpe-user=nagios \
    --with-nrpe-group=nagios \
    --with-nagios-user=nagios \
    --with-nagios-group=nagios \
    --enable-ssl
```

If running the `configure` script failed, it is probably because one or more of the required packages are missing. If this happens, verify whether all the packages mentioned earlier in the chapter have been installed, and then try again. Also, if you know that the package is properly installed, it may require additional options to be passed. In such cases, it is recommended to check for the exact error code on the Internet. The next step is to actually build the NRPE client and daemon. To do this, run the following command:

```
make all
```

This command will build both the binaries and then create the sample configuration files for the NRPE daemon.

It is a very common problem that the build fails, claiming that the `get_dh512` function could not be found. The problem is not obvious. In this case, please make sure that the `openssl` command is installed, the directory where it is located is added to the `PATH` environment variable, and then run all of the steps again—starting with the `configure` script.

The problem is that the `configure` script tries to generate a Diffie-Hellman key if a problem exists during this step. Then the script itself does not fail to complete, but the build process eventually fails. Please make sure that somewhere at the end of the output from the `configure` script, a text similar to the one that follows is printed out:

```
*** Generating DH Parameters for SSL/TLS ***
Generating DH parameters, 512 bit long safe prime, generator 2
This is going to take a long time
+..............+..........+........++*+*++*++*++*++*
```

If the `openssl` command is not present, the following error will show up instead:

```
*** Generating DH Parameters for SSL/TLS ***
configure: line 6703: /usr/bin/openssl: No such file or directory
```

If the compilation process fails for any other reason, it is most probably due to the missing libraries or header files. In this case, installing the packages mentioned earlier will help.

Assuming that the build succeeded, the next step is to install either the NRPE client or the daemon. On the machine that is running the Nagios daemon, we need to install the client `check_nrpe` command. To do this, type the following command:

```
make install-plugin
```

This command will copy the `check_nrpe` command to the `/opt/nagios/plugins` directory. NRPE does not require any configuration file for the NRPE client, and hence, no additional file needs to be copied. For all of the remaining machines, please run the following command to install the NRPE daemon:

```
make install-daemon
```

This command will copy the `nrpe` binary to the `/opt/nagios/bin` directory.

Because the NRPE daemon requires configuration, it is recommended that you copy the `sample-config/nrpe.cfg` file as `/etc/nagios/nrpe.cfg`.

Configuring the NRPE daemon

Our NRPE daemon is now built and ready to be deployed on the remote machines. We need to configure it and set up the system so that it accepts connections from other computers.

The NRPE daemon should use a separate user and password. First, let's create a user and a group named `nagios`:

```
groupadd nagios
useradd -g nagios -d /opt/nagios nagios
```

We also need to create a home directory for the user, and it is a good idea to lock out access for that user if no checks are to be performed over SSH. To do this, run the following commands:

```
mkdir /opt/nagios
chown nagios:nagios /opt/nagios
passwd -l nagios
```

There are many ways of setting this up—NRPE can work either as a standalone process that handles incoming connections, or as part of the `inetd` setup (http://en.wikipedia.org/wiki/inetd) or the `xinetd` (http://www.xinetd.org/) setup. In all cases, a configuration file is needed. This file specifies the commands to be used and the additional options to run the NRPE daemon standalone.

The configuration file is similar to the main Nagios configuration file—all parameters are written in the form of `<name>=<value>`. If you have compiled NRPE from the source, then a default configuration can be found in the `sample-config/nrpe.cfg` file.

A sample NRPE configuration script that will work for both standalone installations as well as under `inetd` is as follows:

```
log_facility=daemon
pid_file=/var/run/nrpe.pid
server_port=5666
nrpe_user=nagios
nrpe_group=nagios
allowed_hosts=192.168.2.51
command_timeout=60
connection_timeout=300
debug=0
```

The first series of parameters includes information related to logging. NRPE uses standard Unix logging mechanisms. The `log_facility` parameter specifies the `syslog` facility name to be used for logging. The default value is `daemon`, but it can be set to any of the predefined syslog facility names.

A standalone NRPE daemon also allows the setting up of the IP address and the port to listen, as well as the user and group names to be used. In order to specify that NRPE should listen only on a specific IP address, you need to use the `server_address` parameter. If this parameter is omitted, then the NRPE will listen on all the network interfaces. The `server_port` parameter is used to specify the port number on which NRPE should listen. If NRPE should accept connections only from a predefined list of machines, you need to specify the `allowed_hosts` parameter, which will contain a list of all the IP addresses of these machines, separated by commas.

For security reasons, NRPE usually runs as a separate user. The options to specify the user and group names that should be used by NRPE are `nrpe_user` and `nrpe_group`, respectively.

We can also specify the file to which NRPE should write the PID of the daemon process — this is useful in the startup scripts that can read this file to terminate any NRPE processes during a restart of the service. The option name is `pid_file`.

We can also tell NRPE for how long a command can run. The first option is `command_timeout`, and it tells NRPE how many seconds a command can run before it should be stopped. If a command is running for more than the specified number of seconds, it is terminated and a CRITICAL status is sent back to the NRPE client.

The `connection_timeout` option specifies the time in seconds after which a connection should be closed if no data has been received. This does not change the way the command times out, it only specifies how much time NRPE should wait for a command to be sent.

NRPE also offers a `debug` option that can specify whether it should record a large amount of information in the system log. A value of 1 enables verbose logging and 0 disables it. This should be disabled in production, but can be useful during the initial runs in case you run into a problem.

The next step is to configure the commands that can be used by the other machines. The NRPE commands define aliases for the actual commands that will be executed. All commands have a unique name and the actual command line to be run.

Usually, command names are the plugin names or the plugin names with some description appended. For example, the `check_disk` command that checks the `/home` directory could be called `check_disk_home`.

Each command is defined as `command[<command_name>]=<command_to_execute>`. Each `command_name` can be used only once, and there is no possibility of defining which hosts can run which commands. The same set of commands can be run by all hosts specified in the `allowed_hosts` parameter. An example command definition to use `check_disk` and to verify the space on the root partition is as follows:

```
command[check_disk_sys]=/opt/nagios/plugins/check_disk -w 20% -c 10%
                        -p /
```

It would be a good idea to create a template configuration that will contain the typical checks and the hosts that should be allowed to run the checks. These can be modified later for individual hosts, but using a template makes it easier to deploy the checks for a large number of boxes. A typical set of commands would be as follows:

```
command[check_rootdisk]=/opt/nagios/plugins/check_disk -w 20% -c 10%
                        -p /
command[check_swap]=/opt/nagios/plugins/check_disk -w 40% -c 20%
command[check_sensors]=/opt/nagios/plugins/check_sensors
```

```
command[check_users]=/opt/nagios/plugins/check_users -w 10 -c 20
command[check_load]=/opt/nagios/plugins/check_load -w 10,8,5 -c
                    20,18,15
command[check_zombies]=/opt/nagios/plugins/check_procs -w 5 -c 10 -s
                    Z
command[check_all_procs]=/opt/nagios/plugins/check_procs -w 150 -c
                    200
```

 The parameters for several plugins may be changed according to your preferences, but they do represent reasonable defaults.

In case you need to troubleshoot why a check is failing, it would be a good idea to set the debug parameter to 1 in nrpe.cfg. If NRPE is running in standalone mode, it will need to be restarted for the changes to take effect. An example log from a connection is as follows:

```
Apr 21 20:07:29 ubuntu2 nrpe[5569]: Handling the connection...
Apr 21 20:07:29 ubuntu2 nrpe[5569]: Host is asking for command
    'check_root_disk' to be run...
Apr 21 20:07:29 ubuntu2 nrpe[5569]: Running command:
    /opt/nagios/plugins/check_disk -w 20% -c 10% -p /
Apr 21 20:07:29 ubuntu2 nrpe[5569]: Command completed with return code 0
    and output: DISK OK - free space: / 7211 MB (90% inode=96%);|
    /=759MB;6717;7557;0;8397
Apr 21 20:07:29 ubuntu2 nrpe[5569]: Return Code: 0, Output: DISK OK -
free space: / 7211 MB (90% inode=96%);|  /=759MB;6717;7557;0;8397
```

Another requirement for using NRPE is that the commands need to be specified using the full path to the plugin, and no macro substitution can take place. Not being able to use any macro definitions requires more attention when writing macros. It also requires that any change to the command is edited in the NRPE configuration on the remote machine, and not in the Nagios configurations on the central server. This introduces a very strict security model, but makes NRPE a bit harder to maintain.

In some cases, it is better to be able to pass arguments to NRPE from the Nagios server and have NRPE put these into the command definition. Even though this functionality is disabled for security reasons, it is possible to enable it. How NRPE can be set up to accept parameters from the Nagios server is described in the *Using command arguments with NRPE* section in this chapter.

Setting up NRPE as a system service

The easiest way to get NRPE up and running is to add it to startup in a standalone mode. In this case, it will handle listening on the specified TCP port and changing the user and group by itself. To do this, simply run the NRPE binary with the following parameters:

`/opt/nagios/bin/nrpe -c /etc/nagios/nrpe.cfg -d`

You can also add NPRE to the `init.d` file so that NPRE will start automatically at system start. Usually, this file is located in `/etc/init.d/nrpe` or `/etc/rc.d/init.d/nrpe`.

The NRPE source code provides two `init.d` scripts: `init-script.debian` that can be used for Ubuntu and Debian distributions and `init-script.suse` that can be used for SUSE/openSUSE Linux distributions. The scripts can be found in the NRPE source directory and are customized as a part of configuring the NRPE sources so that they contain appropriate paths.

If you are running a different Linux distribution, it may be worth checking if either of the scripts work properly in your case. If not, a simple script that starts up and shuts down NRPE is as follows:

```sh
#! /bin/sh

case "$1" in
  start)
        echo -n "Starting NRPE daemon..."
        /opt/nagios/bin/nrpe -c /etc/nagios/nrpe.cfg -d
        echo " done."
        ;;
  stop)
        echo -n "Stopping NRPE daemon..."
        pkill -u nagios nrpe
        echo " done."
        ;;
  restart)
        $0 stop
        sleep 2
        $0 start
        ;;
  *)
```

```
        echo "Usage: $0 start|stop|restart"
        ;;
 esac


 exit 0
```

The script does not have proper error handling or verification that the process is terminated, but should work properly on all Linux distributions. The next step is to set up a system to stop and start this service when changing to appropriate run levels. Depending on your system, the command to add `nrpe` as a service can be one of the following:

```
chkconfig --add nrpe ; chkconfig nrpe on
update-rc.d nrpe defaults
```

NRPE can also be run either from `inetd` or `xinetd`. To do this, we first need to add the following line to the `/etc/services` file:

```
nrpe 5666/tcp
```

This will indicate that the TCP port 5666 maps to the service name, `nrpe`. This specification is used by both `inetd` and `xinetd` to map the service name to the actual protocol and port definition.

If we're using `inetd`, we need to add the following service configuration to the `/etc/inetd.conf` file—a sample definition is as follows:

```
nrpe stream tcp nowait nagios /opt/nagios/bin/nrpe -c /etc/nagios/nrpe.
cfg -i
```

The preceding entry should be stored as a single line. Next, we should restart `inetd` by running the following command:

```
/etc/init.d/inetd reload
```

This will make `inetd` reload the service definition. The NRPE daemon should now be accepting connections whenever one comes on TCP port 5666.

Configuring the NRPE daemon for `xinetd` can be done similarly. We will need to create a file called `/etc/xinetd.d/nrpe` with the following contents:

```
service nrpe
{
        flags           = REUSE
        socket_type     = stream
        wait            = no
```

```
        user            = nagios
        group           = nagios
        server          = /opt/nagios/bin/nrpe
        server_args     = -c /etc/nagios/nrpe.cfg -i
        log_on_failure  += USERID
        disable         = no
}
```

Next, we need to reload `xinetd` by running the following command:

```
/etc/init.d/xinetd reload
```

As with the previous reloading of `inetd`, the NRPE daemon should now accept connections on port 5666.

When NRPE is working under `inetd` or `xinetd`, the server ignores the `server_address`, `server_port`, `nrpe_user`, and `nrpe_group` parameters from the configuration files. This is because `inetd` and `xinetd` handle these internally.

NRPE also ignores the `allowed_hosts` directive when it is running from any `inetd` flavor. In this way, you can configure which hosts are allowed to access this particular service in the `inetd`/`xinetd` file. For `xinetd`, this can be done by using the `only_from` statement in the service definition. For `inetd`, this can be done using the `tcpd` wrapper (`http://linux.about.com/library/cmd/blcmdl8_tcpd.htm`) to achieve this.

Configuring Nagios for NRPE

The next step is to set up Nagios to use NRPE for performing checks via a remote machine. Using NRPE to perform checks requires the creation of one or more commands that will use the `check_nrpe` plugin to send actual check requests to a remote machine.

The syntax of the plugin is as follows:

```
check_nrpe -H <host> [-n] [-u] [-p <port>] [-t <timeout>]
           [-c <command>] [-a <arglist...>]
```

The following table describes all of the options accepted by the plugin. The items required are marked in bold:

Option	Description
-H, --host	This provides the hostname or IP address of the machine to connect; this option must be specified
-c, --command	This is the name of the command that should be executed; the command needs to be defined in the nrpe.cfg file on the remote machine
-n, --no-ssl	This disables SSL for communication
-p, --port	This connects to the specified port; defaults to 5666
-t, --timeout	This is the number of seconds after which a connection will be terminated; defaults to 10
-u, --unknown-timeout	If a timeout occurs, this will return an UNKNOWN state; if not specified, then CRITICAL status is returned in case of timeout

The only two required attributes are -H and -c, which specify the host and the command alias to run on that machine, respectively.

The next thing we should do is make sure that the NRPE server on the remote machine is working correctly. Assuming that check_swap is a valid command defined in NRPE on a remote machine, we can now try to connect from the Nagios server. The first thing that's worth checking is whether calling check_nrpe directly works:

```
$ /opt/nagios/plugins/check_nrpe -H 192.168.2.52 -c check_swap
SWAP OK - 100% free (431 MB out of 431 MB) |swap=431MB;86;43;0;431
```

In our example, 192.168.2.52 is the IP address of the remote computer. As the connection was successful, NRPE passed the actual plugin output to the standard output. After a successful check, we can now define a command in the Nagios configuration that will perform a check over NRPE.

```
define command
{
  command_name    check_swap_nrpe
  command_line    $USER1$/check_nrpe -H "$HOSTADDRESS$"
                  -c "check_swap"
}
```

We can then use the check_swap_nrpe command in a service definition. NRPE has a much lower overhead as compared to SSH. So, in some cases, it would be a good idea to use NRPE even for performing local checks.

In case we are defining a service for a group of hosts, we can use the same trick as those for checks over SSH to perform checks on a local machine by using the plugins directly and checking all of the remaining machines using NRPE. This will reduce the overhead related to monitoring the local machine and remove the need to install NRPE on the local host.

The following is a sample configuration that defines a check for swap usage locally for the computer on which it is defined, and over NRPE for all the remaining machines:

```
define service
{
   use                   generic-service
   host_name             localhost
   service_description   SWAP
   check_command         check_swap
   normal_check_interval 15
}
define service
{
   use                   generic-service
   host_name             !localhost
   hostgroup_name        linux-servers
   service_description   SWAP
   check_command         check_swap_nrpe
   normal_check_interval 30
}
```

Using command arguments with NRPE

By default, NRPE is configured to run only the predefined commands, and it is not possible to pass any arguments to the commands that will be run. In some cases, for example with a large number of partitions mounted on various servers, this is hard to manage as changes to the command configurations need to be done at the remote machine level, and not at the central Nagios server level.

In such cases, it might be worth investigating an option included in NRPE to pass arguments to commands. This option is disabled by default as it is considered to be a large security concern. This is because it is possible to send malicious arguments to a check command and make it perform actions other than the ones it should be doing. It is recommended that you keep the option disabled as this is a more secure option.

However, if lowering the level of security is not a concern, it is possible to enable this functionality within the NRPE daemon. This allows easier management of NRPE and the Nagios configuration.

The first thing that needs to be done is the rebuilding of the NRPE daemon with this option enabled. To do this, run the `configure` script again with the `--enable-command-args` flag added. For the same invocation that was used previously to build NRPE, the command would be:

```
sh configure \
    --sysconfdir=/etc/nagios \
    --libexecdir=/opt/nagios/plugins \
    --prefix=/opt/nagios \
    --localstatedir=/var/nagios \
    --with-nrpe-user=nagios \
    --with-nrpe-group=nagios \
    --with-nagios-user=nagios \
    --with-n agios-group=nagios \
    --enable-command-args \
    --enable-ssl
```

Of course, it is also necessary to rebuild the NRPE daemon and reinstall the binary. If you are running NRPE as a standalone daemon, then you need to restart the daemon after overwriting the binary. Only the daemon on remote machine needs to be reconfigured and recompiled. It is not necessary to rebuild the NRPE client as it always supports the passing of arguments to the NRPE daemon.

The next step is to add the `dont_blame_nrpe` option to the `nrpe.cfg` file and set it to `1`. This option, despite its strange name, enables the functionality to use arguments in the command definitions. When both NRPE is compiled with this option and the option is enabled in the NRPE configuration, this option is enabled.

After that, it is possible to use the `$ARGn$` macros in the NRPE configuration, similar to how they are defined in Nagios. This works in the same way as Nagios, where `$ARG1$` indicates the first argument, `$ARG2$` the second one, and so on for up to 16 arguments. For example, a `check` command that checks the disk space on any partition looks like the following:

```
command[check_disk]=/opt/nagios/plugins/check_disk -w $ARG1$ -c $ARG2$ -p
$ARG3$
```

This requires that the warning and critical levels are passed during the check. The actual path to the mount point, which is specified as a third parameter, is essential. Arguments are passed to check_nrpe by specifying the -a flag and passing all required arguments after it, with each argument as a separate parameter. An example invocation of the check command as a standalone command would be as follows:

```
$ /opt/nagios/plugins/check_nrpe -H 10.0.0.1 -c check_disk -a 10% 5% /usr
DISK OK - free space: /usr 7209 MB (90% inode=96%)
```

After making sure that the check works, we can now define a command and the corresponding service definition. The command will pass the arguments specified in the actual service definition:

```
define command
{
    command_name     check_disk_nrpe
    command_line     $USER1$/check_disk -H "$HOSTADDRESS$"
                     -c "check_disk" -a $ARG1$ $ARG2$ $ARG3$
}
```

And, the actual service definition is as follows:

```
define service
{
    use                  generic-service
    host_name            !localhost
    hostgroup_name       linux-servers
    service_description  Disk space on /usr
    check_command        check_disk_nrpe!10%!5%!/usr
}
```

This way, you can define multiple partition checks without any modifications on the remote machines. Of course, arguments can also be used for various plugins, for example, to be able to configure the load, user, and process thresholds in a central location.

Passing arguments to NRPE is a very useful feature. However, it comes at the price of a lower security level. If the machines you deploy NRPE do not require very strict limitations, then it would be a good idea to enable it.

Having a strict source IP address policy in both the firewalls and the remote machine is a good way of limiting security issues related to the passing of arguments down to the actual check commands.

Troubleshooting NRPE

Our NRPE configuration should now be complete and working as expected. However, in some cases, for example, if there is a firewall issue or an issue of invalid configuration, the NRPE-based checks may not work correctly. There are some steps that you can take to determine the root cause of the problem.

The first thing that should be checked is whether Nagios server can connect to the NRPE process on the remote machine. Assuming that we want to use NRPE on `192.168.2.1`, we can check if NRPE accepts connections by using `check_tcp` from the Nagios plugins. By default, NRPE uses port 5666, which we'll also use in the following example that shows how to check:

```
$ /opt/nagios/plugins/check_tcp -H 192.168.2.1 -p 5666
TCP OK - 0.009 second response time on port 5666|time=0.00879
4s;;;0.000000;10.000000
```

If NRPE is not set up on the remote host, the plugin will return `Connection refused`. If the connection could not be established, the result will be `No route to host`. In these cases, you need to make sure that the NRPE server is working and the traffic that the TCP port NRPE is listening is not blocked by the firewalls.

The next step is to try to run an invalid command and check the output from the plugin. The following is an example that assumes that `dummycommand` is not defined in the NRPE configuration on the remote machine:

```
$ /opt/nagios/plugins/check_nrpe -H 192.168.2.1 -c dummycommand
NRPE: Command 'dummycommand' not defined
```

If you received a `CHECK_NRPE: Error - Could not complete SSL handshake` error or something similar, it means that NRPE is not configured to accept connections from your machine — either via the `allowed_hosts` option in the NRPE configuration or in the `inetd` configuration.

In order to check this, log on to the remote machine and search the system logs for `nrpe`. For example, on most systems, to check if the NRPE is configured we need to execute the following command:

```
# grep nrpe /var/log/syslog /var/log/messages
(...)
ubuntu1 nrpe[3023]: Host 192.168.2.13 is not allowed to talk to us!
```

This indicates that your Nagios server is not added to the list of allowed hosts in the NRPE configuration. Add it in the `allowed_hosts` option and restart the NRPE process.

Another error message that could be returned by the `check_nrpe` command is
`CHECK_NRPE: Received 0 bytes from daemon. Check the remote server logs for`
`error messages`. This message usually means that you have passed arguments or
invalid characters in the command name and the NRPE server refused the request
because of these. Looking at the remote server's logs will usually provide more
detailed information:

```
# grep nrpe /var/log/syslog /var/log/messages
(...)
ubuntu1 nrpe[3023]: Error: Request contained command arguments!
ubuntu1 nrpe[3023]: Client request was invalid, bailing out...
```

In this situation, you need to make sure that you enable arguments or change
the Nagios configuration to not to use arguments over NRPE. Another possibility
is that the check returns `CHECK_NRPE: Socket timeout after 10 seconds`
or a similar message. In this case, the check command has not been completed
within the configured time. You may need to increase `command_timeout` in the
NRPE configuration.

Comparing NRPE and SSH

Both SSH and NRPE are used to perform checks on remote machines. They can be set
up to perform the same tasks; however, there are some differences and each solution
is better in certain conditions. Depending on what the critical issues are for your
network, the choice is usually to either use SSH or NRPE to perform the checks on
other machines.

The first is easier to set up from a network and administrative perspective. All
that is needed is to put a set of plugins on the machine, create a public key-based
authentication, and you are all set to go! The main advantage of this method is that
it uses the existing network protocol, which is usually running and enabled on all
Unix-based machines. This way, it is not necessary to configure firewalls to pass
traffic related to the Nagios checks if the server that Nagios is running on can
already connect to other hosts using the SSH protocol.

Security and performance are the trade-offs. As SSH is a generic protocol, the
Nagios server can run any command on any of the machines that it can access.
Many institutions may consider using a generic service such as SSH. One way
of limiting this problem is to set up a restricted shell for the user that performs
the checks, which will make sure that only Nagios plugins are run.

Another problem with this approach is that SSH is a complex protocol, and the overheads related to connecting to a remote machine and running a plugin are high. The main problem occurs where one central Nagios server performs a large volume of tests over SSH. The problem will not be significant on remote computers, but the central server will require more processing power to handle all of the checks in a timely manner.

NRPE is an alternative to SSH. It is a daemon that is installed on remote computers that allow the running of checks. The main advantage of this approach is that it offers much better security. The administrator of the remote computer can configure NRPE to accept connections only from certain IP addresses and to allow the execution of only predefined commands. By default, it is not even possible to pass any arguments to them. So, there is very little chance of a security issue on account of NRPE. Another advantage is that the NRPE protocol requires much less overhead and frequent checks do not affect the central Nagios server too much.

There are some downsides to NRPE. The first one is that it needs to be set up on all of the machines that will be monitored in a remote manner. In addition, all configurations for the checks are kept on the remote machines. In such cases, it is much harder to maintain changes in the configuration when monitoring multiple computers.

There are many other options for monitoring machines and the services on them. They are not as popular, but they can be also used to get the job done. There are various agent-based systems that offer to run commands remotely. They can be used to create check commands that are executed on remote machines. Another approach is to use existing protocols such as HTTP for deploying checks on the remote host. Common solutions, such as PHP, CGI, or various scripting languages, can be leveraged to perform these kinds of tests. This is mainly useful if you already have a stable web server that is also used for other purposes. All that is needed is to install the scripts and configure the server to accept connections, either from all addresses or just from specific ones.

Usually, it is quite obvious which solution should be used in which case. There may be cases where it's easier to use the existing SSH daemons. In other cases, security or performance is more of an issue and NRPE is a better choice. In some other cases, a custom solution will work best. How you should proceed is a matter of knowing the best tool for a particular case. In all cases, doing checks from the remote computers is not as easy as doing it locally. But, it is also not very difficult if you are using the right tools.

Alternatives to SSH and NRPE

This chapter focuses mainly on using SSH and NRPE for performing the remote checks. This is because Nagios is widely used to perform checks on the remote machines. There are also various alternate approaches that people take to invoke checks remotely. A very popular approach is to use frameworks for working remotely. In such cases, you might need to create some scripts or jobs that perform the checks, but the entire network communication along with authentication and authorization are already implemented in them.

One such framework is the **Software Testing Automation Framework (STAF)** available at `http://staf.sourceforge.net/`. This is a peer-to-peer-based framework that allows you to write code that performs specific jobs on remote machines. As the system is not centralized, there is no critical resource that can make your entire system malfunction if it is down.

STAF can be used from various languages such as Java, Perl, Python, Tcl, and Ant. This means that pieces of the checks can be done in languages that best fit a specific scenario. Another approach is to use `check_http` and web-based communication. This is a very common scenario when doing a check for web applications. This way, you can invoke a specific URL that will perform a check on the remote machine and provide the results over the HTTP protocol.

In such a case, an application can have a URL that is accessible only from specific IP addresses and returns diagnostic information about the website. This can mean performing a test SQL query to the database and checking the file permissions and available disk space. The application can also perform a sanity check of critical data either in the files or in a database.

The web page can return a predefined string if all of the tests are passed correctly and will return an error message otherwise. In this case, it is possible to perform the check with the `check_http` plugin.

A typical scenario is when a check is done for both the string preset in the answer and a page size range. For example, a check for the OK string combined with a page size ranging from two to eight will check whether the result contains information about the correct test and will also detect any additional messages preset in the output.

Summary

Checking whether a service is available over a network can be done from a single machine. In such cases, using a single, dedicated machine to do all of these checks would be a good idea as it also reduces the load to be on just a single computer on your network. In reality, this is not enough for a robust computer and failure monitoring solution.

In this chapter, we have learned how to perform checks on the remote machines using the SSH protocol. We have set up our SSH private key, added the corresponding public key to remote machine, and performed the checks using this approach. We have also learned how to perform multiple checks over the SSH protocol using a single check invocation, which can be used to reduce the number of connections and load on the remote machine.

This chapter also covers the NRPE protocol and how to set up the NRPE server and client. We have configured an NRPE server that allows specific checks from the remote machines. We have also learned how to use NRPE to perform checks and how to pass arguments to the checks, such as using a single check definition to allow checking the disk space for multiple volumes. The chapter also discussed the differences between the SSH-based and NRPE-based approaches and when it is better to use one or the other. It also mentions other less popular alternatives to automate performing remote checks.

The next chapter talks about **Simple Network Management Protocol (SNMP)**, which is a protocol for monitoring and managing various types of devices connected to a network. The protocol supports both querying the device as well as receiving information from the devices regarding the failure. The SNMP protocol is used by a large variety of devices, from network switches and routers to mainframe servers.

9
Monitoring using SNMP

The previous chapter talked about different approaches to verify remote computers and the services they offer. This chapter covers another way to monitor remote machines and devices.

Simple Network Management Protocol (SNMP) is designed to monitor and manage various devices connected to a network. Its main purpose is to create a standardized way to get and set parameters, regardless of the underlying hardware. The protocol allows the retrieval of information from a device and the setting of options, and covers the means for a device to notify other machines about a failure.

In this chapter, we will learn what SNMP is and how it works. We will also learn to configure SNMP on various types of machines and how to retrieve information using Nagios plugins.

Introducing SNMP

SNMP is an industry standard and all major hardware and software vendors support it. All commonly used operating systems can provide information using SNMP. Microsoft offers SNMP for its Windows platform. UNIX systems have SNMP daemons that receive requests from other machines.

SNMP also offers a standardized, hierarchical way to group and access information, called **Management Information Base (MIB)**, which defines the attributes that can be accessed and the data types associated with them. This allows the creation of attributes that all devices should use to provide information on standard parameters, such as network configuration, usage, and potential threats. It also allows custom parameters to be created so that they do not interfere with other devices' data.

Most operating systems come with various utilities that allow communication with other devices over SNMP. These utilities can be used to verify which attributes are available on specific devices and what their values are at the moment.

SNMP is designed so that it is easy to implement and can provide a uniform way to access information on various machines. It is designed so that the footprint of the SNMP services is minimal. This allows devices with very limited storage size and operating memory to use the protocol. SNMP uses **User Datagram Protocol (UDP)** (`http://en.wikipedia.org/wiki/User_Datagram_Protocol`) that requires much fewer resources than TCP. It also uses one packet for sending a single request or response operation, so the protocol itself is stateless.

Each machine that is managed by SNMP has an application that responds to requests from local machines and remote computers. Such an application is called an **agent**. For UNIX systems, it is usually a daemon working in the background. Many devices with embedded systems have SNMP support included in the system's core. In all of these cases, a device needs to listen for SNMP requests and respond accordingly.

All agents are usually managed by one or more machines called the SNMP **managers**. This is a computer that queries agents for data and may set their attributes. Usually, this is an application running in the background that communicates over SNMP and stores the information in a data storage.

By default, SNMP uses UDP port 161 to communicate with the agent and port 162 to send information from the agent to the manager. In order to use SNMP, these ports need to be passed correctly by all network routers and should not be filtered by the firewalls.

There are two types of communication used by SNMP: the first is when a manager sends requests to an agent. These can be GET requests in which the manager wants to retrieve information from an agent. If the information needs to be modified, a SET request is sent out.

Another type of communication is when an agent wants to notify a manager about a problem. In such cases, an SNMP **trap** is sent out. An agent needs to know the IP address of the manager to send out the information. A manager needs to listen for SNMP traps and should react to the issue.

The following is an illustration of possible SNMP communication types:

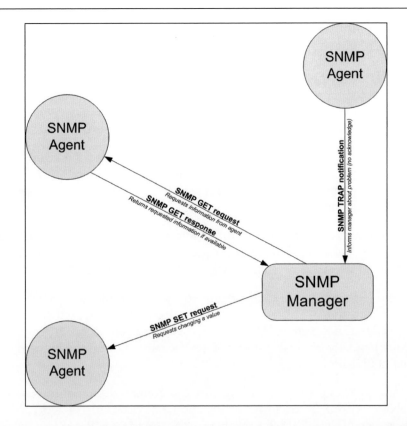

SNMP has several versions through which an agent can communicate. **SNMPv1** was the first version of the protocol that featured GET, SET, and TRAP operations. The standard defines scalar data objects, which is a single value as well as tabular objects, which are a table of objects. It also featured the GETNEXT operation that allows iterating over the tables of data objects.

The security model related to SNMPv1 is relatively unsophisticated. A GET, SET, or GETNEXT request is authenticated based on the IP address of the manager and the community string that it uses. All SNMP devices communicating over SNMPv1 use the community string to verify that a request—whether none, only GET, or both GET and SET operations—can be performed. By default, the private community string allows reading and writing information, while the public community string only allows reading.

SNMP Version 2 introduced improvements in terms of both performance and security. Instead of using GET and GETNEXT, it used a GETBULK operation that allows the retrieval of all entries in a table in a single operation. It also introduced an **inform** packet—this is a trap that requires an acknowledgement from the manager. This tackles the problem of a single UDP packet getting lost, thus preventing a trap from being received by the manager. This version also introduced a party-based security model, which did not gain wide acceptance due to its complexity.

The most common Version 2 implementation is **Community-Based Simple Network Management Protocol 2 (SNMPv2c)**. It uses the features of Version 2 without implementing the new security model, but uses the community string mechanism that was introduced in SNMPv1.

User-Based Network Management Protocol version 2 (SNMPv2u) is another variant of SNMP Version 2. This includes greater security than SNMPv2c, but does not include all of the security features originally developed for SNMPv2.

SNMP Version 3 introduced a more improved security model than SNMPv2 and includes authentication, privacy, and access control; one of the security frameworks uses the functionalities from SNMPv2u. This standard is now gaining more attention than SNMPv2, mostly because it offers better security without the high-level complexity of SNMPv2.

Most SNMP server implementations that are integrated with operating systems support SNMPv1, SNMPv2c, and SNMPv3. Some devices only support SNMPv1, while others also offer SNMPv2. Packets from different SNMP versions are incompatible, so a device using only SNMPv1 will not recognize a SNMPv2c packet.

In many cases, devices that are used across your network will offer a different subset of the versions they support. There are multiple ways to work in such an environment.

The best approach is to use a proxy agent. A proxy agent is usually an application on a computer or a physical device. Some SNMP management software use SNMPv3, and devices that do not support this version will need to have the packets translated. In such cases, all requests from the manager are received by the proxy agent; the proxy agent translates all packets and passes them to the actual agent, and sends the results back to the manager. The proxy agent receives traps from the actual agent. It then passes them to the manager as a trap or translates the packet using a newer SNMP version.

Often, SNMP managers allow the configuration of the SNMP version that should be used for specific devices.

Understanding data objects

SNMP uses **Object Identifiers (OIDs)** (http://en.wikipedia.org/wiki/Object_identifier) to identify the data objects that it refers to. OIDs define a unique object for a specified SNMP agent. The object is identified using a hierarchical definition, similar to how domains work on the Internet.

Object identifiers are a series of numbers separated by periods. Each number represents a part of the tree. Often, the first number in the series is also preceded by a period to indicate that this is an OID—this is not necessary though. An example of an OID is .1.3.6.1.2.1.1.5.0, which maps to the system name of a machine.

As it is very hard to memorize, read, and compare OIDs written as a series of numbers, there is a standard for naming and describing the MIB tree. The standard is called **Management Information Base (MIB)** (http://en.wikipedia.org/wiki/Management_Information_Base). It describes how various parameters are defined—how they are named, as well as what types of values these objects may return. Each MIB definition is a text file written in a subset of the ASN.1 notation (http://en.wikipedia.org/wiki/ASN.1). A file can describe a small or large subset of the MIB trees. Currently, the standard is MIB SMIv2 that defines all commonly used attributes along with additional information, which can be used by visualization applications.

MIB files describe fields that can be used in SNMP and define parent nodes in the hierarchy, the numeric identifier, and the type of data that this field is associated with. SNMP uses the following basic data types:

- **String**: A string, written as bytes, that can have 0 to 65535 bytes
- **Integer and Integer32**: A signed 32-bit integer value
- **Counters32 and Counter64**: These are nonnegative integers that increase and are reset to 0 after they reach the maximum value
- **Gauges**: These are nonnegative integers that can increase and decrease within a defined minimum-maximum range
- **Time tick**: This defines a time span, where the value of 100 represents one second
- **IP address**: This represents an address from the IP protocol family; SNMPv1 only supports IPv4, while Version 2 and 3 support both IPv4 and IPv6

In many cases, an enumeration field is returned as an integer. This means that some predefined numbers represent several predefined values. A good example is the `ifType` field when defining network interfaces — this specifies the type of network interface. Some examples are `23` for a **Point-to-Point Protocol (PPP)** (`http://en.wikipedia.org/wiki/Point-to-Point_Protocol`) connection and `6` for Ethernet interfaces.

An example OID is `.1.3.6.1.2.1.1.5.0`. The following table describes each element, both as string and as corresponding numbers:

Identifier	Description
1	**iso**: This is the iso standard tree
3	**org**: Organizations — this node is a placeholder for all national and international organizations
6	**dod**: Department of Defense — this is the node for the U.S. Department of Defense
1	**internet**: Subnode for the Internet — since the Internet was originally a project for the U.S. military defense, its placeholder is under the **dod** subtree
2	**mgmt.**: This is the Systems management node
1	**mib-2**: This is the Management Information Base and a Version 2 root node
1	**system**: This is the Operating system information
5	**sysName**: This is the name of the machine and is usually a fully qualified domain name
0	This is an index of the elements; in this case, it is always 0

The string representation of this OID is `iso.org.dod.internet.mgmt.mib-2.system.sysName.0`. It is also often referred to as `SNMPv2-MIB::sysName.0`.

The `.1.3.6.1.2.1` part of the OID defines the root elements for all MIB-2 standardized parameters. All of the standard SNMP parameters that various devices use are under this OID node or its descendants. This node is also called the `SNMPv2-MIB` namespace; hence the `SNMPv2-MIB::sysName.0` OID also maps to the same object.

The MIB tree has a few major nodes that are the bases for many other subtrees that may be significant to you under various circumstances, which are as follows:

- `.1.3.6.1.2.1`: This stands for `iso.org.dod.internet.mgmt.mib-2`, which is the base for all of the attributes that are available on a majority of SNMP-aware devices.

- `.1.3.6.1.4.1`: This stands for `iso.org.dod.internet.private. enterprise`, which is the root node for all corporations and companies that use private objects. It is used by companies such as Microsoft, Motorola, and many other hardware and software vendors.

The most important node is `.1.3.6.1.2.1`, which is used by all SNMP-aware devices to report information. This part of the MIB tree is the root node for a majority of standard objects. It is also mandatory for all SNMP-enabled devices to provide at least the basic part of information in this subtree. For example, information such as contact information, location, system name, and the type should be provided by all SNMP-aware devices.

SNMP can be used to retrieve different kinds of information. This information is usually grouped into various categories. All categories also have corresponding aliases with which they are usually referenced to avoid putting the entire structure in every OID definition or MIB name. All applications that offer communication over SNMP allow the specification of attributes using both OID and MIB names. Let's go over a few of the most important sections of the MIB tree.

Information in `IF-MIB`, `IP-MIB`, `IPv6-MIB`, `RFC1213-MIB`, `IP-FORWARD-MIB`, `TCP-MIB`, and `UDP-MIB` describe network connectivity—interfaces, IP configuration, routing, forwarding, and the TCP and UDP protocols. They allow the querying of the current configuration as well as the currently active and listening sockets.

Data contained in `SNMPv2-MIB` and `HOST-RESOURCES-MIB` describes a system's information and the current parameters. This can include information on the disk storage, current processes, installed applications, and hardware that the computer is running on.

Working with SNMP and MIB

Different operating systems can come with different SNMP applications. Many hardware vendors also offer additional software that manage multiple machines using SNMP, for example, HP OpenView or Sun Management Center. For this section and the following ones, we will use the Net-SNMP package (`http://net-snmp.sourceforge.net/`). This package is included in all Linux distributions and works with almost all UNIX operating systems.

In order to install this package on Ubuntu Linux, run the following command:

```
apt-get install snmp
```

For yum-based Linux distributions, the package is called `net-snmp` and the command to install it is as follows:

```
yum install net-snmp
```

The Net-SNMP project homepage also offers binaries for several platforms, including HP-UX and Fedora Linux. Fedora packages should also work on Red Hat Enterprise Linux systems.

It is also possible to build everything from the source for various UNIX operating systems such as AIX, HP-UX, and Solaris. Exact instructions are provided on the project page (`http://net-snmp.sourceforge.net/`).

After a successful installation, we should be able to run any SNMP-related command, such as `snmpget`, and check the Net-SNMP version by using the following command:

```
root@ubuntu:~# snmpget -V
NET-SNMP version: 5.3.1
```

Assuming we do have a host with the SNMP agent set up, and it is accepting the SNMP protocol Version 1, we can now try to communicate with it and query its host name by using the following command:

```
root@ubuntu:~# snmpget -v 1 -c public 192.168.2.2 \
    iso.org.dod.internet.mgmt.mib-2.system.sysName.0
SNMPv2-MIB::sysName.0 = STRING: WAG354G
```

As you can see, the device returned the system name as WAG354G. This is actually a Linksys/Cisco router, and the only way to access its information is over the web interface or SNMP.

The Net-SNMP package comes with a couple of very useful commands that can be used to check the current values as well as dump a part of or the whole MIB tree. These commands vary from simple tools to query a single attribute to very complex ones that print out a report of partitions, which is like `df` on a remote system. There are also commands to display tables and to set parameters remotely.

Throughout this section and the following ones, we'll mainly use SNMP Version 1 as it is supported by almost all SNMP-enabled devices. When using SNMP in production, it's better to check which devices accept the SNMP versions and use one that is most recent and handled correctly by a device.

The first command that's worth getting familiar with is `snmpget`. This allows the querying of a single or multiple attributes over SNMP.

The syntax of the command is as follows:

```
snmpget [options] IP-address OID [OID] ...
```

All of the Net-SNMP commands accept a huge number of parameters. The following parameters are used throughout this chapter and are worth knowing:

Option	Description
-h	This provides help
-V	This prints the Net-SNMP version
-c	This specifies the community name to be used
-v	This specifies the SNMP version to be used; it should be either 1, 2c, or 3
-r	This specifies the number of retries
-t	This indicates the timeout in seconds
-o	This denotes output options and should be one or more of the following:
	n: This prints OIDs as numerical values without expanding them from MIB
	e: This prints enum and OID fields as numbers instead of string values
	v: This prints values only, instead of the name = value format
	f: This prints full OID names and disallows shortcuts such as SNMPv2-MIB

The -o option allows the retrieval of values without having to apply MIB shortcuts, thus giving us the ability to see the entire branch. It also allows output to be changed so that only values along with data types are printed, instead of the object names themselves.

An example of this command is as follows:

```
# snmpget -O ef -v 1 -c public rtr SNMPv2-MIB::sysObjectID.0
.iso.org.dod.internet.mgmt.mib-2.system.sysObjectID.0 =  OID:
  .iso.org.dod.internet.private.enterprises.ucdavis.
  ucdSnmpAgent.linux
```

 All of the previous options can also be used with other Net-SNMP commands.

Net-SNMP also offers a command to iterate through either the entire MIB tree or only a part of it. The snmpwalk command accepts the same options as shown earlier. Most versions of Net-SNMP's snmpwalk command do not require the passing of any OID to work. For older versions, in order to list the entire tree, .1 can be specified as the OID.

The following command will list the entire MIB tree of an SNMPv1 agent:

```
root@ubuntu:~# snmpwalk -v 1 -c public 192.168.2.2
```

Depending on the underlying operating system and the SNMP agent itself, the actual data may be different. Please note that if the device is not on a local network, then this operation may take a very long time to complete.

In order to retrieve only a part of the MIB tree, simply pass the prefix of the tree you are interested in. An example is shown in the following command line:

```
root@ubuntu:~# snmpwalk -v 1 -c public 192.168.2.2 1.3.6.1.2.1.1
```

The preceding command will limit the query to the `iso.org.dod.internet.mgmt.mib-2.system` node and its children. It will also be completed much faster than querying the entire tree.

Walking over a part of a tree is mainly useful when trying to check the objects that are available on a remote device that does not respond quickly to SNMP requests—either because of a network lag or the computations required for some objects. It is also commonly used to find out which values are available in a specified part of the MIB tree.

Another useful utility is the `snmptable` command. It allows the listing of various SNMP tables and shows them in a human-readable form. The syntax is as follows:

```
snmptable [options] IP-address OIDprefix
```

For example, to list all TCP/IP connections, the following command can be used:

```
root@:~# snmptable -v 1 -c public 192.168.2.2 tcpConnTable
SNMP table: TCP-MIB::tcpConnTable
```

connState	connLocalAddress	connLocalPort	connRemAddress	connRemPort
listen	0.0.0.0	23	0.0.0.0	0
listen	0.0.0.0	80	0.0.0.0	0
listen	0.0.0.0	199	0.0.0.0	0

Net-SNMP also allows the setting of new object values that can be used to reconfigure various devices, which can be performed using the `snmpset` command. The syntax for this command is as follows:

```
snmpset [options] IP-address OID type value [OID type value] ...
```

This command accepts all of the same standard options as does the snmpget command. A single command invocation can be used to set more than one parameter by specifying more than one set of OIDs. Each set operation needs to specify the new value along with the data type it should be set to.

The value type can be one of the types listed in the following table:

Type	Description
i	Integer
u	Unsigned integer
s	String
x	Hex string—each letter is specified as 2 hex digits
d	Decimal string—each letter is specified as 1-2 digits
n	NULL object
o	OID—for objects that accept other objects
t	Timeticks
a	IP address
B	Series of bits

The most common types are String, Integer, and OID. The first two require the passing of either a number or text that the object's value should be set to. Setting an OID type of object requires providing either a full OID identifier or a string that can be matched by the MIB definitions.

An example of how to set a system's contact name and host name is as follows:

```
root@ubuntu:~# snmpset -v 2c -c private 192.168.2.2 \
    SNMPv2-MIB::sysContact.0 s admin@net.home \
    SNMPv2-MIB::sysName.0 s RTR
SNMPv2-MIB::sysContact.0 = STRING: admin@net.home
SNMPv2-MIB::sysName.0 = STRING: RTR
```

Some attributes cannot be set via SNMP. For example, it is not possible to modify objects that are used for the monitoring system. These "unsettable" attributes usually include the IP address configuration, counters, or diagnostic information—for example, TCP/UDP connection tables, process lists, installed applications, and performance counters. Many devices tend to support command-line administration over SNMP, and in this case, the parameters may be read-only.

MIB definitions specify which attributes are explicitly read-only. Using a graphical tool to find out which attributes can be modified will ease the automatic device configuration over the SNMP protocol.

Using graphical tools

Using SNMP and the MIB tree is not a simple task. Many people, not very familiar with command-line tools and the large amounts of information returned, may feel a bit overwhelmed by it. This is where graphical tools come in handy. There are lots of freely available tools that can visualize SNMP; however, we will discuss only a few of them here.

The first tool is called **mbrowse** (`http://www.kill-9.org/mbrowse/`). It is a graphical tool used to browse the MIB tree, query attributes, and run a complete or partial walk through the MIB tree. This tool uses the SNMPv1 and the SNMPv2c protocols. It uses the Net-SNMP libraries and shares the same MIB definitions.

The following screenshot shows the tool with a result from a walk and an expanded TCP tree:

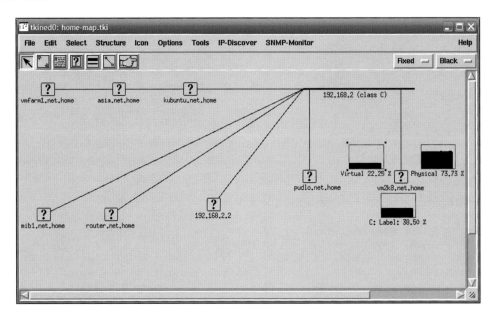

Another interesting tool is **Tcl/tK based Interactive Network EDitor (TkIned)** from the Scotty package (`https://trac.eecs.iu-bremen.de/projects/scotty/`). This is a graphical tool that uses Tk for the graphical interface and Scotty for the SNMP protocol. It allows the browsing of the MIB tree, the monitoring of hosts over SNMP, and the visualization of your network by clicking on the layout.

This tool also has another very interesting feature. Based on one or more IP network addresses, it can automatically detect your networks and try to find hosts that respond to SNMP requests. It uses the default `public`/`private` community pair and communicates over the SNMPv1 and SNMPv2c protocols. This allows the detection of various operating systems and devices that are configured to respond to these communities, which are still default in many cases.

The tool can be configured to monitor various parameters such as disk usage or system load over the SNMP protocol. The results are graphed and updated in real time. This can serve as a backup system to verify up-to-date values for various attributes. Once the SNMP or ICMP checks are set up, they are done periodically until removed from the map.

The following screenshot shows the tool after an **IP-discover** option has been run, where the tool has been configured to monitor the disk and memory usage of a Windows machine:

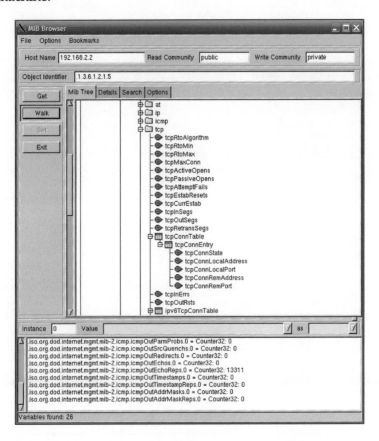

The layout of the machines on the chart can be freely edited. There is also a wide set of icons that can be associated with particular hosts.

Setting up an SNMP agent

The previous section talked about how to communicate with SNMP agents. If you have a network device such as a router or a WiFi, WiMax, or DSL gateway, it is highly probable that it will also come with a built-in SNMP agent.

The next step is to set up the SNMP agent on one or more computers so that we can use SNMP to monitor servers or workstations. In this way, a majority of the networked equipment will allow monitoring from a single machine using the SNMP protocol.

Let's start with various UNIX boxes. The SNMP agent is a part of Net-SNMP, and several distributions usually come with command-line tools, libraries, and the SNMP agent as optional packages.

In our case, we will install the SNMP agent on Ubuntu Linux by running the following command:

```
apt-get install snmpd
```

This will cause the SNMP daemon, which is a part of Net-SNMP, to be installed. By default, the Ubuntu Linux SNMP agent only accepts connections on 127.0.0.1; this is for security reasons. In many cases, an SNMP agent is used mainly by tools such as MRTG to gather usage statistics.

To change this, we will need to either specify the IP address that the SNMP agent should listen on in the SNMPDOPTS variable of the /etc/default/snmpd file, or remove it completely — it should be the last argument in the SNMPDOPTS variable.

If the SNMP agent should listen on all available IP addresses, then the line should look similar to the following example:

```
SNMPDOPTS='-Lsd -Lf /dev/null -u snmp -I -smux -p
  /var/run/snmpd.pid'
```

The preceding options are standard snmpd options and may differ depending on the Linux distribution and version.

Changing this option requires restarting the SNMP agent by invoking the /etc/init.d/snmpd restart command.

After a successful installation, the SNMP agent should be up and running, and making a walk over the entire tree should produce some output.

To verify that the SNMP agent we have just set up is working properly, simply launch the following command on the same machine to see if it will return information retrieved from the localhost:

```
snmpwalk -v 1 -c public 127.0.0.1
```

The agent that we have just installed supports the SNMPv1, SNMPv2c, and SNMPv3 protocol versions. It also features an extensive security model that you can configure to provide a more secure setup.

The Net-SNMP agent allows you to define one or more OIDs along with all the subnodes that can be retrieved by specific security groups. These groups can be mapped to specific communities that originate from all or specific IP addresses. Security groups are also mapped using SNMP versions used by the remote machine.

A sample configuration that allows read-only access from all of the hosts is as follows:

```
com2sec readonly default public
group readonlyGroup v1   readonly
group readonlyGroup v2c readonly
group readonlyGroup usm readonly
view all     included  .1                              80
access readonlyGroup "" any noauth     exact  all    none    none
syslocation Home
syscontact Administrator <admin@yourcompany.com>
```

The first line defines a mapping between the community and a security group—readonly. The next three lines assign readonlyGroup access rights to this group. The next two lines grant read-only access to all objects from the .1 OID node and its children, which is the main OID node. The last two lines specify the system administrator and the location at which the machines are stored.

For the SNMPv3 model, it is also possible to specify one or more users by calling the snmpusm command (http://linux.die.net/man/1/snmpusm). It allows real-time configuration of the user list for local or remote SNMPv3 agents.

SNMP can also be set up on all modern Microsoft Windows operating systems. As with UNIX systems, it is necessary to install an SNMP agent. In order to do this on Windows XP and Windows 2003 Server, we need to perform the following steps:

1. We first need to go to the **Control Panel**.

2. Next, we need to select the **Add or Remove Programs** applet and select the **Add/Remove Windows Components** option. The following window will be displayed:

3. Then, select both **Simple Network Management Protocol** and **WMI SNMP Provider** from the next window (shown in the following screenshot) to proceed with the installation of SNMP management and monitoring tools:

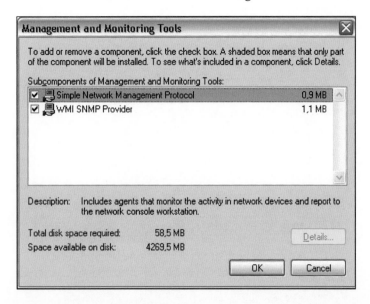

4. Next, we need to select **Management and Monitoring Tools**, as shown in the preceding screenshot. We can also click on the **Details** button and choose **Simple Network Management Protocol**. The **WMI SNMP Provider** allows the retrieval of the SNMP parameters over WMI and can be left unchecked if you do not need it.

The Windows SNMP agent exports information about the system in the same way as other platforms. You can use it to query the underlying hardware, the operating system version, and the network configuration, along with the currently active connections. It is also possible to list active processes and monitor the system load. The Windows SNMP agent also exports details of all of the installed applications along with security patches from Microsoft. This mechanism can be used to monitor whether all critical system patches are installed. It can also be used to track software license monitor compliance by checking installed and/or running software and keeping count of which machines have license-restricted software applied.

After successful installation, we can go to the `Administrative Tools` folder and run the **Services** applet. When selecting **SNMP Service** and choosing **Properties**, the following service properties window, along with the SNMP configuration, is displayed:

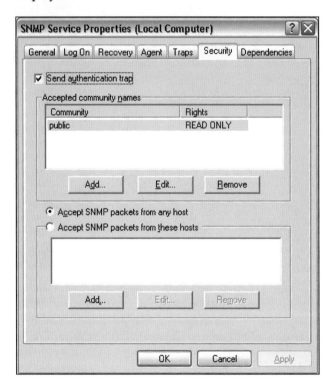

The window has three additional tabs—**Agent**, **Traps**, and **Security**. The **Agent** tab allows you to configure which parts are exported over SNMP and offers the setting up of contact and location information, as shown in the following screenshot:

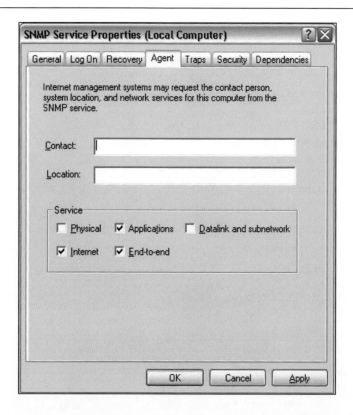

The **Security** tab allows you to configure how SNMP information from this host can be accessed. The Windows SNMP agent offers support for SNMPv1 and SNMPv2c, so the security model is based on a community string and IP addresses for authentication.

The agent can accept SNMP queries either from all hosts or only from the specific hosts listed in the bottom part of the tab. There is also the possibility of specifying one or more readable and writable communities. By default, only queries on the public community string are accepted and allowed read-only access.

The **Traps** tab allows configuration of Windows to send or forward traps to specific IP addresses and indicate which SNMP community is to be used for communication.

Using SNMP from Nagios

Now that we are able to query information from Windows and UNIX boxes, it would be good to know how to integrate SNMP checks with Nagios. The Nagios plugins package comes with a plugin called `check_snmp` for checking SNMP parameters and validating their value. The plugin uses the `snmpget` and `snmpgetnext` commands from Net-SNMP, and it does not work without these commands. The syntax of the `check_snmp` command is as follows:

```
check_snmp -H <ip_address> -o <OID> [-w warn_range] [-c crit_range]
          [-C community] [-s string] [-r regex] [-R regexi]
          [-l label] [-u units] [-d delimiter]   [-D output- delimiter]
          [-t timeout] [-e retries] [-p port-number]
          [-m miblist] [-P snmp version] [-L seclevel] [-U secname]
          [-a authproto] [-A authpasswd] [-X privpasswd]
```

The following table describes the commonly-used options accepted by the plugin. Options that are required are marked in bold.

Option	Description
-H, --hostname	Host name or IP address of the machine to connect to; this option must be specified
-o, --oid	OID to get from the remote machine; can be specified either as dot-separated numbers or as a name, multiple elements can be specified and need to be separated with commas or spaces
-w	Specifies the `min:max` range of values outside of which a warning state should be returned; for integer results only
-c	Specifies the `min:max` range of values outside of which a critical state should be returned; for integer results only
-P, --protocol	Specifies the SNMP protocol version; accepted values are 1, 2c, and 3
-C, --community	Specifies the community string to be used; for SNMPv1 and SNMPv2c, this defaults to `public`
-s, --string	Returns a critical state unless the result is an exact match to the value specified in this parameter
-r, --regex	Returns a critical state if the result does not match the specified regular expression; is case sensitive
-R, --eregi	Returns a critical state if the result does not match the specified regular expression; is case insensitive
-t, --timeout	Specifies the period in seconds after which it is assumed that no response has been received and the operation times out

Option	Description
-e, --retries	Specifies the number of retries that should be performed if no answer is received
-n, --next	Uses the `getnext` request instead of `get` to retrieve the following attribute after the specified one
-d, --delimiter	Specifies the delimiter which should be used to match values in the output from the Net-SNMP commands; defaults to an equal sign(=)
-D, --output-delimiter	Specifies the character used to separate output if multiple OIDs are provided

Depending on which exact flags are passed, the plugin behavior is different. In all cases, the plugin will return `critical` if the SNMP agent could not be contacted or if the specified OID does not exist. If none of the `-s`, `-r`/`-R`, `-w`, and `-c` flags are specified, the plugin will return OK as long as the OID is not retrieved. Specifying `-s` will cause the check to fail if the value returned by the SNMP `get` request is different from the value supplied to this option. It is worth noting that this option uses an exact match, not a substring.

An example would be to make sure that the exact location is specified in an SNMP agent. This can be checked by the following command:

```
root@ubuntu:~# /opt/nagios/plugins/check_snmp -H 10.0.0.1 -P 2c \
    -o SNMPv2-MIB::sysLocation.0 -s "Miami Branch"
SNMP OK - VMware | SNMPv2-MIB::sysLocation.0=Miami Branch
```

Matching a part of text can be done with the `-r` or `-R` option. The first one is a case-sensitive match. The latter option ignores the case while matching the resulting value. Similarly, to make sure that the contact information field contains e-mail information, the following command can be used:

```
root@ubuntu:~# /opt/nagios/plugins/check_snmp -H 10.0.0.1 -P 2c \
    -o SNMPv2-MIB::sysContact.0 -r "@"
SNMP OK - root@company.com | SNMPv2-
  MIB::sysContact.0=root@company.com
```

It is also possible to match the specific value ranger for integer results, in which case the values indicate acceptable ranges for specific values. If the result is outside of a specified range, a WARNING or CRITICAL state is returned. It is possible to specify separate ranges for critical and warning checks.

Typical usage can be to monitor system load or the number of processes running on a specific host.

The following is an example of how to check whether the number of system processes is less than 20:

```
root@ubuntu:~# /opt/nagios/plugins/check_snmp -H 10.0.0.1 -P 2c \
    -o HOST-RESOURCES-MIB::hrSystemProcesses.0 -w 0:20 -c 0:30
SNMP CRITICAL - *33* | HOST-RESOURCES-MIB::hrSystemProcesses.0=33
```

The check will return CRITICAL status if the number of processes is 30 or more. A WARNING status will be returned if the number of processes is 20 or more. If the number is less than 20, an OK status will be returned.

In all cases, it is advised that you first use the snmpwalk command and check which objects can be retrieved from a specific agent.

Nagios also comes with SNMP plugins written in Perl that allow the checking of network interfaces and their statuses. These plugins require the installation of the Perl Net::SNMP package. For Ubuntu Linux, the package name is libnet-snmp-perl.

The syntax of the plugins is as follows:

```
check_ifstatus -H hostname [-v version] [-C community]
check_ifoperstatus -H hostname [-v version] [-C community]
                   [-k index] [-d name]
```

The following table describes the options accepted by the plugins. Required options are marked in bold:

Option	Description
-H, --hostname	The host name or the IP address of the machine to connect to; this option must be specified
-v, --snmp_version	Specifies the SNMP protocol version to be used; acceptable values are 1 and 2c
-C, --community	Specifies the SNMP community string to be used
-k, --key	Specifies the index of the network interface to be checked (ifIndex field)
-d, --descr	Specifies the regular expression to match the interface description (ifDescr field) against

The `check_ifstatus` plugin simply checks whether the status of all of the interfaces is up or whether they are down for administrative purposes. If at least one interface is down, a critical status is reported even if all other interfaces are set up properly.

The `check_ifoperstatus` plugin allows you to check the status of a specific network interface. It is possible to specify either the index of the interface or an expression to match the device name against. An example to check the `eth1` interface is as follows:

```
root@ubuntu:~# /opt/nagios/plugins/check_ifoperstatus -H 10.0.0.1 \
    -d eth1
OK: Interface eth1 (index 3) is up.
```

As we also checked the index that `eth1` is associated with, we can now use the `-k` option to check the interface status, as follows:

```
root@ubuntu:~# /opt/nagios/plugins/check_ifoperstatus
  -H 10.0.0.1 -k 3
OK: Interface eth1 (index 3) is up.
```

The main difference is that by using the `-d` flag, you make sure that changes to the indexes of the network interfaces shifting your configuration are not affected. On the other hand, using the `-k` flag is faster. If you are sure that your interfaces will not change, it's better to use `-k`; otherwise, you should use `-d`.

The next step is to configure the Nagios commands and services for the SNMP usage. We will define a command and a corresponding service. We will also show how custom variables can be used to standardize command definitions.

The following is a generic command used to query SNMP:

```
define command
{
  command_name check_snmp
  command_line $USER1$/check_snmp -P 1 -H $HOSTADDRESS$
               -o $ARG1$ $ARG2$
}
```

Using the Nagios 3 functionality, we can also define the _SNMPVERSION and _ SNMPCOMMUNITY parameters in the host object for all of the SNMP-aware devices and use them in the command as follows:

```
define host
{
  use                       generic-host
  host_name                 linuxbox01
  address                   10.0.2.1
  _SNMPVERSION              2c
  _SNMPCOMMUNITY            public
}
define command
{
  command_name check_snmp
  command_line $USER1$/check_snmp -H $HOSTADDRESS$ -o $ARG1$
            -P $_HOSTSNMPVERSION$ -C $_HOSTSNMPCOMMUNITY$
$ARG2$
}
```

Next, we should define one or more services that will communicate over SNMP.

Let's check for a number of processes and add some constraints that we want monitored, as shown in the following commands:

```
define service
{
  use                   generic-service
  hostgroup_name        snmp-aware
  service_description   Processes
  check_command         check_snmp!HOST-RESOURCES-
                        MIB::hrSystemProcesses.0!-w 0:250
                        -c   0:500
}
```

Please note that the preceding check_command statement needs to be specified on a single line. This check will monitor the number of processes running on a system.

It's worth mentioning that for Microsoft Windows systems, the number of processes that should trigger a warning and critical state should be much lower than shown in the preceding example.

Receiving traps

SNMP traps work in an opposite way to GET and SET requests. That is, the agent sends a message to the SNMP manager, as a UDP packet, when a problem occurs. For example, a link down or system crash message can be sent out to the manager so that administrators are alerted instantly. Traps differ across versions of the SNMP protocols. For SNMPv1, they are called *traps* and are messages that do not require any confirmation by the manager. For SNMPv2, they are called *informs* and require the manager to acknowledge that they have received the *inform* message.

In order to receive traps or informs, the SNMP software needs to accept incoming connections on UDP port 162, which is the standard port for sending and receiving SNMP trap/inform packets. In some SNMP management software, trap notifications are handled within separate applications, while in others, they are integrated into an entire SNMP manager backend.

For a Net-SNMP trap, the daemon is a part of the SNMP daemons, but is a separate binary, called snmptrapd. By default, it is not started. To change this, we will need to modify the /etc/default/snmpd file and change the TRAPDRUN variable to yes, as shown in the following command:

```
TRAPDRUN=yes
```

Changing this option requires restarting the SNMP agent by invoking the service snmpd restart command.

On Ubuntu Linux, the trap listening daemon configuration file is /etc/snmp/snmptrapd.conf. For other systems, it may be in a different location.

The daemon can log specified SNMP traps/informs. It can be configured to run predefined applications or to forward all or specific packets to other managers.

A sample configuration that logs all incoming traps but only if they originate from the SNMPv1 and SNMPv2c private community would look like this:

```
authCommunity log,execute,net private
```

This option enables the logging of traps from the private community originating from any address. It also allows the execution of handler scripts and forwarding traps to other hosts. But this requires additional configuration directives.

Each change in the snmptrapd.conf file requires a restart of the snmpd service.

Usually, traps will be received from a device such as a network router or another computer from which we want to receive traps. We will need two machines with Net-SNMP installed—one for sending the trap and another that will process it. We can use any machine for sending the traps. However, the one processing it should be the one where Nagios is installed, so we can pass it on later. For the purpose of this section, we will use another computer and define a test MIB definition.

We need to create an MIB file called `NAGIOS-TRAP-TEST-MIB.txt` that will define the types of traps and their OIDs. On Ubuntu, the file should be put in `/usr/share/snmp/mibs`; for other platforms, it should be in the same location as the `SNMPv2-SMI.txt` file.

The contents of the file should be as follows:

```
NAGIOS-TRAP-TEST-MIB DEFINITIONS ::= BEGIN
      IMPORTS enterprises FROM SNMPv2-SMI;

 nagiostests OBJECT IDENTIFIER ::= { enterprises 0 }
 nagiostraps OBJECT IDENTIFIER ::= { nagiostests 1 }
 nagiosnotifs OBJECT IDENTIFIER ::= { nagiostests 2 }

 nagiosTrap TRAP-TYPE
      ENTERPRISE nagiostraps
      VARIABLES { sysLocation }
      DESCRIPTION "SNMPv1 notification"
      ::= 1

 nagiosNotif NOTIFICATION-TYPE
      OBJECTS { sysLocation }
      STATUS current
      DESCRIPTION "SNMPv2c notification"
      ::= { nagiosnotifs 2 }
   END
```

This contains definitions for both the SNMPv1 trap called `nagiosTrap` and the inform packet for SNMPv2c called `nagiosNotif`. The file should be copied to all of the machines that will either send or receive these trap/inform packets. In this example, we are using a subtree of the enterprises branch in SNMPv2-MIB, but this should not be used in any production environment as this is a reserved part of the MIB tree.

In order to send such a trap as an SNMPv1 packet, we need to invoke the following command on the machine that will send the traps, replacing the IP address with the actual address of the machine that is running the `snmptrapd` process:

```
root@ubuntu2:~# snmptrap -v 1 -c private 192.168.2.51 \
    NAGIOS-TRAP-TEST-MIB::nagiostraps "" 6 nagiosTrap "" \
    SNMPv2-MIB::sysLocation.0 s "Server Room"
```

Sending an SNMPv2c notification will look like this:

```
root@ubuntu2:~# snmptrap -v 2c -c private 192.168.2.51 "" \
    NAGIOS-TRAP-TEST-MIB::nagiosNotif \
    SNMPv2-MIB::sysLocation.0 s "Server Room"
```

Please note that, in both the cases, there is no confirmation that the packet was received. In order to determine this, we need to check the system logs — usually the `/var/log/syslog` or `/var/log/messages` files. The following command should return log entries related to traps:

```
root@ubuntu:~# grep TRAP /var/log/syslog /var/log/messages
```

Now that we know how to send traps, we should take care so that we handle them properly. The first thing that needs to be done is to add scripts as event handlers for the traps that we previously defined. We need to add these handlers on the machine that has the Nagios daemon running.

To do this, add the following lines to `snmptrapd.conf` and restart the `snmpd` service:

```
traphandle NAGIOS-TRAP-TEST-MIB::nagiostraps
  /opt/nagios/bin/passMessage
traphandle NAGIOS-TRAP-TEST-MIB::nagiosnotifs
  /opt/nagios/bin/passMessage
```

We now need to create the actual `/opt/nagios/bin/passMessage` script that will forward information about the traps to Nagios (as seen in the following code):

```
#!/bin/sh

CMD=/var/nagios/rw/nagios.cmd

read ORIGHOSTNAME
read ORIGIP
# parse IP address
IPADDR='echo "$ORIGIP" | sed 's,^...: \[,,;s,\]:.*$,,''
HOST=""
```

```
# map IP address to host and service definition
case $IPADDR in
  192.168.2.52)
    HOST=ubuntu2
    SVC=TrapTest
    ;;
  esac

if [ "x$HOST" = "x" ] ; then
  exit 1
fi

# send check result to Nagios
CLK='date +%s'
echo "[$CLK] PROCESS_SERVICE_CHECK_RESULT;$HOST;$SVC;2;Trap received"

exit 0
```

When used for a volatile service, this offers a convenient way to track SNMP traps and notifications in Nagios. Such a service will remain in a critical state until a problem is acknowledged via the web interface.

Using Nagios to track SNMP traps also allows you to merge it with powerful event handling mechanisms inside Nagios. This can cause Nagios to perform other checks or try to recover from the error when a trap is received.

Using additional plugins

NagiosExchange hosts a large number of third-party plugins under the **Check Plugins**, **Software**, **SNMP** category (visit http:// exchange.nagios.org/ directory/Plugins/Network-Protocols/SNMP). These allow the monitoring of the system load over SNMP, the monitoring of processes and storage space, and the performance of many other types of checks. You can also find checks that are dedicated to specific hardware, such as Cisco or Nortel routers. There are also plugins for monitoring bandwidth usage. There are also dedicated SNMP-based check plugins that allow the monitoring of many aspects of Microsoft Windows without installing dedicated Nagios agents on these machines. This includes checks for the IIS web server, checking whether WINS and DHCP processes are running, and so on.

The Manubulon website (http://nagios.manubulon.com/) also offers a very wide variety of SNMP plugins. These offer checks for specific processes that are running and monitoring the system load, CPU usage and network interfaces, and options specific to routers.

Another interesting SNMP use is to monitor the network bandwidth usage. In this case, Nagios can be integrated with the **Multi Router Traffic Grapher (MRTG)** package (see `http://www.mrtg.org/`). This is a utility that allows the creation of graphs of bandwidth usage on various network interfaces that also use SNMP to gather information on traffic. Nagios offers a `check_mrtg` plugin (see `http://nagiosplugins.org/man/check_mrtg`) that can be used to retrieve bandwidth usage information from the MRTG log files.

Most companies that need bandwidth monitoring already use MRTG as it is the most popular solution for this task. That is why it is a good idea to integrate Nagios if you already have MRTG set up. Otherwise, it is better to use a dedicated bandwidth monitoring system.

Summary

SNMP can be used by Nagios in various ways. As the protocol is widely supported by operating systems and network devices, it is a great choice for monitoring a wide variety of machines. SNMP features a standardized way of describing typical parameters that describe a device—hardware, network connectivity, applications and services, and much more. This makes accessing this information from Nagios very easy. SNMP is enabled by default on many operating systems and on most network devices, which makes it very easy to monitor such devices in Nagios.

In this chapter we learned what SNMP is and saw the different versions of the protocol—SNMPv1, SNMPv2c, and SNMPv3. We also learned what OIDs are and how they are used to access data over SNMP. This chapter also covered how to access SNMP data graphically using various tools. This can be of great help when starting with SNMP in order to better understand it.

We learned how to use SNMP from Nagios—both for querying various SNMP-enabled devices as well as for receiving SNMP traps from other devices on the network. We also looked at additional Nagios plugins that can be used to query data over SNMP.

The next chapter will talk about monitoring Microsoft Windows machines using NSClient++. It will also describe setting up multiple Nagios instances and distributed monitoring.

10
Advanced Monitoring

The previous chapter provided information about **Simple Network Management Protocol (SNMP)** and how it can be used to monitor various devices with Nagios.

This chapter describes solutions that can be used to monitor a Microsoft Windows host and its services by installing and configuring a dedicated agent in the operating system. It shows how to communicate from the Nagios server to Windows machines, as well as the other way around.

This chapter also talks about how Nagios can be configured so that it notifies other Nagios instances about the current status of all hosts and services. These techniques can be used to create a central Nagios server that receives notifications from other machines.

In addition, this chapter covers the basics of setting up Nagios so that it handles problems when receiving information from other Nagios instances. If one of your Nagios monitoring systems is down or unreachable, you will want another Nagios instance to detect this and report it to you.

In this chapter, we will cover the following settings:

- Setting up NSClient++, an agent for Microsoft Windows machines that allows them to be monitored from Nagios
- Running tests using the check_nt plugin and using the NRPE protocol
- Scheduling checks from NSClient++ and sending results using the NSCA protocol
- Setting up multiple Nagios instances for monitoring
- Sending notifications about host and/or service status changes from one Nagios instance to another
- Using templates to ease the process of configuring multiple Nagios instances

Monitoring Windows hosts

Nagios was originally designed to monitor UNIX operating systems. The plugins package developed along with Nagios cannot be used on Microsoft Windows systems. As mentioned in the previous chapter, SNMP can be used to monitor Windows, and this requires the installation of an SNMP agent on the system.

The SNMP agent on a Microsoft Windows system allows you to check for a large number of parameters. There are, however, things that cannot be easily checked using SNMP and cannot be monitored remotely using the standard Nagios plugins. This includes running external processes, gathering information unavailable via SNMP, and checking the status of multiple parameters in a single check.

An alternative to SNMP on Microsoft Windows workstations and servers is to install a dedicated agent that is used to monitor these systems from Nagios. The most commonly used agent is NSClient++ (http://www.nsclient.org/), the first Windows agent to be designed to work strictly with Nagios.

This agent allows you to query various parameters from Nagios using a special plugin. NSClient++ can also report results directly to Nagios using the **Nagios Service Check Acceptor** (**NSCA**) protocol described in *Chapter 7, Passive Checks and NSCA*. It is possible to set up the types of checks that should be performed, the frequency of the checks, and whether they should be reported as host or service checks. The agent will also need to know the hostname of the Nagios server, the NSCA port, the encryption method, and the password.

Setting up NSClient++

NSClient++ (**NSCP**) is a project that is based on and extends the NSClient concept. The original concept was to create an agent for Windows that, once installed, allows the querying of system information. NSClient has created a de facto standard protocol that offers the ability to query variables with parameters. NSClient++ uses the same protocol, but also offers the ability to perform more complex checks using the NRPE protocol.

Installing NSClient++ requires you to pass the path where it will be installed and choose the features to install. Unless you need to install NSClient++ in a specific location, it is best to use the default path of C:\Program Files\NSClient++. The next step is to choose the features that you want installed. The following image shows the setup with choice of features to install:

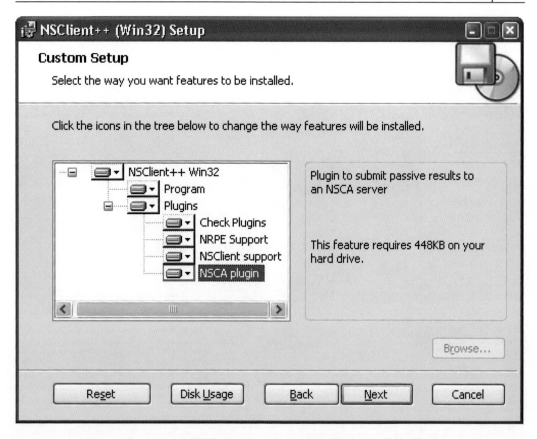

NSClient++ comes with multiple features, such as various plugins, that can be installed. NSClient++ can also be set up to act as the NRPE daemon and run external checks. It is also possible to make it send results over NSCA. This option is mainly useful if your network is set up in such a way that it is not possible to establish outgoing connection to the workstations. If not, it is better for the Nagios daemon to query NSClient++.

After a successful installation, NSClient++ registers itself as a Windows service. The service will be started after rebooting the system, or by going to the **Services** management console in **Administrative Tools**, finding the NSClient++ service and starting it, as shown in the following screenshot:

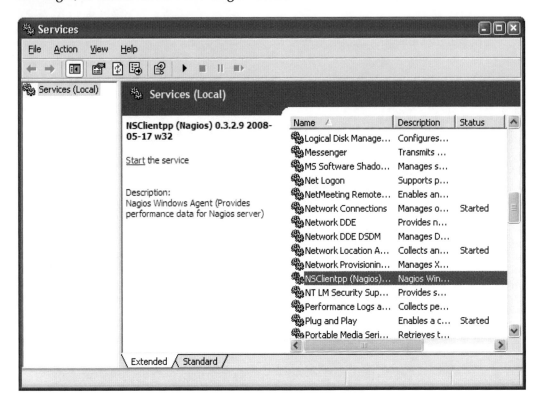

 The screenshots are taken using Windows 2003/XP, but the look and feel of the installer as well as the **Services** management console in **Administrative Tools** is the same across all Windows versions.

In order to start the service, select the **NSClientpp** service and click on the **Start the service** action on the left. NSClient++ comes with the main engine, the plugin that accepts checks over the network, the NRPE daemon, and the ability to perform checks and report results automatically via NSCA. It is best to select all of the features at the time of installation. These features need to be explicitly enabled in the configuration file.

Once installed, NSClient++ needs to be configured. By default, the configuration file NSC.ini is located in the application folder, that is, C:\Program Files\ NSClient++\NSC.ini. After a fresh installation, a default configuration is installed. This configuration file contains a list of all the available parameters along with comments for them. It also has all of the features disabled, so enable only the ones you need. We will now enable the features we want to use.

The configuration is split into several sections. Each section begins with a section name enclosed in brackets; for example, the first section begins with [modules]. This section defines which modules should be loaded by simply specifying each DLL. The Settings section is used to specify global parameters. The most important is allowed_hosts, which is a list of IP addresses or IP ranges that can connect to the agent. The password option specifies the password that will be used to authenticate Nagios checks. If a password is not specified, then all checks will be accepted. The NSClient and NRPE sections are used to configure the acceptance of requests from the Nagios daemon.

If you plan to use NSCA, then the NSCA Commands section allows the definition of one or more checks that should be performed and reported to the Nagios daemon over NSCA. Connectivity with the NSCA daemon can be configured in the NSCA Agent section.

The following is a sample configuration file that loads all types of checks, loads the NSCA agent, and sets up NSClient and NSCA:

```
[modules]
FileLogger.dll
CheckSystem.dll
CheckDisk.dll
CheckEventLog.dll
CheckHelpers.dll
CheckWMI.dll
CheckExternalScripts.dll
NSClientListener.dll
NRPEListener.dll
NSCAAgent.dll

[Settings]
allowed_hosts=192.168.0.0/16
use_file=1

[NSClient]
port=12489
```

```
[NRPE]
port=5666
[NSCA Agent]
interval=60
encryption_method=1
password=mysecret
hostname=windows1
nsca_host=192.168.2.51
nsca_port=5667

[NSCA Commands]
CPU Usage=checkCPU warn=80 crit=90 time=20m time=10s time=4
```

If you are not interested in using NSCA, all you need to do is to comment out the NSCAAgent.dll line in the modules section.

Performing tests using check_nt

NSClient++ offers a uniform mechanism to query system information. Basic system information can be retrieved using the check_nt command from a standard Nagios plugins package.

The syntax and options of the command is as follows:

```
check_nt -H <host> [-p <port>] [-P <password>] [-w level]
        [-c level] -v <variable> -1 <arguments>
```

Option	Description
-H, --hostname	This option must be specified to denote the hostname or IP address of the machine to connect to.
-p, --port	This specifies the TCP port number to connect to. For NSClient++, it should be set to 1248, which is the default port.
-P, --password	This specifies the password to use for authentication. This is optional and is needed only if a password is set up on the Windows agent.
-v, --variable	This is the variable to query. The possible variables are described further in this section.
-1, --arguments	This is the arguments to be passed to the variable and is optional.
-w, --warning	This specifies the return values above which a warning state should be returned.
-c, --critical	This specifies the return values above which a critical state should be returned

The variables that can be checked are predefined. Most checks return both the string representation and an integer value. If an integer value is present, then the -w and -c flags can be used to specify the values that will indicate a problem.

The first variable is CPULOAD that allows the querying of processor usage over a specified period of time. The parameters are one or more series of <time>, <warning>, and <critical> levels, where time is denoted in minutes and the warning/critical values specify, in percentage, the CPU usage that can trigger a problem, as seen in the following example:

```
# check_nt -h 192.168.2.11 -v CPUUSAGE -l 1,80,90
CPU Load 2% (1 min average) |   '1 min avg Load'=2%;80;90;0;100
```

The USEDDISKSPACE variable can be used to monitor space usage. The argument should be a partition letter. The -w and -c options are used to specify the percentage of used disk space that can trigger a problem, as seen in the following example:

```
# check_nt -h 192.168.2.11 -v USEDDISKSPACE -l C -w 80 -c 90
C:\ - total: 24.41 Gb - used: 17.96 Gb (74%) - free 6.45 Gb (26%)
  | 'C:\ Used Space'=17.96Gb;0.00;0.00;0.00;24.41
```

System services can also be monitored using the SERVICESTATE variable. The arguments must specify one or more internal service names, separated by commas. Internal service names can be checked in the **Services** management console, as seen in the following example:

```
# check_nt -h 192.168.2.11 -v SERVICESTATE -l NSClientpp,Schedule
OK: All services are running.
```

The same as with monitoring services, it is also possible to monitor processes running on a Windows machine. The PROCSTATE variable can be used to achieve this. The variable accepts a list of executable names separated by commas, as seen in the following example:

```
# check_nt -h 192.168.2.11 -v PROCSTATE -l winword.exe
OK: All processes are running.
```

Similarly, the monitoring of memory usage can be checked. Use the MEMUSE variable to perform this kind of check. This does not require any additional arguments. The -w and -c arguments are used to specify the warning and critical limits, as seen in the following example:

```
# check_nt -h 192.168.2.11 -v MEMUSE -w 80 -c 90
Memory usage: total:5891.77 Mb - used: 846.01 Mb (14%) - free:
  5045.75 Mb (86%) | 'Memory
  usage'=846.01Mb;4713.41;5302.59;0.00;5891.77
```

Another thing that can be checked is the age of a file using the FILEAGE variable. This variable allows the verification of whether a specified file has been modified within a specified time period. The arguments, -w and -c, are used to specify the warning and critical limits. Their values indicate the number of minutes within which a file should have been modified—a value of 240 means that a warning or critical state should be returned if a file has not been modified within the last four hours, as seen in the following example:

```
# check_nt -h 192.168.2.11 -v FILEAGE -l \
  "C:\\Program Files\\NSClient++\\NSC.log" -w 5 -c 10
  0 years 0 mon 0 days 0 hours 0 min 0 sec
```

It is also possible to check the version of the agent. This makes the maintenance of upgrades and new versions much easier. The CLIENTVERSION variable allows the retrieval of version information, as seen in the following example:

```
# check_nt -h 192.168.2.11 -v CLIENTVERSION
NSClient++ 0.3.2.9 2008-05-17
```

It is also possible to use check_nt to query the Windows counters for information. However, this method has deprecated as querying **Windows Management Instrumentation (WMI)** (http://en.wikipedia.org/wiki/Windows_Management_Instrumentation), which is available as NRPE, is a much more powerful feature. We describe NPRE in the next section.

WMI is a mechanism that allows applications to access the system management information using various programming languages. WMI offers an extensive set of information that can be retrieved. It describes the hardware and operating system as well as the currently-installed applications and the running applications. WMI also offers a query language (http://en.wikipedia.org/wiki/WQL) very similar to the **Structured Query Language (SQL)** (http://en.wikipedia.org/wiki/SQL) that makes the retrieval of specific information very easy.

Performing checks with NRPE protocol

Another way to communicate with NSClient++ is over NRPE (detailed in *Chapter 8, Monitoring Remote Hosts*). UNIX machines offer a way to run external commands via NRPE. In this case, the protocol can be used to query internal functions as well as run external commands or scripts.

NSClient++ requires the modification of the NSC.ini configuration file in order to query data over NRPE. First, enable NRPEListener.dll and CheckExternalScripts.dll in the modules section. NRPEListener.dll is responsible for handling the NRPE protocol, while CheckExternalScripts.dll allows the creation of aliases for internal commands and external scripts.

NSClient++ can be configured to use both internal commands and external scripts to perform actual checks. Internal commands define aliases for checks that will be done internally, without launching external applications. NSClient++ allows the definition of aliases that are used later on when invoking the check_nrpe command from the Nagios server. The External Alias section in the NSClient++ configuration allows the definition of aliases for the actual commands.

The following are some examples of the aliases:

```
[External Alias]
check_cpu=checkCPU warn=80 crit=90 time=5m time=1m
check_mem=checkMem MaxWarn=80% MaxCrit=90% ShowAll type=physical
check_no_ie= CheckWMI -a 'Query:load=SELECT Caption FROM
  Win32_Process' +filter-string:Caption=iexplore.exe MaxCrit=1
```

The check_no_ie alias needs to be put in a single line in the configuration file. The first alias is used to monitor CPU usage. The second one allows the monitoring of memory. The third example uses the WMI command to list processes and find iexplore.exe. The command will return a critical state if at least one iexplore.exe process is found.

In order to perform a check from Nagios, the following command can be used:

```
# check_nrpe -h 192.168.2.11 -c check_cpu
OK CPU Load ok.|'5m'=48;80;90; '1m'=45;80;90; '30s'=45;80;90;
```

The $IP argument is the IP address of the remote host against which a check should be performed. It is also possible to use direct NSClient++ NRPE commands without aliases. This requires you to set the allow_arguments option to 1 in the NRPE section in the NSC.ini file.

With the arguments enabled for NRPE, it is possible to do the following:

```
# check_nrpe -h $IP -c check_cpu -a warn=80 crit=90 time=5m time=1m
OK CPU Load ok.|'5m'=48;80;90; '1m'=45;80;90; '30s'=45;80;90;
```

This will pass arguments specified after -a argument to the check command. The commands that can be used both directly and when defining aliases in the External Alias configuration section can be found in the commands' documentation (http://trac.nakednuns.org/nscp/wiki/CheckCommands).

NSClient++ also allows the execution of external commands, similar to the UNIX NRPE implementations. This can be used to run various types of scripts as well as executables. The default configuration comes with some sample definitions.

The following are a few examples that show how to use the various scripting languages:

```
[External Scripts]
check_vbs_sample=cscript.exe //T:30 //NoLogo scripts\check_vb.vbs
check_tcl_test=tclsh.exe scripts\check_tcl.tcl
check_python_test=python.exe scripts\check_python.py
```

The first check uses the standard Windows Script Host mechanism to run a Visual Basic script. In order to run Tcl or Python scripts on Windows, a distribution of these languages needs to be installed. The most popular ones are ActiveTcl (available for download at http://www.activestate.com/Products/activetcl/) and ActivePython (available for download at http://www.activestate.com/Products/activepython/), both maintained by the ActiveState company.

Running external commands does not differ from running internal ones. This makes it possible to dynamically change between internal checks and external scripts when necessary.

For example an external command is run similarly to internal one by specifying check name with -c:

```
# check_nrpe -h $IP -c check_tcl_test
OK from Tcl 8.4.19 as C:/Tcl/bin/tclsh.exe (pid 1234)
```

As with other NRPE implementations, NSClient++ allows the passing of parameters to commands that are to be executed.

For example, the following alias allows the monitoring of the CPU adaptively by specifying warning and critical values:

```
[External Alias]
check_cpu2=checkCPU warn=$ARG1$ crit=$ARG2$ time=5m time=1m
```

The following command needs to be run to perform the check:

```
# check_nrpe -h $IP -c check_cpu2 -a 80 90
OK CPU Load ok.|'5m'=48;80;90; '1m'=45;80;90; '30s'=45;80;90;
```

Performing passive checks using NSCA Protocol

NSClient++ offers a way for Windows machines to send results to the Nagios server using the NSCA protocol. This is done by incorporating the sending mechanism in the agents. A very common situation is where network routers or firewalls filter out communication to the Windows machines. It is impossible to communicate using the check_nt and check_nrpe plugins. In such cases, the only option is to send results over NSCA.

Setting up the NSCA functionality is very simple. First, enable the `NSCAAgent.dll` library in the `modules` section. It is also necessary to configure the `NSCA Agent` section. This configures the intervals (in seconds) at which the checks will be performed and the connection options—encryption, password, NSCA host, and port. For details on the NSCA connectivity, please refer to *Chapter 7, Passive Checks and NSCA*.

The NSCA section of the configuration file also specifies the local hostname that should be used when reporting to the NSCA daemon. The `NSCA Commands` section specifies the list of commands to be checked and the services they should be reported as. The hostname and services need to reflect the actual names used in the Nagios configuration. Otherwise, the reports from NSClient++ will be discarded by Nagios.

The following is an example of such a configuration:

```
[NSCA Agent]
interval=300
encryption_method=1
password=test
hostname=windows1
nsca_host=192.168.2.51
nsca_port=5667

[NSCA Commands]
check_cpu=checkCPU warn=80 crit=90 time=20m time=10s time=4
check_no_ie= CheckWMI -a 'Query:load=SELECT Caption FROM
    Win32_Process' +filter-string:Caption=iexplore.exe MaxCrit=1
```

The alias definitions of an NSCA check are the same as the NRPE aliases. The commands that can be used in NSClient++ to define the NSCA commands can be found in the commands documentation at `http://trac.nakednuns.org/nscp/wiki/CheckCommands`.

In order for Nagios to accept information from the Windows machine, we need to create a corresponding service for it.

The following is an example that has active checks disabled and allows only passive checks to be received:

```
define service
{
    use                         generic-service
    host_name                   windows1
    service_description         check_cpu
    active_checks_enabled       0
    passive_checks_enabled      1
}
```

We also need to have the NSCA server running on the Nagios server. This is detailed in *Chapter 7, Passive Checks and NSCA*.

Understanding distributed monitoring

There are many situations in which you may want to have more than one Nagios instance monitoring your IT infrastructure. One reason can be a firewall blocking all but a few machines in your company. Another reason could be the need to load balance all checks so that they don't require an enterprise-class server. Others may need to monitor machines in different physical locations from separate machines to check what is wrong within a branch, even if the links to the central servers are temporarily down.

Regardless of the reason, you may want or need to have the execution of checks split across multiple computers. This type of setup might sound complicated and hard to configure, but it is not as hard as it seems. All that's necessary is to set up multiple Nagios instances along with the NSCA agents or daemons.

There are subtle differences in how various instances need to be configured. Usually, there are one or more Nagios instances that report information to a central Nagios instance. An instance that reports information to another Nagios machine will be referred to as a **slave**. A Nagios instance that receives reports from one or more slaves will be called a **master**.

Let's consider a simple organization that has four branches and a headquarters. Each branch is connected to the main office and has a local set of computers. A typical scenario is that a local instance of Nagios monitors the computers and routers in a single branch. The results are then sent to the central Nagios server over an NSCA protocol. These are instances of slave Nagios. If a connection to one of the branches is broken, the local administrators will continue to have access to the status of the local machines. This information is not propagated to the master Nagios server. Setting up the services on the central Nagios server to use freshness checks will cause the central Nagios server to generate an alert when no results are received within a predetermined time frame. Combining this with parent configurations will allow Nagios to accurately determine the root cause of the problems.

The following figure shows how a typical setup in a multiple branch configuration is done. It shows the network topology: which machines are checked by which Nagios servers, and how this information is reported to the central Nagios server.

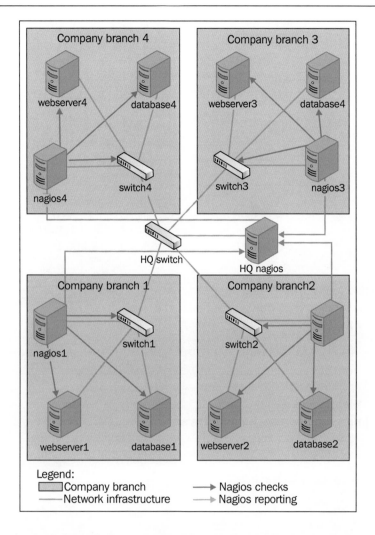

In this example, each branch has a Nagios slave server that monitors and logs information on the local computers. This information is then propagated to the master Nagios server.

Introducing obsessive notifications

Monitoring IT infrastructure using multiple Nagios instances requires a way to send information from slave servers to one or more master servers. This can be done as event handlers that are triggered when a service or a host state changes, however, this has a huge drawback: it necessitates the setup of an event handler for each object. Another disadvantage is that the event handlers are only triggered on actual changes and not after each test is done.

Nagios offers another way to do this through **obsessive notifications**. These provide a mechanism to run commands when a host or service status is received, regardless of whether it is a passive or an active check result. The mechanism is also set up across the system, which means that the object definitions do not need to be changed in any way for Nagios to send information about their status changes.

Setting up obsessive notifications requires a couple of changes in your configuration. The first one is to define a command that will be run for each notification. An example of this is shown as follows:

```
define command
{
    command_name    send-ocsp
    command_line    $USER1$/send-ocsp 192.168.1.4 $SERVICESTATE$
                    $HOSTNAME$ '$SERVICEDESC$' '$SERVICEOUTPUT$'
}
```

The code needs to be entered in a single line in your configuration file. Also, put the actual IP address of the central Nagios server instead of `192.168.1.4` in the preceding example.

We now need to write commands that simply pass the results to the other server over NSCA.

A sample script is as follows:

```
#!/bin/sh

# args: nsca-server status hostname svcname output

# map status to return code
RC=-1
case "$2" in
    OK)
        RC=0
        ;;
    WARNING)
        RC=1
        ;;
    CRITICAL)
        RC=2
        ;;
esac

echo -e "$3\t$4\t$RC\t$5" | /opt/nagios/bin/send_nsca \
    -H $1 -c /etc/nagios/send_nsca.cfg

exit 0
```

The script first converts the status from text (OK, WARNING, or CRITICAL) to exit codes. It then passes the hostname, service name, exit code, and output from the check to the send_nsca command that sends it to Nagios. The name of the host to send it to is passed as the first argument.The next step is to enable obsessive notifications for services and set up the correct commands to be run in the main Nagios configuration file.

The following are the required parameters along with the sample values that should be set in the main Nagios configuration file (nagios.cfg):

```
obsess_over_services=1
ocsp_command=send-ocsp
```

The command name should match the name in the command definition.

That's it! After reloading your Nagios configuration, the send-ocsp script will be run every time a check result comes in.

Configuring Nagios to send host status information is very similar to setting up a service status to be sent. The first thing to do is set up the command that will be run for each notification, which is as follows:

```
define command
{
    command_name    send-ochp
    command_line    $USER1$/send-ochp 192.168.1.4 $HOSTSTATE$
                    $HOSTNAME$ '$HOSTOUTPUT$'
}
```

Please note that the command_line directive in the preceding example needs to be specified in a single line.

The script to send information will look exactly like the one for sending the host status information, except that the actual command sent over NSCA will be generated a bit differently. It also converts the status from text to exit codes and passes the hostname (without the service name), exit code, and output from the check to the send_nsca command that sends it to Nagios by sending only the hostname to indicate that it's a host check result:

```
echo -e "$3\t$RC\t$4" | /opt/nagios/bin/send_nsca \
    -H $1 -c /etc/nagios/send_nsca.cfg
```

In order for Nagios to send notifications to another Nagios instance, we need to enable *obsessing* over hosts and specify the actual command to use.

Here are some sample directives in the main Nagios configuration file (nagios.cfg):

```
obsess_over_hosts=1
ochp_command=send-ochp
```

Restart Nagios after these changes have been made to the configurations. When it restarts, Nagios will begin sending notifications to the master server.

A good thing to do is to verify the `nagios.log` file to see if notifications are being sent out after a check has been made. By default, the file is in the `/var/nagios` directory. If the notifications are not received, it may be a good idea to make the scripts responsible to send messages to log this information in either the system log or in a separate logfile. This is very helpful when it comes to debugging instances where the notifications sent out by slave Nagios instances are lost. Writing information to the system log can be done using the `logger` command (for more details, visit `http://linux.die.net/man/1/logger`).

Configuring Nagios instances

Setting up multiple servers to monitor infrastructure using Nagios is not easy, but it is not too hard either. It only requires a slightly different approach as compared to setting up a single machine. That said, there are issues with the configuration of hosts and services. It is also necessary to set up all slave and master servers correctly and in a slightly different way.

Distributed monitoring requires a more mature change control and versioning process for Nagios configurations. This is necessary because both the central Nagios server and its branches need to have a partial or complete configuration available, and these need to be in sync across all machines.

Usually, it is recommended that you make the slave servers query both the service and the host status. It is also recommended that you disable service checks on the master Nagios server, but keep host checks enabled. The reason is that host checks are not usually scheduled and are done only when a service check returns a `warning`, `critical`, or `unknown` status. Therefore, the load required to only check the hosts is much lower than the load required to perform regular service checks. In some cases, it is best to also disable host checks. Either the host checks need to be performed regularly or the security policies should disallow checks by the central server.

To maintain Nagios configurations, we recommend that you set up a versioning system such as Git (`http://git-scm.com/`), Subversion (`http://subversion.tigris.org/`), or **Concurrent Versions System (CVS)** (`http://www.cvshome.org/`). This allows you to keep track of all the Nagios changes and makes it much easier to apply configuration changes to multiple machines. We can store and manage the configuration similar to how we had done it previously. Hosts, services, and the corresponding groups should be kept in directories and separate for each Nagios slave—for example, `hosts/branch1` and `services/branch1`. All other types of objects, such as contacts, time periods, and check commands, can be kept in global directories and reused in all branches—for example, the single `contacts`, `timeperiods`, and `commands` directories.

It's also a good idea to create a small system to deploy the configuration to all the machines, along with the ability to test new configuration before applying it in production. This can be done using a small number of shell scripts. When dealing with multiple computers, locations, and Nagios instances, doing everything manually is very difficult and can get problematic over the long term. This will cause the system to become unmanageable and can lead to errors in actual checks caused by out-of-sync configurations between the slave and master Nagios instances. A very popular tool that is recommended for this purpose is **cfengine** (http://www.cfengine.com/). There are other tools that can be used for automating configuration deployment, such as **Chef** (http://www.getchef.com/), **Puppet** (http://www.puppetlabs.com/), or **Ansible** (http://www.ansible.com/). They can be used to automate configuration deployment and to ensure that Nagios is up-to-date on all the machines. It also allows for customization; for example, a set of files different from the set on the master server can be deployed on slave servers. If you are already familiar with such tools, we recommend that you use them to manage Nagios deployments. If not, try them out and choose one that best suits you.

The first step in creating a distributed environment is to set up the master Nagios server. This will require you to install Nagios from a binary distribution or build it from sources. Details related to Nagios installation are described in *Chapter 2, Installing Nagios 4*.

The main changes in a single Nagios set up for a master server are defined in the main Nagios configuration file—nagios.cfg. This file must contain the cfg_dir directives for objects related to all of the slave servers. If not, the master Nagios instance will ignore the reports related to hosts that it does not know about.

We'll also need to make sure that Nagios accepts passive check results for services and that the master Nagios instance does not independently perform active checks. To do this, set the following options in the main Nagios configuration file on the master server:

```
check_external_commands=1
accept_passive_service_checks=1
execute_service_checks=0
```

If you also want to rely on passive check results for host checks, you will also need to add the following lines to your main Nagios configuration:

```
accept_passive_host_checks=1
execute_host_checks=0
```

You will also need to set up the NSCA daemon on the master Nagios server. Details of how to set this up are described in *Chapter 7, Passive Checks and NSCA*.

The next step is to set up the first slave server that will report to the master Nagios instance. This also means that you will need to set up Nagios from a binary or source distribution and configure it properly.

All of the slave Nagios instances also need to have the `send_nsca` command from the NSCA package in order to communicate changes with the master instance. After setting up the NSCA client, we also need to create a configuration to send notifications. It is also a good idea to check whether the sending of dummy reports about an existing host and an existing service works is done correctly.

All of the slave instances need to be set up to send obsessive notifications to the master Nagios server. This includes setting up the OCSP and OCHP commands and enabling them in the main Nagios configuration file. (Obsessive notifications have already been described earlier in the chapter, in the *Introducing obsessive notifications section.*)

After setting up everything, it's best to run notification commands directly from the command line to see if everything works correctly. Next, restart the slave Nagios server. After that, it is good idea to check the Nagios logs to see if the notifications are being sent out.

It would also be a good idea to write down or automate all the steps needed to set up a Nagios slave instance. Setting up the master is done only once, but large networks may require you to set up a large number of slaves.

Performing freshness checking

We now have set up distributed monitoring set up and the slave Nagios instances should report the results to the master Nagios daemon. Everything should work fine, and the main web interface should report up-to-date information from all of the hosts and services being monitored.

Unfortunately, this is not always the case. In some cases, network connectivity can be down or, for example, the NSCA agents and daemon on the network might fail temporarily, and the master Nagios instance may not even know about it. Based on our assumption that the master Nagios instance is not responsible for monitoring the IT infrastructure, it needs to rely on other systems to do it. Configuration, as described earlier, does not take into account a situation where checks are not sent to the master instance.

Nagios offers a way to monitor whether results have come within a certain period of time. If no report comes within that period, we can specify that Nagios should treat this as a critical state and warn the administrators about it. This makes sense as obsessive notifications are sent out very frequently. So if no notification has come within half an hour, there is a problem with some part of the distributed monitoring configuration.

Implementing this in the master Nagios configuration requires a slightly different approach to the one mentioned in the previous section. The approach in the previous section was to disable service checks completely. This is why all services and/or hosts needed to have their active checks reconfigured for the new approach to work correctly. In this case, it is necessary to enable service checks (and host, if needed) on a global basis in the `nagios.cfg` file.

For the reasons given above, all of the services and/or hosts that receive notifications from slave Nagios instances need to be defined differently in the master configuration from the definitions that are set for the Nagios slaves.

The first change is that active checks for these objects need to be enabled, but should not be scheduled, that is, the `normal_check_interval` option should not be set. In addition, the `check_freshness` and `freshness_threshold` options need to be specified. The first of these options enables you to monitor whether results are up-to-date and the second one specifies the number of seconds after which the results should be considered outdated.

This means that Nagios will only run active checks if there has been no passive check result for a specified period of time. It is very important that the host and service definitions on both the master and slave instances have the same value specified for the `check_period` directive. Otherwise, the master Nagios instance will raise an alert only for services that are checked during specific time periods. An example could be the `workinghours` time period, which is not checked on weekends.

For example, the following service definition will accept passive checks but will report an error if they are not present:

```
define service
{
    use                          generic-service
    host_name                    linuxbox02
    service_description          SSH
    check_command                no-passive-check-results
    check_freshness              1
    freshness_threshold          43200
    active_checks_enabled        1
    passive_checks_enabled       1
}
```

The `freshness_threshold` option specifies the number of seconds after which an active check should be performed. In this case, it is set to 12 hours.

It is also necessary to define a command that will run if no passive check results have been provided.

The following command will use the `check_dummy` plugin to report an error:

```
define command
{
   command_name          no-passive-check-results
   command_line          $USER1$/check_dummy 2 "No passive check
                         results"
}
```

It is important to make sure that all of the services and/or hosts are defined, so only dummy checks that report problems (and not actual active checks) are performed. This is different from our previous approach that made sure active checks were not performed.

Using passive checks for regular reporting, and performing active checks when no passive results have been provided, is described in more detail in *Chapter 7, Passive Checks and NSCA*. The main difference is that in our case, no actual checks will be performed if passive results are not available.

The main drawback of this approach is that it makes the management of configurations on master and slave instances more difficult. We need to maintain the configuration for the master Nagios instance with the service that contains only the dummy freshness checks. However, slave configurations need to have complete check definitions in place.

Using templates for distributed monitoring

In order to avoid reconfiguring all of the objects and managing two sets of configurations, it is possible to use multiple inheritances to manage the configurations efficiently. It can be used to separate parts that are common to both master and slave Nagios instances from information that is local to each Nagios instance. We'll assume each location will have a single Nagios instance, and it will either be a master or a slave.

For each location, there will be `local` and `remote` templates. Slave instances will load the `local` template for its own location and not load the configuration for other locations. Master instance(s) will load the `remote` template for each location that will report information to this machine.

The actual objects will inherit a template for a specific check—such as the CPU load or the service template monitoring the HTTP server. They will also inherit a location's template— local or remote, as they are the first items in the inheritance list. This will allow the location templates to override all the configuration options.

The local and remote templates will define whether regular checks will be done or if the passive check results should be used. Each Nagios instance will load the local or remote definition of the location template.

For the example mentioned in previous sections, the following would be loaded in branch 1:

```
cfg_dir=global_configuration
cfg_dir=branch1
cfg_dir=branch1_local
```

This will cause Nagios to load the definition for the global configuration, which may include users, time periods, generic hosts, and service templates. It will also load the local templates and the definition of objects for branch1. All other branches' configurations will load their respective branch objects.

For master Nagios instances, the loaded configurations will be as follows:

```
cfg_dir=global_configuration
cfg_dir=branch1
cfg_dir=branch1_remote
cfg_dir=branch2
cfg_dir=branch2_remote
cfg_dir=branch3
cfg_dir=branch3_remote
cfg_dir=branch4
cfg_dir=branch4_remote
```

This will load the global configuration objects, definitions of objects for all branches, and each branch's remote templates.

Creating the host and service objects

For the example mentioned in previous sections, a typical host definition will be in the `branch1` directory and will look as follows:

```
define host{
        use                     branch1-server
        host_name               branch1:webserver
        hostgroups              branch1-servers
        address                 192.168.0.1
}
```

The `branch1-server` will be defined in both the `branch1_local` and `branch1_remote` directories. The definition in the `branch1_local` directory will be as follows:

```
define host{
        register                0
        use                     generic-server
        name                    branch1-server
        contact_groups          branch1-admins
        obsess_over_host        1
        }
```

The definition for the remote location will be as follows:

```
define host{
        register                0
        use                     remote-server
        name                    branch1-server
        contact_groups          branch1-admins
        }
```

The `generic-server` can be a typical host template. The `remote-server` uses this definition, but disables active checks and enables the accepting of passive check results. An example definition of `generic-server` is as follows:

```
define host{
        register                0
        use                     generic-server
        name                    remote-server

        active_checks_enabled   0
        passive_checks_enabled  1

        notifications_enabled   0
        }
```

With this definition, the host for a local branch will perform active checks if it is alive. The obsess_over_host will cause results to be sent to the master Nagios instance. For remote locations, it will only accept remote check results and will not send any notifications, so each host that is down is only reported from the local Nagios instance.

A typical service is defined as follows:

```
define service{
        use                          branch1-service,service-
    http
        host_name                    branch1:webserver
        service_description          HTTP
        }
```

The service-http service will define a check using check_http and optionally additional options for the check itself.

The local definition for branch1-service will be similar to the following code:

```
define service{
        register                     0
        name                         branch1-service
        contact_groups               branch1-admins
        obsess_over_service          1
        }
```

For the remote, it should be as follows:

```
define service{
        register                     0
        name                         branch1-service
        use                          remote-service
        contact_groups               branch1-admins
        }
```

The local definition does not perform many changes in the service. It specifies the default contact group to use for all services and enables obsession over the service — so status updates are sent to the master Nagios instance.

The `remote` directory uses the `remote-service` definition, which will disable active checks unless no passive check result is received. For example a `remote-service` definition can be as follows:

```
define service{
        register                        0
        name                            remote-service
        active_checks_enabled           0
        check_freshness                 1
        freshness_threshold             43200
        check_command                   check_dummy!3!No recent
passive check result
        notification_options            u
        event_handler_enabled           0
        }
```

This runs an active check in case no passive result is received for 12 hours. The active check will simply report an unknown status.

Notification for remote services is only enabled for an unknown status. This send out notifications whenever no active check results are received by the master Nagios instance, but prevents sending of notifications to statuses sent by the slave server as passive check results.

The `check_dummy` command simply invokes the `check_dummy` plugin, which reports an UNKNOWN status and a message that no recent result was received. The `check_dummy` command definition is as follows:

```
define command{
   command_name    check_dummy
   command_line    $USER1$/check_dummy $ARG1$ "$ARG2$"
}
```

This way, the host and service definitions can be shared for all Nagios instances and the templates for each location determine whether the active checks should be run.

The `remote-server` and `remote-service` templates are shared across all Nagios instances, which can be helpful in managing configurations that consist of many branches.

Customizing checks with custom variables

This approach has a downside: each service check has to be defined as a template. However, Nagios custom variables can be used to allow the fine-tuning of the service check for each object. For example, for the HTTP check, it could be as follows:

```
define command{
  command_name  check_http_port
  command_line  $USER1$/check_http -H $ARG1$ -p $ARG2$
}

define service{
        use                             generic-service
        name                            service-http
        register                        0
        check_command
    check_http_port!$_SERVICEHOSTNAME$!$_SERVICEHTTPPORT$
        _HTTPPORT                       80
        }
```

This allows us to override the port to use the HTTP checks by specifying _HTTPPORT in the actual service as follows:

```
define service{
        use                   branch1-service,service-http
        host_name             branch1:webserver
        service_description   HTTP on port 8080
        _HTTPPORT             8080
        }
```

Summary

Nagios offers multiple ways of monitoring the Microsoft Windows workstations and servers. These vary from monitoring computers remotely and querying SNMP, to installing dedicated agents. Another very interesting feature of Nagios is its ability to effortlessly configure multiple machines in order to perform monitoring and to have a single place where the results are easily available.

In this chapter, we have learned how to install the NSClient++ agent that can be used to monitor Microsoft Windows based machines and using Nagios.

We have also learned different ways in which checks can be performed — for example, using the `check_nt` plugin, using the NRPE protocol, or scheduling the checks on the agent and sending the results using the NSCA protocol.

This chapter also covered how to set up multiple Nagios instances and a Nagios instance so that it reports all host and services status updates to another Nagios instance. This can be used to split the load related to actually performing the checks. It can also be a solution to the firewall and security policies. A local instance can query all the machines in the same location and report to the central server.

We have also learned how to use templates and multiple inheritance to create a single configuration for all types of Nagios instances — both slaves that send status updates and a master instance that receives the status update, but does not independently perform checks.

The next chapter will talk about how to write your own Nagios plugins to monitor services that require customized checks. It will also describe how to create your own plugins using various programming languages.

11
Programming Nagios

The previous chapter provided information about monitoring Microsoft Windows machines and several approaches for more advanced monitoring using Nagios.

This chapter focuses on extending Nagios using various programming languages. One of the key features of Nagios is its extensibility. There are multiple ways in which Nagios can be tailored to suit your needs. It is also possible to integrate Nagios tightly with your applications and benefit from a powerful mechanism to schedule and perform checks.

In this chapter, we will cover the following topics:

- Understanding what aspects of Nagios can be customized
- Writing plugins that perform active checks
- Monitoring cloud environments (VMware and Amazon Web Services machines)
- Creating commands to send custom notifications
- Managing Nagios and reading its status information
- Using passive checks for long-running tests

Introducing Nagios customizations

The most exciting aspect of using Nagios is the ability to combine your programming skills with the powerful engine offered by the Nagios daemon. Your own pieces of code can be plugged into the Nagios daemon, and they can communicate with it in various ways.

One of the best things about Nagios is that, in most cases, it does not force you to use a specific language. Whether the language of your choice is PHP, Perl, Tcl, Python, Ruby, or Java, you can easily use any one with Nagios. This is a fundamental difference between Nagios and the majority of monitoring applications. Usually, an application can only be extended in the language in which it is written.

Our code can cooperate with Nagios in various ways, for example, by implementing commands, by sending information to the Nagios daemon, and so on. The first case means that we can create a script or executable that will be run by Nagios, and its output and exit code will be processed by Nagios. Running external commands is used to perform active checks, send notifications, and trigger event handlers. By using the macro substitutions and variables available in the current context (see `http://nagios.sourceforge.net/docs/nagioscore/4/en/macrolist.html`), we will be able to pass down all of the information that's needed for the command to do its job.

The alternative method of extending Nagios is to send information to it from other applications. The first option is that external applications (such as web or typical user interface) allow the configuration and management of the Nagios system. This is done by sending control commands to Nagios over the UNIX sockets. Because this involves opening and writing to a Unix socket, which works just like a file, it can be done in any programming language that handles I/O.

Yet another option is that the other applications reporting to your application or a system scheduling mechanism, such as **cron**, are responsible for running the checks. A test needs to be carried out on its own and the application itself is responsible for sending the results back to Nagios. Results can be sent directly via a Unix socket or via a **Nagios Status Check Acceptor (NSCA)** protocol. Luckily, even sending over a network with NSCA is simple, as results can be sent directly to the standard input of the `send_nsca` command.

Your software can also get information related to Nagios easily. All that's needed is to monitor Nagios' `status.dat` file for changes, and read it as if it contains all object definitions along with the current soft and hard states. The format of the file is quite simple, and the task of writing a parser for it is quite easy. The file format and how to parse its content is described later in this chapter.

There are ready-to-use Nagios status file parsers for multiple languages—for example, **Pynag** for Python (available at `http://pynag.org/`), **nagios_analyzed** for Ruby (available at `https://github.com/jbbarth/nagios_analyzer`), and so on. Also, there are multiple ready-to-use PHP solutions to parse statuses—for example, **Naupy** (available at `http://sourceforge.net/projects/naupy/`).

Over the course of this chapter, we will use various programming languages, such as PHP (`http://www.php.net/`), Ruby (`http://www.ruby-lang.org/`), Python (`http://www.python.org/`), Perl (`http://www.perl.org/`), Tcl (`http://www.tcl.tk/`), Java (`http://www.oracle.com/technetwork/java/`), and C/C++. Even though many people do not know all of these languages, the code will only use the basic functionality of the languages so that it is understandable to nontechnical users.

Assuming that you need to write a piece of code on your own, the first thing you should start with is choosing the programming language. If you already know a language that would fit this task, stick to it. Otherwise, there are a few candidates to consider. The languages I will recommend are Ruby, Python, or Tcl.

Ruby is a very popular dynamic language that has a large variety of uses. It has a very natural syntax that makes the code easy to read. Python is another popular dynamic language, and its syntax makes it easy to write check commands. Both languages have a wide range of libraries that can be used to interact with other software.

Tcl, on the other hand, is less popular, but a very powerful language in its own way. This is usually my first choice for a programming language. It features a very simple, but very powerful syntax. Tcl is tightly integrated with an event loop that is handy when programming event-driven applications. This is perfectly suitable for communicating with the Nagios server. It also comes with a huge set of protocols and libraries to use, especially the **ActiveTcl** distribution from ActiveState (`http://www.activestate.com/`). Throughout this book, Tcl examples will be using the packages available with ActiveTcl distributions. If your Tcl interpreter does not have one or more of these packages, it is recommended that you install the ActiveTcl distribution.

People who are only familiar with PHP can also feel safe about it. It's possible to create various commands and passive check scripts in this language. It is also possible to integrate Nagios with error reporting for your web applications.

Nagios is known to integrate very well with Perl. This chapter teaches us how both Perl and other languages can be easily integrated with Nagios so that the readers familiar with other languages will also benefit from it, and will learn Perl just for the purpose of extending Nagios.

Even though we'll focus only on few languages, almost any technology can be used. Nagios mainly uses basic functionality for interaction—exit codes, reading a program's output, and passing commands via a pipe. Also, all of its interaction is in text mode, and both active check output and command pipe use very basic formats.

Programming in C with libnagios

Nagios 4 comes with `libnagios`. It is a C library that provides various functionality that are used in Nagios, and which could also be reused in other programs. This section will talk about the library, how to install it, and how to use it in your programs. If you are not interested in the development of Nagios-related applications in C, you may skip this section.

The functions in the library also make it easier to create software that interact with Nagios, such as plugins, event handlers, or programs that send passive check results. The library is built as a part of the Nagios compilation and is created as a statically linked library only (please visit `http://en.wikipedia.org/wiki/Static_library` for more details). This means, in order to use the library, it will be included in the application, so we do not have look for it in the shared libraries directory such as `/usr/lib`.

In order to install the application, go to the source directory of Nagios and run the following commands:

```
# make install-lib
# make install-headers
```

For an installation performed according to the steps given in *Chapter 2, Installing Nagios 4*, the library will be copied to `/opt/nagios/lib` and the header files will be placed in `/opt/nagios/include`.

The `libnagios` library provides multiple platform-independent functions and algorithms that are used throughout Nagios and can be reused.

As an example of using `libnagios`, let's write a simple program that communicates with a query handler that was introduced in Nagios 4. It will query for information about core scheduling queue:

```c
#include <stdio.h>
#include <stdlib.h>
#include <unistd.h>
#include <libnagios.h>

main()
{
    // socket descriptor
    int sd;
    // buffer for reading output
    char buf[16384];
    // buffer size, last value and iterator
    int bufsize, last = 0, i;
```

```
// open socket to Nagios query handler
sd = nsock_unix("/var/nagios/rw/nagios.qh", NSOCK_TCP |
    NSOCK_CONNECT);
if (sd < 0)
{
    printf("Unable to connect to Nagios socket\n");
    exit(3);
}

// send "squeuestats" query to core handler
nsock_printf_nul(sd, "@core squeuestats");
// read result until \0 is received
while (bufsize < sizeof(buf))
{
    if (read(sd, buf + bufsize, 1) == 1)
    {
        // check if this is end of response
        if (buf[bufsize] == '\0')
            break;
        bufsize++;
    }
}
buf[bufsize] = 0;

// read all values separated by semi-colon
for (i = 0 ; i < bufsize ; i++)
{
    if (buf[i] == ';')
    {
        buf[i] = '\0';
        printf("%s\n", buf + last);
        last = i + 1;
    }
}

// print last value
printf("%s\n", buf + last);

// close socket
close(sd);
}
```

The program sends a command to the query handler, reads the response, and then prints each individual result that is returned.

To compile the program, simply run the following command:

```
# gcc -o query_squeue query_squeue.c \
    -I/opt/nagios/include/nagios/lib \
    -L/opt/nagios/lib -lnagios
```

Here, `query_squeue` is the output binary name and `query_squeue.c` is the name of the source code file. The paths for `-I` and `-L` options are valid for installations performed according to the steps given in *Chapter 2, Installing Nagios 4*, the library will be copied to `/opt/nagios/lib`, and the header files will be placed in `/opt/nagios/include`. If you have installed Nagios to your Linux distribution or to another location, the paths may be different.

Once it is built successfully, we can now run it using the following command:

```
# ./query_squeue
```

If the command fails to create the socket, please make sure that the command is run by the user that has write access to `/var/nagios/rw/nagios.qh` file; for example, a `nagios` user, a member of `nagioscmd` group, or as `root`.

After running, the code will print a result similar to the following output:

```
SERVICE_CHECK=22
COMMAND_CHECK=0
LOG_ROTATION=1
PROGRAM_SHUTDOWN=0
PROGRAM_RESTART=0
CHECK_REAPER=1
ORPHAN_CHECK=1
RETENTION_SAVE=1
STATUS_SAVE=1
SCHEDULED_DOWNTIME=0
SFRESHNESS_CHECK=1
EXPIRE_DOWNTIME=0
HOST_CHECK=4
HFRESHNESS_CHECK=0
RESCHEDULE_CHECKS=0
EXPIRE_COMMENT=0
CHECK_PROGRAM_UPDATE=1
SLEEP=0
USER_FUNCTION=0
SQUEUE_ENTRIES=33
```

The code communicates with the Nagios query handler that can be used for many interesting things such as receiving information about host and/or service check results. The query handler and its possible uses are described in more detail in *Chapter 12, Using the Query Handler*.

Creating custom active checks

One of the most common areas where Nagios can be suited to fit your needs is that of **active checks**. These are the checks that are scheduled and run by the Nagios daemon. This functionality is described in more detail in *Chapter 2, Installing Nagios 4*.

Nagios has a project that ships the commonly-used plugins and comes with a large variety of checks that can be performed. Before thinking about writing anything on your own, it is best to check for the standard plugins (described in detail in *Chapter 4, Using the Nagios Plugins*).

> The Nagios Exchange (http://exchange.nagios.org) website contains multiple ready-to-use plugins for performing active checks. It is recommended that you check whether somebody has already written a similar plugin for your needs.

The reason for this is that even though active checks are quite easy to implement, sometimes a complete implementation that handles errors and command line options parsing is not very easy to create. Typically, proper error handling can take a lot of time to implement. Another thing is that plugins that have already existed for some time have often been thoroughly tested by others. Typical errors would have been already identified and fixed; and sometimes the plugins have been tested in a larger environment, under a wider variety of conditions. Writing check plugins on your own should be preceded by an investigation to find out whether anybody has encountered and solved a similar problem.

Active check commands are very simple to implement. They simply require a plugin to return one or more lines of check output to the standard output stream, and return one of the predefined exit codes—OK (code 0), WARNING (code 1), CRITICAL (code 2), or UNKNOWN (code 3). How active check plugins work is described in more detail at the beginning of *Chapter 4, Using the of Nagios Plugins*.

Testing the correctness of the MySQL database

Let's start with a simple plugin that performs active checks. We'll implement a simple check that connects to a MySQL database and verifies whether the specified tables are structurally correct. It will also accept connection information from command line as a series of arguments. We'll write the script in Python.

From a technical point of view, the check is quite simple—all that's needed is to connect to a server, choose the database, and run the CHECK TABLE (https://dev.mysql.com/doc/refman/5.7/en/check-table.html) command in SQL.

The plugin requires installation of the MySQLdb package for Python (http://sourceforge.net/projects/mysql-python/). We will also need a working MySQL database that we can connect to for testing purposes. It is a good idea to install the MySQL server on your local machine and set up a dummy database with tables to test.

In order to set up a MySQL database server on Ubuntu Linux, install the mysql-server package using the following command:

```
# apt-get install mysql-server
```

In Red Hat and Fedora Linux, the package is called mysql-server and the command to install it is as follows:

```
# yum install mysql-server
```

After that, you will be able to connect to the database locally as root, either without a password or with the password supplied during database installation.

If you do not have any other database to run the script against, you can use mysql as the database name, as this is a database that all instances of MySQL have.

The following is a sample script that performs the test. It needs to be run with the hostname, username, password, database name, and the list of tables to be checked as arguments. The table names should be separated by commas.

```python
#!/usr/bin/env python

import MySQLdb
import sys, string

# only perform check if we're loaded as main script
if __name__ == '__main__':
    dbhost = sys.argv[1]
    dbuser = sys.argv[2]
    dbpass = sys.argv[3]
    dbname = sys.argv[4]
    tables = sys.argv[5]
    errors = []
    count = 0
```

```
# connect to the database
conn = MySQLdb.connect(dbhost, dbuser, dbpass, dbname);
cursor = conn.cursor()

# perform check for all tables in the table list
# (splits the table names by ",")
for table in string.split(tables, ","):
    cursor.execute("CHECK TABLE %s" % (table))
    row = cursor.fetchone()
    count = count + 1
    if row[3] != "OK":
        errors.append(table)

# handle output - if any errors occurred, report 2, otherwise 0

if len(errors) == 0:
    print "check_mysql_table: OK %d table(s) checked" % count
    sys.exit(0);
else:
    print "check_mysql_table: CRITICAL: erorrs in %s" % \
        (string.join(errors, ", "))
    sys.exit(2);
```

The code consists of four parts: initialization, argument parsing, connection, and checking each table. The first part consists of the import statements that load various required modules and make sure that the code is run from the command line. In the second part, the arguments passed by the user are mapped to the various variables. After that, a connection to the database is made. If the connection succeeds, for each table specified when running the command, a CHECK TABLE command (http://dev.mysql.com/doc/refman/5.0/en/check-table.html) will be run. This makes MySQL verify that the table structure is correct.

To use it, let's run it by specifying the connection information and tables tbl1, tbl2, and tbl3:

```
root@ubuntu:~# /opt/nagios/plugins/check_mysql_table.py \
    127.0.0.1 mysqluser secret1 databasename tbl1,tbl2,tbl3
check_mysql_table: OK 3 table(s) checked
```

As you can see, the script seems quite easy and usable.

Monitoring local time with a time server

The next task is to create a check plugin that compares the local time with the time on a remote machine and issues a warning or critical state if the difference exceeds a specified number. We will use Tcl for this job.

We'll use Tcl's time package (http://tcllib.sourceforge.net/doc/ntp_time.html) to communicate with remote machines. This package comes bundled with ActiveTcl and is a part of the tcllib package available in many Linux distributions.

If you do not have the tcllib and/or time packages, you will need to install them. On Ubuntu Linux, the package is called tcllib and the following command installs it:

```
apt-get install tcllib
```

The script will accept the hostname and the warning and critical thresholds in number of seconds. The script will use these to decide on the exit status. It will also output the difference in number of seconds, for informational purposes.

The following is a script to perform a check of the time on a remote machine:

```
#!/usr/bin/env tclsh

package require time

# retrieve arguments for the script
set host [lindex $argv 0]
set warndiff [lindex $argv 1]
set critdiff [lindex $argv 2]

# retrieve times
set handle [time::gettime $host]
set remotetime [time::unixtime $handle]
time::cleanup $handle
set localtime [clock seconds]

# calculate difference
set diff [expr {abs($remotetime - $localtime)}]

# decide which exit code should be used
if {$diff > $critdiff} {
    puts "check_time CRITICAL: $diff seconds difference"
    exit 2
} elseif {$diff > $warndiff} {
    puts "check_time WARNING: $diff seconds difference"
    exit 1
} else {
    puts "check_time OK: $diff seconds difference"
    exit 0
}
```

This command is split into three parts: initializing, parsing arguments, and checking status. The first part loads the `time` package and the second maps the arguments to variables. After that, a connection to the remote host is made, the time on the remote machine is received, and this remote time is compared with the local time. Based on what the difference is, the command returns either a CRITICAL, WARNING, or OK status.

And now, let's run it against a sample machine using the following command:

```
root@ubuntu:~# /opt/nagios/plugins/check_time.tcl \
    ntp2a.mcc.ac.uk 60 120
check_time WARNING: 76 seconds difference
```

As shown in the preceding output, the script works properly and returns a WARNING state as the difference is higher than 60, but lower than 120.

Another example may be using `libnagios` to monitor the Nagios 4 query handler and use the `@echo` handler for this purpose. This is a query handler that returns whatever is sent to it and is meant mainly for testing the query handler.

The following C code can be used to monitor whether the Nagios query handler is working properly:

```
#include <string.h>
#include <stdio.h>
#include <stdlib.h>
#include <unistd.h>
#include <libnagios.h>

main(int argc, char *argv[])
{
    // socket descriptor
    int sd;
    // buffer for reading output
    char buf[16384];
    // buffer size, last value and message size
    int bufsize, last = 0, test_message_size;
    char *test_message;
    char *qh;

    // get arguments from command line
    if (argc != 3)
    {
        printf("Usage: %s path/to/nagios.qh mesasge\n", argv[0]);
        exit(1);
    }
```

```
qh = argv[1];
test_message = argv[2];
test_message_size = strlen(test_message);

// open socket to Nagios query handler
sd = nsock_unix(qh, NSOCK_TCP | NSOCK_CONNECT);
if (sd < 0)
{
    printf("check_qh: Unable to connect to Nagios socket %s\n",
        qh);
    exit(3);
}


// send "squeuestats" query to core handler
nsock_printf_nul(sd, "@echo %s", test_message);
if (read(sd, buf, test_message_size) != test_message_size)
{
    printf("check_qh: Invalid returned message size\n");
    exit(2);
}

if (memcmp(buf, test_message, test_message_size) != 0)
{
    printf("check_qh: Invalid message returned\n");
    exit(2);
}
else
{
    printf("check_qh: Correct message received\n");
    exit(0);
}
}
```

The code connects to the Nagios query handler, sends the specified message to
the `@echo` query handler, and reads the same amount of bytes returned. The query
handler functionality and how to use it is described in more detail in *Chapter 12,
Using the Query Handler*.

If the message is not the same, or an invalid number of bytes is read, the program
returns an error. If Nagios does not return sufficient number of bytes, either the
closed socket will cause `read()` to return a smaller number of bytes or, if Nagios
will not close the closed socket, Nagios will detect an active check's timeout that has
elapsed and consider the test as invalid.

Writing plugins correctly

We have already created a few sample scripts, and they're working. So, it is possible to use them from Nagios. However, these checks are very far from being complete. They lack error control, parsing, and argument verification.

It is recommended that you write all the commands in a more user-friendly way. The reason is that in most cases, after some time, someone else will take over using and/or maintaining your custom check commands. You might also come back to your own code after a year of working on completely different things. In such cases, having a check command that is user-friendly, has proper comments in the code, and allows debugging, will save a lot of time. The standard Nagios plugins guidelines (available at `https://nagios-plugins.org/doc/guidelines.html`) documents good practices for standard Nagios plugins package developers. While some parts may be specific to C language, it is worth reading them when developing in other languages as well.

The first thing that should be done is to provide proper handling of arguments—this means using functionality such as the `getopt` package for Python (`http://www.python.org/doc/2.5/lib/module-getopt.html`) or the `cmdline` package for Tcl (`http://tcllib.sourceforge.net/doc/cmdline.html`) to parse the arguments. This way, functionalities like the `--help` parameter will work properly and in a more user-friendly way. The majority of programming languages provide such libraries, and it is always recommended to use them.

Another thing worth considering is proper error handling. If connectivity to a remote machine is not possible, the check command should exit with a critical or unknown status. In addition, all other pieces of the code should be wrapped to catch errors depending on whether an error suggests a failure in the service being checked, or is due to a problem outside of a checked service.

Using the example of the first check plugin, we can redesign the beginning of the script to parse the arguments correctly. The reworked plugin sets the values of all of the parameters to their default value and then parses the options and corresponding values based on what the argument is. The script also allows specification of the `--verbose` flag to tell the plugin that it should report more information on what it is currently doing.

Finally, the connection is wrapped in the `try ... except` Python statements to catch exceptions when connecting to the MySQL server. This statement is used to detect errors when running the commands between `try` and `except`. In this case, if a connection to the database could not be established, the script will handle this and report an error, instead of returning a Python error report.

It's also a good practice to wrap the entire script in a `try ... except` statement so that all potential errors or unhandled situations are sent to Nagios as a general error. In addition, if the `--verbose` flag is specified, more information should be displayed. This should ease the debugging of any potential error.

The following code extract shows the rewritten beginning of a Python script that uses `getopt` to parse arguments and has used `try ... except` to handle errors in connectivity:

```python
# only perform check if we're loaded as main script
if __name__ == '__main__':
    dbhost='localhost'
    dbuser=''
    dbpass=''
    dbname=''
    tables=''
    verbose = False

    try:
        options, args = getopt.getopt(sys.argv[1:],
            "hvH:u:p:d:t:", ["help", "verbose", "hostname=",
                "username=", "password=", "dbname=", "tables="]
            )
    except getopt.GetoptError:
        usage()
        sys.exit(3)

    for name, value in options:
        if name in ("-h", "--help"):
            usage()
            sys.exit(0)
        if name in ("-H", "--hostname"):
            dbhost = value
        if name in ("-u", "--username"):
            dbuser = value
        if name in ("-p", "--password"):
            dbpass = value
        if name in ("-d", "--dbname"):
            dbname = value
        if name in ("-v", "--verbose"):
            verbose = True
        if name in ("-t", "--tables"):
            tables = value

    if verbose:
        print "  Connecting to %s@%s (database %s)" % \
            (dbuser, dbhost, dbname)

    try:
```

```
    conn = MySQLdb.connect(dbhost, dbuser, dbpass, dbname);
except Exception:
    print "Unable to connect to database"
    sys.exit(3)
```

This code also requires the defining of a usage function that prints the usage syntax. This has been left out of our example and is left as an exercise for the reader.

Another change would be to add the reporting of what is currently being done if the --verbose flag is passed. This helps to determine whether the script is idle or is currently trying to check specific table contents.

Similarly, for Tcl, we should use the cmdline package to parse arguments. It's also a good idea to check if all arguments have been specified correctly:

```
package require cmdline

array set opt [cmdline::getoptions argv {
    {host.arg      "127.0.0.1" "Host to connect to"}
    {warntime.arg "300"        "Warning threshold (seconds)"}
    {crittime.arg "600"        "Critical threshold (seconds)"}
}]

set host $opt(host)
set warntime $opt(warntime)
set crittime $opt(crittime)

if {![string is integer -strict $warntime] || $warntime <= 0} {
    puts stderr "Invalid warning time specified"
    exit 3
}

if {![string is integer -strict $crittime] || $crittime <= 0} {
    puts stderr "Invalid critical time specified"
    exit 3
}
```

The preceding code should replace the three lines that read the argv variable in the original script earlier. The remaining part of the check script should stay the same.

Of course, the changes mentioned here are just small examples of how plugins should be written. It's not possible to cover all possible aspects of what plugins should take into account. It's your responsibility as the command's author to make sure that all scenarios are covered in your plugin.

Typically, this means correct error handling—usually related to catching all of the exceptions that the underlying functions might throw. There are also additional things to take into account. For example, if you are writing a networked plugin, the remote server can return error messages that also need to be handled properly.

An important thing worth considering is the proper handling of timeouts.

Usually, a plugin tries to connect in the background. If it fails within a specified period of time, the plugin will exit the check and report an error status. This is usually done through the use of child threads or child processes. In event-driven languages, this can be done by scheduling an event that exits with a timeout message after a specified time interval.

Checking websites

Nagios ships with a very powerful `check_http` plugin that allows you to monitor websites in a simple way. This plugin should be enough for a large variety of tasks. However, there are often situations where using only this plugin is not enough.

If you are running a website that is critical to your business, checking only whether the main page is showing up correctly may not be enough. In many cases, you might actually want to be sure that the users are able to log in, orders can be sent out, and reports can be generated correctly.

In such cases, it is not sufficient just to check if a couple of pages work correctly. It might be necessary to write a more complex check that will log you into the website, fill out an order form, send it, and verify whether it shows up in the order history. You may also want to check that a specified text is present on specific pages.

This task is very common when performing automated tests during the development of a site. Not many people perform such tests regularly when the site is in production. A downside of this is that if version control of your website is not very strict, then small bug fixes can break things in a different part of the website and those may go unnoticed for a long time.

One may question whether this is a task for system monitoring or for the testing phase of the development and maintenance cycles. For a number of reasons, this task should be common to both development and maintenance, but it should also be a part of system monitoring. The first reason is that such tests make sure that the overall functionality of the site is working as expected. It can also be used to detect defacing or other unauthorized modification of the page. It can also be used to monitor the response time. Monitoring the web page's functionality should normally be performed rarely, but checks for the web server and the main page should be done more often.

There are a couple of approaches to this problem, depending on what you actually want to monitor. The first one is using the `http` or `https` protocol directly using various libraries—**requests** for Python (`https://github.com/kennethreitz/requests`), **http** for Tcl/Tk (`http://www.tcl.tk/man/tcl8.4/TclCmd/http.htm`), and **LWP** for Perl (`http://search.cpan.org/~gaas/libwww-perl/lib/LWP.pm`). By deciding on the appropriate approach, you will need to hardcode your URLs along with the queries to send and, in some cases, also implement cookie handling on your own.

Another approach is to use automated test frameworks. This includes **mechanize** for Python (`http://wwwsearch.sourceforge.net/mechanize/`), **webautotest** for Tcl (`http://sourceforge.net/projects/dqsoftware/`) for Tcl, and **WWW::Mechanize** for Perl (`http://search.cpan.org/dist/WWW-Mechanize/`). There are also multiple Java frameworks for this, such as **HttpUnit** (`http://httpunit.sourceforge.net/`) and **HtmlUnit** (`http://htmlunit.sourceforge.net/`). These packages offer the automated parsing of HTML, reading of the DOM tree, and operating similar to how a browser would work. This allows scripts to be written at a higher level without having to care about low-level things such as reading and passing values from all fields. A typical script would consist of going to a URL, locating forms, setting values, and sending these values.

The last approach is to use packages that take advantage of Internet Explorer over **Component Object Model (COM)**, which is available at `http://www.microsoft.com/com/`. This approach uses an entire browser and, therefore, is the most accurate method of testing a website's correctness. It also requires a much larger setup to accomplish the same task—tests need to be performed on a Microsoft Windows system and require a separate account for proper cookie management. For example, in the cases where tests need to start after all of the cookies have been removed, Perl offers the ability to automate Internet Explorer using the **PAMIE** package (`http://pamie.sourceforge.net/`), while for Python it is **SAMIE** (`http://samie.sourceforge.net/`). Tcl offers Internet Explorer automation in the **autoie** package (`http://sourceforge.net/projects/dqsoftware/`). For Ruby, the most popular utility is called **Watir** (`http://wtr.rubyforge.org/`). In order to use IE- and COM-based automation, you should set up all the checks on a Microsoft Windows-based machine and set it up so that the results are sent back via NSCA.

Usually, the best choice is to use automated web testing frameworks. These require fewer overheads when developing the code to perform checks, and tend to react nicely to small changes in the way your website works.

As an example, we will write a simple script in Tcl that communicates with a website using the **webautotest** package. The plugin logs into the backend of a **Joomla!** content management system (`http://www.joomla.org/`) and makes sure that it works correctly. This test also checks that all Joomla! mechanisms are working correctly.

The following is the source code of the plugin:

```
package require http

# initialize Webautotest object
package require webautotest::httpclient
set o [webautotest::httpclient ::#auto]

if {$argc != 3} {
    puts "Usage: check_joomla_backend URL username password"
    exit 3
}

set url [lindex $argv 0]
set username [lindex $argv 1]
set password [lindex $argv 2]

if {[catch {
    # go to your company's Joomla backend
    $o navigate $url

    # log in and submit form
    $o setForm -name login
    $o setFormValue username $username
    $o setFormValue password $password
    $o setFormValue lang en-GB
    $o submitForm

    # check if "Logged in Users" text can be found on the page
    set result [$o regexpDataI "Logged in Users"]
} error]} {
    puts "JOOMLA UNKNOWN: error occurred during check."
    exit 3
}

if {[llength $result] > 0} {
    puts "JOOMLA OK: Administrative panel loaded correctly."
    exit 0
} else {
    puts "JOOMLA CRITICAL: Administrative panel does not work."
    exit 2
}
```

To check the plugin, simply run the following command:

```
root@ubuntu:~# /opt/nagios/plugins/check_joomla_backend \
    http://joomla.yourcompany.com/administrator/ admin adminpassword
JOOMLA OK: Administrative panel loaded correctly.
```

Virtualization and clouds

Nowadays, more and more IT systems are moving into private or public cloud solutions. Clouds allow the more efficient use of resources and movement from smaller to bigger CPU power, memory, or storage capacity instantly.

Clouds can be divided into two forms:

- **Public clouds**: These are clouds hosted by external companies and allow the use of their machines as a service. There are a few public cloud providers that are most popular and commonly used — AWS from Amazon and Azure from Microsoft.
- **Private clouds**: These are setups where the company that wants to use the system also hosts it.

Both have their advantages and disadvantages, and sometimes both types of clouds are used. There are multiple free and commercial technologies to set up private clouds — VMware being a very popular one in enterprise IT infrastructure.

Nagios provides many ready-to-use plugins for various types of clouds. If possible, it is always a good idea to use the already-existing plugins. However, often we will need to either retrieve specific information or monitor specific data, in which case, we will need to create our own plugins.

Monitoring VMware

For Intel-based platforms, VMware virtualization (`http://www.vmware.com/`) is one of the most popular technologies. This spans from desktop solutions to server products. VMware also offers a free virtualization platform called VMware Server (`http://www.vmware.com/products/server/`).

Although Nagios does not offer a large variety of plugins to monitor VMware ESX and ESXi systems, VMware offers a Perl API that can easily be used to query virtual machines, along with a few of their parameters. On Windows operating systems, there is also the VmCOM API that allows interaction with VMware products.

These functions allow the querying of the virtual machine's status and guest parameters, as well as checking whether the virtual machine is working correctly.

The following code contains a script written in Perl that allows the querying of a particular virtual machine's state as well as make sure that it is working correctly. The script can easily be expanded to monitor CPU usage on a particular machine by querying the `cpu.cpusecs` parameter by using the `get_resource()` function from a virtual machine object.

Even though the script is configured to connect to a local machine, it is possible to specify different connection parameters so that it will query remote machines. In such a case, it is also necessary to specify the username and password of a user who can log in to the VMware system.

For the script to work, it is necessary that the VmPerl API is configured in your Perl interpreter. In order to check this, please run the following command:

```
root@ubuntu:~# perl -e 'use VMware::VmPerl;'
```

If VmPerl libraries are correctly installed, then this command should pass without any warnings or errors being generated. Otherwise, a configuration of VMware might be needed — VmPerl needs to be recompiled on each minor and major upgrade of Perl.

```perl
#!/usr/bin/perl

require VMware::VmPerl::VM;
require VMware::VmPerl::ConnectParams;

if (@ARGV != 2)
{
  printf "Usage: check_vmstatus <machine> <command>\n";
  exit(1);
}
($vmpath, $cmd) = @ARGV;
my $params = VMware::VmPerl::ConnectParams::new();
my $vm = VMware::VmPerl::VM::new();
$vm->connect($params, $vmpath);
my $title = $vm->get_config("displayName");

if ($cmd eq "state")
{
  if ($vm->get_execution_state() != 1)
  {
    printf "CRITICAL: %s is not running\n", $title;
    exit(2);
  }
  else
```

```
    {
      printf "OK: %s is running\n", $title;
      exit(0);
    }
  }
  if ($cmd eq "heartbeat")
  {
    my $hb0 = $vm->get_heartbeat();
    sleep(5);
    my $hb1 = $vm->get_heartbeat();
    if ($hb0 == $hb1)
    {
      printf "CRITICAL: %s does not respond to events\n", $title;
      exit(2);
    }
    else
    {
      printf "OK: %s is alive\n", $title;
      exit(0);
    }
  }

  printf "UNKNOWN: invalid command\n", $cmd;
  exit(3);
```

In order to test the script, simply run the following command:

```
# /opt/nagios/plugins/check_vm "/path/to/Solaris.vmx" state
OK: Solaris 10 test machine is running
```

You will need to specify the full path to the `.vmx` file, and the virtual machine needs to be added to the VMware.

Monitoring Amazon Web Services

Amazon Web Services (AWS) is a public cloud. It provides large variety of services such as storage, CDN, computing, and running of servers. It also provides a monitoring service called **CloudWatch**, which can easily be integrated with Nagios using the plugins available on Nagios Exchange (visit `http://exchange.nagios.org/` for more details). AWS provides a very easy-to-use API and client libraries exist for all popular programming languages. For some languages such as Java, Ruby, or Python, Amazon provides the client library themselves. For many other languages, there are unofficial libraries available. For example, there are complete libraries available for Perl and Tcl.

Elastic Compute Cloud (EC2) is an AWS service that allows the running of Linux- or Windows-based virtual machines in the cloud (visit http://aws.amazon.com/ec2/ for more details). A very basic thing that we can do is write code to test whether specific EC2 instance is currently running or not. For this example, we'll use Ruby. First, we need to install official APIs in Ruby, we can use the API. To install it, simply run the following command:

```
# gem install aws-sdk
```

The gem command is a command from **RubyGems** package (visit http://rubygems.org for more details), and it is a standard way to install additional modules for Ruby.

It will install the SDK for AWS. For testing purposes, it is enough to set AWS_ACCESS_KEY_ID and AWS_SECRET_ACCESS_KEY environment variables, for example:

```
# export AWS_ACCESS_KEY_ID=XXXXXXXXXXXXXXXXXXXXX
# export
AWS_SECRET_ACCESS_KEY=XXXXXXXXXXXXXXXXXXXXXXXXXXXXXXXXXXXXXXXXX
```

This is where the values can be retrieved from the AWS console of the **IAM** section at https://console.aws.amazon.com/iam/home. For production, the values should be stored in a file that only a nagios user can read and should be loaded from the script.

We'll now create a simple script to check instance statuses that will take the values from the command-line options:

```ruby
#!/usr/bin/env ruby

# load Amazon Web Services API
require 'aws-sdk'

# parse options
require 'optparse'

# default values for options
options = {instance: nil, status: :running}

# parse command line options
OptionParser.new do |opts|
  opts.banner = \
    "Usage: check_ec2_instance options"
```

```
    # instance has to be in form of i-XXXXXXXX
    opts.on("-i", "--instance ID",
      /^i-[0-9A-Fa-f]{8}$/,
      "Instance to test") do |v|
      options[:instance] = v
    end

    # status can be running or stopped (there are
    # other statuses as well, but we check those only)
    opts.on("-s", "--status running|stopped",
      [:running, :stopped],
      "Expected status") do |v|
      options[:status] = v.to_sym
    end
  end.parse!

  # verify instance ID is specified, exit otherwise
  if options[:instance].nil?
    puts "UNKNOWN Instance must be specified"
    exit 3
  end

  # create an EC2 instance and get instance status
  ec2 = AWS::EC2.new
  i = ec2.instances[options[:instance]]
  # check that instance exists and its status matches expected
  if !i.exists?
    puts "CRITICAL Instance #{i.id} does not exist"
    exit 2
  elif i.status == options[:status]
    puts "OK Instance #{i.id} is #{i.status}"
    exit 0
  else
    puts "CRITICAL Instance #{i.id} is #{i.status}"
    exit 2
  end
```

The preceding example will return an appropriate message and status, for example:

```
# ./check_ec2_instance.rb -i i-12345678 -s running
CRITICAL Instance i-12345678 is running
$ ./check_ec2_instance.rb -i i-12341234 -s stopped
CRITICAL Instance i-12341234 is running
```

Amazon Web Services (AWS) also provides EC2 as spot instances. These are the same as normal EC2 instances, but the pricing model works by bidding, which is similar to how stock markets operate. When requesting a spot instance, you can specify the maximum price you can pay. If the current price is lower, your machine gets started or continues running and you get charged for the current price. When the current price is higher than the specified one, the machine gets stopped. This allows calculations, tests, or other activities that can be done at any time, at a lower price than regular instances, for example, analyzing historical data. Visit `http://aws.amazon.com/ec2/spot-instances/` to find out more about spot instances.

If you are using spot instances, it may be a good idea to monitor spot pricing of EC2 instances and show a warning if it exceeds a certain value for some time.

The following code is a complete example that fetches the history for specified availability zone (the price is different for each instance type in each availability zone) and compares it with the maximum values for warning and critical results:

```ruby
#!/usr/bin/env ruby

# load API
require 'aws-sdk'

# parse options
require 'optparse'

options = {
  zone: "us-east-1a",
  type: "m1.small",
  hours: 4
}

OptionParser.new do |opts|
  opts.banner = \
    "Usage: check_ec2_instance options"

  opts.on("-z", "--availability_zone zone",
    "Availability zone price to check") do |v|
    options[:zone] = v
  end
  opts.on("-t", "--type type",
    "Availability zone price to check") do |v|
    options[:type] = v
  end
```

```ruby
  opts.on("-h", "--hours",
    "Number of hours to request history for") do |v|
    options[:hours] = v.to_i
    # make sure at least 2 hours are used
    options[:hours] = 2 if options[:hours] < 2
  end
  opts.on("-w", "--warning price", Float,
    "Warning threshold price") do |v|
    options[:warning] = v.to_f
  end
  opts.on("-c", "--critical price", Float,
    "Critical threshold price") do |v|
    options[:critical] = v.to_f
  end
end.parse!

# get pricing history
ec2 = AWS::EC2.new
history = ec2.client.describe_spot_price_history(
  instance_types: [options[:type]],
  start_time: (Time.now - 3600*options[:hours]).iso8601,
  availability_zone: options[:zone]
)

# get list of prices and calculate average value
prices = history[:spot_price_history_set]
  .map{|i| i[:spot_price].to_f}

avg = prices.inject(0.0) {|s,i| s+i} / prices.size

# format message and print it along with proper status
msg="Average %s price in %s is %.3f" % \
  [options[:type], options[:zone], avg]
if options[:critical] && (avg > options[:critical])
  puts "CRITICAL #{msg}"
  exit 2
elsif options[:warning] && (avg > options[:warning])
  puts "WARNING #{msg}"
  exit 1
else
  puts "OK #{msg}"
  exit 0
end
```

This will retrieve the pricing history for a specified amount of time, calculate average value using the `inject` method (this is described in more details `http://apidock.com/ruby/Enumerable/inject`), and check if the values are above specified thresholds, for example:

```
# ./check_spot_pricing.rb -w 0.015 -c 0.02 -t m1.small
OK Average m1.small price in us-east-1a is 0.013
# ./check_spot_pricing.rb -w 0.015 -c 0.02 -t m1.large
CRITICAL Average m1.large price in us-east-1a is 0.327
```

AWS provides a large variety of services and options how those services can be used. If you are using AWS for anything more than just basic functionality, it is a good idea to create custom Nagios plugins to monitor metrics specific to your operations.

Writing commands to send notifications

Another part of Nagios that can be extended to fit your needs are notifications. These are messages that Nagios sends out whenever a problem occurs or is resolved.

One way in which Nagios' notification system can be expanded is to create template-based e-mails. These will send notifications as both plain text and HTML messages. The template of the e-mail will be kept in separate files.

We will use Tcl for this purpose as it contains libraries for MIME (`http://tcllib.sourceforge.net/doc/mime.html`) and SMTP (`http://tcllib.sourceforge.net/doc/smtp.html`) functionality. The first one allows the creation of structured e-mails, whereas the latter one is used to send these using an SMTP server.

E-mails that contain content in multiple formats need to be wrapped in the `multipart/alternative` MIME type. This type will contain two subparts: first the plain text version and then the HTML version. This order makes e-mail clients choose HTML over plain text if both the types are supported.

This part can then be wrapped in a `multipart/related` MIME type. This allows the embedding of additional files such as images, which can then be used from within an HTML message. This is not used in the example shown on the next page, but can easily be added, in the same manner as text and HTML parts are embedded inside the `multipart/alternative` MIME type.

In the same way that macro substitution works in Nagios commands, templates will replace certain strings such as $HOSTSTATE$ within the template. For example, the following script can be used in a HTML template:

```
<tr><td>Notification type</td>
<td><b>$TYPE$</b></td></tr>
```

Similar macros can be used in plain text templates and will be substituted as well.

The following script will allow users to be notified in HTML format through the use of templates:

```
#!/usr/bin/env tclsh

package require mime
package require smtp
package require fileutil

# map arguments
set mappings {TEMPLATE EMAIL TYPE
    HOSTNAME HOSTSTATE HOSTOUTPUT}

if {[llength $argv] != [llength $mappings]} {
    puts stderr "Usage: [info script] [join $mappings]"
    exit 1
}

# handle arguments
set template [lindex $argv 0]
set to [lindex $argv 1]
foreach name $mappings value $argv {
    lappend map "\$$name\$" $value
}

# read template files and map variables accordingly
set textbody [string map $map \
    [fileutil::cat $template/body.txt]]
set htmlbody [string map $map \
    [fileutil::cat $template/body.html]]
set mailsubject [string map $map \
    [fileutil::cat $template/subject.txt]]
```

```
# create a list of alternate formats (plain text and html)
set parts [list]
lappend parts [mime::initialize -canonical text/plain \
    -encoding 8bit -string $textbody]
lappend parts [mime::initialize -canonical text/html \
    -encoding 8bit -string $htmlbody]

# wrap all parts inside multipart/alternative
set parts [mime::initialize -canonical multipart/alternative \
    -header [list Subject $mailsubject] \
    -header [list To "\"$to\" <$to>"] \
    -header [list From "\"Nagios\" <nagios@yourcompany.com>"] \
    -parts $parts]

smtp::sendmessage $parts \
    -recipients $to \
    -originator "nagios@yourcompany.com" \
    -servers {localhost}

exit 0
```

To test it, simply run the following command:

```
root@ubuntu:# /opt/nagios/plugins/notify-email-html template1 \
    jdoe@yourcompany.com RECOVERY myhost1 OK "OK: host is alive"
```

This should cause an e-mail to be sent to jdoe@yourcompany.com.

We can now define a command that will send a notification for the host, for example:

```
define command{
    command_name    notify-host-by-email-html
    command_line    $USER5$/notify-email-html
                    template1 '$CONTACTEMAIL$'
                    '$NOTIFICATIONTYPE$' '$HOSTNAME$'
                    '$HOSTSTATE$' '$HOSTOUTPUT$'
    }
```

It will pass the appropriate arguments for the user's e-mail address, notification type, hostname, state, and output from the host check. The command can then be used for one or more contacts by setting the host_notification_commands option, for example:

```
define contact{
    name                        jdoe
    host_notification_period    24x7
    host_notification_options   d,u,r,f,s
    host_notification_commands  notify-host-by-email-html
    (...)
    }
```

Managing Nagios

Your application might also want to have some control over Nagios. You might want to expose an interface for users to take control of your monitoring system, for example, a web interface or a client-server system. You might also want to handle custom authorization and the access control list, but this is something that is beyond the functionality offered by the web interface that Nagios comes with.

In such cases, it is best to create your own system to read the current status, as well as to send commands directly over the external command pipe. In both cases, this is very easy to do from any programming language.

The first thing we can do is to show Nagios' current status. This requires the reading of the `status.dat` file, parsing it to any data format, and then manipulating it. The format of the file is relatively simple — each object is enclosed in a section and each section contains one or more `name=value` directives. For example, the following is a definition of information about the `status.dat` file:

```
info
{
    created=1388002190
    version=4.0.1
}
```

All hosts, services, and other objects are defined in the same way as the preceding definition. There can be multiple instances of a specified object type, for example, each `hoststatus` object definition specifies a single host along with its current status.

Sending commands to Nagios also seems easy. The details of the most commonly used commands were given in *Chapter 6, Notifications and Events*. Sending commands simply involves opening a pipe to write and send commands, and close the pipe again.

Controlling Nagios from an external application is commonly done in PHP to create web applications. Implementing the reading of the current status as well as sending commands to Nagios is relatively easy to do in PHP, as the language offers convenient functions for string manipulation and regular expressions. Your web application also needs to limit commands that a user is able to send to Nagios, as it might be a security risk if your application offers functionalities such as disabling and enabling checks for hosts and/or services.

The following function reads the Nagios status file and returns it as an array of types of objects:

```
function readStatus($filename)
{
    $rc = array();
    $fh = fopen($filename, "r");
    $objname = "";
    while (!feof($fh))
    {
        $line = fgets($fh);
        $line = substr($line, 0, strlen($line)-1);

        // match beginning of an object
        if (ereg("^(.*) +\{$", $line, $ereg_output))
        {
            // if object data was previously read, store it
            if ($objname != "")
                $rc[$objname][] = $object_info;
            $objname = $ereg_output[1];
            $arguments = array();
        }
        else if (ereg("^(.*)=(.*)$", trim($line),
          $ereg_output))
        {
            $object_info[trim($ereg_output[1])] =
                $ereg_output[2];
        }
    }
    // if object data was previously read, store it
    if ($objname != "")
        $rc[$objname][] = $object_info;
    return $rc;
}
```

The function reads the file and looks for a line that starts with a text and is followed by one or more spaces and ends with a curly bracket open character ({). This will match the beginning of an object definition and store the object name. For lines matching the `name=value` pattern, the name and value are stored if a beginning of an object was previously read.

Whenever a new object is read or when an end of file is reached, information about the previously read object is stored. In this way, the returned value is an array that contains a list of all object types, such as the `info` definition mentioned above.

It's also relatively easy to write a function that allows you to search for objects by their type so that they match the specified criteria, for example, all of the services associated with a host. A sample code to do this is as follows:

```
function findObject($status, $object_type, $matching_fields)
{
    $rc = array();
    // iterate over all objects of said type
    foreach ($status[$object_type] as $object)
    {
        $ok = true;
        // iterate over all matching fields query and
        // check if they are all set and match value
        foreach ($matching_fields as $name => $value)
        {
            if ($object[$name] != $value)
                $ok = false;
        }
        // if all fields matched criteria, add to output list
        if ($ok)
            $rc[] = $object;
    }
    return $rc;
}
```

The function takes all objects of the specified type and checks whether all of the fields and expected values passed as $matching_fields. The current $object is added to the output list only if it has all of the required fields and their values matched expected values

Next, we can test this by reading the status and finding all of the services on the localhost machine that have critical statuses. This is done by invoking the following sample code:

```
$s = readStatus("/var/nagios/status.dat");
print_r(findObject($s, "servicestatus",
    array("host_name" => "localhost", "last_hard_state" => "2")));
```

This code will print out an array of all services matching the predefined criteria. This can be used to perform complex searches and show the status depending on many configuration options.

Sending commands to Nagios from PHP is also a very simple thing to do. The following is a class that offers internal functions for sending commands, as well as two sample commands that cause Nagios to schedule the next host or service check on the specified date. If the date is omitted, then the check is run immediately. Please check the following code:

```
class Nagios
{
    var $pipefilename = "/var/nagios/rw/nagios.cmd";
    function writeCommand($str)
    {
        $f = fopen($this->pipefilename, "w");
        fwrite($f, "[" . time() . "] " . $str . "\n");
        fclose($f);
    }
    function scheduleHostCheck($host, $when = "")
    {
        if ($when == "")
            $when = time();
        $this->writeCommand("SCHEDULE_FORCED_HOST_CHECK;" .
            $host . ";" . $when);
    }
    function scheduleServiceCheck($host, $svc, $when = "")
    {
        if ($when == "")
            $when = time();
        $this->writeCommand("SCHEDULE_FORCED_SVC_CHECK;" .
            $host . ";" . $svc . ";" . $when);
    }
}
```

A small section of code to test the functionality is as follows:

```
$n = new Nagios();
$n->scheduleHostCheck("linux1");
$n->scheduleServiceCheck("localhost", "APT", strtotime("+1 day"));
```

The preceding code initializes an instance of the Nagios class, and then schedules a host check for the linux1 machine immediately. Next, it schedules the APT service check on the localhost machine to occur one day from now.

Implementing additional commands should be as simple as specifying new functions that send commands (http://www.nagios.org/developerinfo/ externalcommands/) to Nagios over the external command pipe. Usually, the functionality base grows as the project grows. Hence, we should not define unused functions on a *just-in-case* basis.

Using passive checks

Nagios offers a very powerful mechanism to schedule tests. However, there are many situations where you might want to perform tests on your own and just tell Nagios what the result is. One of the typical scenarios to use passive tests can be when performing the actual test takes very little time, but the startup overhead is large. This is normal for languages such as Java, whose runtime initialization requires a lot of resources.

Another reason might be that checks are done on different machines where the Nagios instance is running. In many cases, due to security issues, it is not possible to schedule checks directly from Nagios. This is because communications not initiated by those machines are blocked. In this case, it's often best to schedule checks on your own and simply submit the results back to Nagios. In cases where such tests are going to be written by you, it's wise to integrate them with a mechanism to send the results over to NSCA directly.

Passive checks are responsible for scheduling and performing tests on their own. They can also be started by Nagios event handlers and be run as part of other applications. After a passive check is done, the result needs to be sent to the Nagios server. There are a couple of ways to do this. The easiest way is to send results over the external commands pipe, which is similar to managing Nagios. In this case, the application needs to send proper commands to submit either service or host check results. Nagios will then take care of incorporating the results into its database.

Another approach is to use NSCA. This is a protocol for sending results over the network. NSCA provides a command to send the results over the network and requires the passing of the configuration file that specifies the protocol, password, and other information. It is described in more detail in *Chapter 7, Passive Checks and NSCA*.

The next page contains an example of an application that periodically performs tests and sends its results to Nagios over the external command pipe. This code consists of a method to supply information to Nagios and a main loop that performs tests every 5 minutes. It does not contain the actual test that should be performed as this might vary depending on your needs. The following is a sample Java code to perform the test and report its results using Nagios external commands pipe:

```
/* write check status to Nagios pipe */
private static void writeStatus(String host, String svc,
   int code, String output) throws Exception
{
    long time = System.currentTimeMillis() / 1000;
    FileWriter fw = new FileWriter("/var/nagios/rw/nagios.cmd");
```

```
        fw.write("[" + time +"] PROCESS_SERVICE_CHECK_RESULT;" +
            host + ";" + svc + ";" + code + ";" + output + "\n");
        fw.close();
    }
    public static void main(String[] args)
    {
        while (true)
        {
            int code;
            StringBuffer output = new StringBuffer();
            /* perform actual test and report error if it failed */
            try
            {
                code = performTest(output);
            }
            catch (Exception e)
            {
                code = 3;
                output = new StringBuffer("Error: "+e.getMessage());
            }
            try
            {
                writeStatus("hostname","serviceDescription",
                    code, output.toString());
            }
            catch (Exception e)
            {
                System.out.println("Problem sending command to Nagios:" +
                    e.getMessage());
            }
            /* wait for 5 minutes between performing tests */
            Thread.sleep(300*1000);
        }
    }
    private static int performTest(StringBuffer buf)
    {
        return 0;
    }
}
```

Please note that the actual implementation of the performTest method will perform real tests. The following is a sample test function to connect over JDBC:

```
int performTest(StringBuffer output)
{
    String url = "jdbc:mysql://localhost:3306/mysql";
    String username = "root";
    String password = "yourpassword";
    Connection conn;
    try {
        conn = java.sql.DriverManager.
```

```
        getConnection(url, username, password);
        conn.close();
    }
    catch (Exception exception) {
        output.append("JDBC CRITICAL: Unable to connect");
        return(2);
    }
    output.append("JDBC OK: Connection established");
    return(0);
}
```

To run the tests, you will first need to compile the class. Assuming the source code is called `PerformTests.java`, run the following command:

`javac PerformTests.java`

Now, you can run the actual test using the following command:

`java -cp . PerformTests`

This will send reports to Nagios, so you can check the Nagios log file to see whether it has received information from your test checker.

Very often, you will need to create or extend applications to perform checks on remote machines. In this case, NSCA is used to send the check results to the Nagios server.

The following code is a Python class for sending service and host results over NSCA. It uses the **Subprocess** API (http://docs.python.org/2/library/subprocess. html) and allows configuration of the path to the command, and the configuration, host, and port:

```python
import subprocess

class nscawriter:
    def __init__(self):
        self.nscacommand = "/opt/nagios/bin/send_nsca"
        self.nscaconfig = "/etc/nagios/send_nsca.cfg"
        self.nscahost = "10.0.0.1"
        self.nscaport = 5667

    def open(self):
        process = subprocess.Popen(
            "\"" + self.nscacommand + "\"" +
            " -H \"" + self.nscahost + "\"" +
            " -p \"" + str(self.nscaport) + "\"" +
            " -c \"" + self.nscaconfig + "\"")
        self.nscain = p.stdin
        self.nscaout = p.stdout
```

```
def serviceResult(self, host, svc, code, output):
    self.nscaout.write(host + "\t" + svc +
        "\t" + str(code) + "\t" + output + "\n")
    self.nscaout.flush()

def hostResult(self, host, code, output):
    self.nscaout.write(host +
        "\t" + str(code) + "\t" + output + "\n")
    self.nscaout.flush()

def close(self):
    self.nscaout.close()
```

In order to test it, we can run the following code. This will send out a host notification about the linux1 machine and submit a result for the APT service on that host.

```
if __name__ == "__main__":
    nsca = nscawriter()
    nsca.open()
    nsca.hostResult("linux1", 0, "Host is reachable")
    nsca.serviceResult("linux1", "APT", 0, "No upgrades available")
    nsca.close()
```

You have to open and close the handle on your own. This is because the send_nsca command has an internal timeout handling to read results from the standard input. For the same reason, it is not possible to use the same NSCA instance to submit results over long periods of time.

Summary

Nagios has many places where it can be extended with external scripts or applications. We have also learned that Nagios is not bound to any specific language and that its real power comes from the fact that you can choose the language you'll use to program your code.

In this chapter, we learned how to create our own plugins to perform active checks. Adding our own commands makes it possible to perform checks using techniques that might not be available using the default Nagios plugin commands. We have also learned how it can be used to create various types of plugins—checking database consistency, monitoring system time differences, websites, and cloud environments.

This chapter also covered how to use passive checks and supply the check results to Nagios. In such a case, we are responsible for performing the test and sending results to Nagios. Nagios will then handle all of the results of the new status for a host or service, such as triggering event handlers and sending notifications.

We also covered how to send results to Nagios in two different ways. For tests that are running on the same machine where the Nagios process is running, results can be sent using the external commands pipe. If the test is running on another machine, this can be done using NSCA protocol.

We have created a custom notification command that sends e-mails using a predefined template. This can be used to send HTML and plain text notifications using Nagios; these are more readable and nicer than plain, text-only e-mails.

This chapter also discusses how Nagios stores its status information and how it can be read, to present it to the user or perform processing of the data.

Of course, this chapter does not cover all of the aspects in which Nagios can be customized. Nagios offers an event handling mechanism that you can use for tasks such as automatic recovery or the deployment of backup configuration.

The next chapter talks about using the query handler and **Nagios Event Radio Dispatcher (NERD)** to communicate with the Nagios process and receive real-time updates about host and service statuses.

12
Using the Query Handler

The last chapter talked about the extension of Nagios using multiple approaches, including writing your own plugins or commands to send notifications, and performing passive checks and sending the results to Nagios.

Nagios 4 provides a new interface called **query handler**, which is a general purpose mechanism that allows other processes to communicate with Nagios. It allows two-way communication, so it is possible to both send commands to the Nagios, similar to external commands pipe, and to receive information—either answers to a command that was previously sent to the query handler or asynchronous notifications, such as information about changes in the host and/or service status.

In this chapter, we will cover the following topics:

- Understanding the query handler
- Learning the services currently available in the query handler
- Communicating with various services
- Using the **Nagios Event Radio Dispatcher (NERD)** service to receive real-time notifications about changes in the host and service statuses

Introducing the query handler

The query handler is a major new feature of Nagios 4. It allows two-way communication between Nagios internal processes and external applications, and is designed to be extensible. The future versions of Nagios may provide more functionality using the query handlers.

The query handler communicates using Unix domain sockets (for more details, visit `http://en.wikipedia.org/wiki/Unix_domain_socket`). These are meant for communication between processes on same machine. Unix domain sockets use filesystems as names for remote addresses. For example, `/var/nagios/rw/nagios.qh` is the path to the query handler's Unix domain socket for an installation performed according to the steps given in *Chapter 2, Installing Nagios 4*. Filesystem permissions are used to determine whether a process can connect to the other side—so it is possible to limit the access to the query handler to specific operating system users or groups.

Unix domain sockets are very similar to named pipes, such as the Nagios external commands pipe; however, it is not possible to use named pipes for a two-way communication with more than one client. Another difference is that you cannot open Unix domain sockets as a file and/or send commands to the socket using shell commands such as `echo`, which is possible with named pipes such as the Nagios external commands pipe.

Nagios provides its functionalities through the query handlers using services. There are several built-in services, and the ones that are public are described throughout this chapter. The future versions of Nagios (or third-party software) may provide additional services. Each command sent to Nagios is prefixed with its service name, so each service may use any name for its subcommands.

Nagios uses the query handlers internally to distribute jobs to worker processes. Child processes connect to the query handler and receive tasks that should be performed. This is one of the reasons the query handler was originally created—to control the worker processes. The worker processes use the `wproc` service, which is an internal service and should only be used by Nagios processes.

Nagios also provides services that can be used by external applications. The first and most basic one is `echo`, which simply responds with the data that was sent to it. It is mainly a useful tool to learn how to communicate with Nagios.

The `core` service allows the querying of information about Nagios processes and scheduled jobs. The `nerd` service allows you to subscribe to events and can be used to receive real-time updates about changes on the Nagios host and/or service status.

Communicating with the query handler

The location (address) of the Nagios query handler is similar to the Nagios external command pipe—which is called `nagios.qh` and by default, resides in the same directory as the external commands pipe. The path to the query handler is `/var/nagios/rw/nagios.qh` for an installation performed according to the steps given in *Chapter 2, Installing Nagios 4*.

Let's begin to understand the query handler by communicating with it from the shell. There are multiple commands that allow us to connect to the Unix domain sockets, for example, **Netcat** (for more details, visit `http://netcat.sourceforge.net/`) and **socat** (for more details, visit `http://www.dest-unreach.org/socat/`). Both can be used to send commands to the Nagios query handler. To install the tools, simply run the following command on Ubuntu:

```
# apt-get install socat netcat
```

For Red Hat Enterprise Linux, CentOS, and Fedora Core, you can run the following command:

```
# yum install socat nc
```

For Red Hat Enterprise Linux, the **socat** package is available as part of **Extra Packages for Enterprise Linux (EPEL)** (for more details, visit `https://fedoraproject.org/wiki/EPEL`). This package will not be available unless EPEL is installed. It will install both of the tools, which will be used later to check the communication with the query handler. The communication protocol for query handler is simple. There is no initial message, so post connection, we can simply send the commands to the query handler.

All commands that are sent to the query handler are prefixed with the name of the handler and are sent using the following command:

```
@service command\0
```

In the preceding command, `@service` is the name of the service prefixed with the `@` character, `command` is the command (and parameters) to be sent, and `\0` is a character with the ASCII code of 0 that indicates the end of the command. Nagios may also send information—responses to commands or notifications. The format of the response varies by the service that implements it.

Many commands return an answer or send notifications after it is invoked. However, some commands, for example, to modify settings, will return an exit code. The code is modeled after the HTTP status codes (visit `http://en.wikipedia.org/wiki/List_of_HTTP_status_codes`), where codes starting with `200` indicate success and those starting with `400` indicate an error.

Nagios provides the @echo service that can be used to test the connectivity to the query handler. It will return the same message that was sent to it. To test the connectivity, we can simply run the following command:

```
# echo -e '@echo Query handler is working properly!\0' | \
    socat - UNIX-CONNECT:/var/nagios/rw/nagios.qh
```

The first line generates a command to be sent to the @core service. The -e option passed to the echo command enables the interpretation of backslash escapes, which changes \0 to the ASCII character 0.

Next, the output from the echo command is sent to the socat command, which sends its output to the query handler and prints out the result to the standard output. The socat command takes two arguments, which are the channels to relay data for. The hyphen (–) indicates using standard input/output and the UNIX-CONNECT:/var/nagios/rw/nagios.qh argument specifies the Unix domain socket path to connect to—in our case the Nagios query handler.

If the command succeeds, its output should look like this: **Query handler is working properly!**

If the current user does not have access to connect to the socket, the output will indicate an error as follows:

```
socat E connect(3, AF=1 "/var/nagios/rw/nagios.qh", 26): Permission
denied
```

For netcat, the command is similar:

```
# echo -e '@echo Query handler is working properly!\0' | \
    nc -U /var/nagios/rw/nagios.qh
```

The first line of the command is identical to the previous example. The -U option for the netcat command allows it to connect to the Unix domain socket with its address specified in the command line.

A single connection to Nagios can be used to send multiple commands and/or receive multiple types of information. However, as the formats of the responses can vary, it is best to use a single connection for a single service, that is, use one connection to manage the Nagios load and another to get notifications about the host and/or service check results.

Using the query handler programmatically

Now that we know how to communicate with the Nagios query handler, we can do so programmatically. Almost all languages provide a mechanism to communicate using the Unix domain sockets.

For example, to send a test message using Python, we can use the `socket` module (described in more detail at http://docs.python.org/library/socket.html) to communicate with the query handler using the following code:

```python
#!/usr/bin/env python

# path to query handler and message to send
nagios_qh = "/var/nagios/rw/nagios.qh"
test_message = "TestMessage"

# load required modules
import socket, sys, os

# connect using stream-based Unix socket
s = socket.socket(socket.AF_UNIX, socket.SOCK_STREAM)
s.connect(nagios_qh)

# send message to @echo query handler
s.sendall("@echo " + test_message + "\0")

# read result and close the socket
test_result = s.recv(len(test_message))
s.close()

# check whether the test message was sent back as expected
if test_result == test_message:
    print "Return message matches sent message"
    exit(0)
else:
    print "Return message does not match"
    exit(1)
```

The preceding code sends a test message to the @echo query handler service and retrieves the result. As the @echo service handler does not provide an end-of-message indicator, the code simply reads the same amount of bytes that were sent.

For Ruby, the `UNIXSocket` class (described in more detail at `http://ruby-doc.org/stdlib/libdoc/socket/rdoc/UNIXSocket.html`) can be used to connect to the query handler. An example similar to the preceding code is shown as follows:

```ruby
#!/usr/bin/env ruby

require 'socket'

nagios_qh = "/var/nagios/rw/nagios.qh"
test_message = "Test message"

s = UNIXSocket.new(nagios_qh)

s.send "@echo #{test_message}\0", 0
test_result = s.recv(test_message.length)

if test_result == test_message
  puts "Return message matches sent message"
  exit 0
else
  puts "Return message does not match"
  exit 1
end
```

PHP also supports the Unix domain sockets using the `stream_socket_client` function. It is documented in more detail at `http://www.php.net/manual/function.stream-socket-client.php`.

For example, to write a message and read it, we can use the following PHP code:

```php
<?php
test_message = "TestMessage";
$sock = stream_socket_client('unix:///var/nagios/rw/nagios.qh');
fwrite($sock, '@echo '.test_message."\0");
echo fread($sock, strlen(test_message))."\n";
fclose($sock);
?>
```

While programming in Perl, the **IO::Socket::UNIX** module (described in more detail at `http://perldoc.perl.org/IO/Socket/UNIX.html`) can be used to communicate with the query handler. For example, to connect to the Nagios query handler, use the following code:

```
use IO::Socket::UNIX;

my $qh_socket = IO::Socket::UNIX->new(
    Type => SOCK_STREAM,
    Peer => '/var/nagios/rw/nagios.qh',
);

$message = "Test Message";
print $qh_socket "\@echo $message\0";

$qh_socket->recv($output, length($message));
print "Read:\n$output";
```

Java does not natively support the Unix domain sockets, but there are multiple projects that use **Java Native Interface (JNI)** to provide Unix sockets. These include **jnr-unixsocket** available at `https://github.com/jnr/jnr-unixsocket` and **juds** project at `https://github.com/mcfunley/juds`.

Also, Tcl does not provide native support for Unix sockets. However, the **ceptcl** package (described in detail at `http://wiki.tcl.tk/ceptcl`) provides mechanisms to connect to the Nagios query handler.

Regarding programs written in C, it is best to use `libnagios` and its `nsock_unix` API to connect to the Nagios query handler. *Chapter 11, Programming Nagios,* demonstrates how to use the C language and the `libnagios` library to connect to the Nagios query handler and query the `@core` service.

For other programming languages, support for the Unix domain sockets may be built-in or require additional modules or packages. But as the technology is quite ubiquitous, commonly used languages should provide support for it.

Using the core service

The Nagios query handler provides the @core service, which can be used to get and set information about the Nagios process.

For all commands handled by the @core service, the result is a text that ends with the \0 character — to read a response, all we need to do is continue reading until we receive \0, which indicates the end of the response.

It allows you to query information about the queue of scheduled jobs, such as the next active check or background operation to be performed. The command name is squeuestats and the full command to be sent is as follows:

```
@core squeuestats\0
```

The result is a string with multiple statistics information in the form of name=value, separated by semicolons — name1=value1;name2=value2;....

For example, to print all information, we can simply use the following code:

```python
#!/usr/bin/env python

import socket, sys, os

nagios_qh = "/var/nagios/rw/nagios.qh"

s = socket.socket(socket.AF_UNIX, socket.SOCK_STREAM)
s.connect(nagios_qh)

s.sendall("@core squeuestats\0")
result = ""
while True:
    b = s.recv(1)
    if ord(b) == 0:
        break
    result += b
s.close()

result = sorted(result.split(";"))
print "\n".join(result)
```

The code connects to the Nagios socket, sends the `@core squeuestats` command, and reads the response until the `\0` character is sent. The `ord` function returns the code of the currently read character as an integer number (documented in detail at `http://docs.python.org/2/library/functions.html#ord`), and if the read data is not 0, it is added to the result string as a character. Then, the result is split by a semicolon, sorted, and finally, printed as a text, where each element of the list is joined by a newline character (`\n`).

Another command that the `@core` service provides is `loadctl`, which can be used to get values for all available load control settings or change one of their values. The syntax for the command is as follows:

```
@core loadctl
@core loadctl setting=value
@core loadctl setting1=value1;setting2=value2;...
```

The first form returns a list of all load control settings in the form of options, such as `setting=value`, separated by semicolons. For example, look at the following output:

```
backoff_change=1168;backoff_limit=5.00;changes=0;jobs_limit=3896;jobs
_max=3896;jobs_min=40;jobs_running=0;load=0.00;nofile_limit=1024;npro
c_limit=46272;options=0;rampup_change=292;rampup_limit=1.60
```

If the `loadctl` command has any setting specified, it can be changed and the command returns whether it succeeded or failed as result.

For example, we can change the `jobs_max` setting using the following command:

```
# echo -e '@core loadctl jobs_max=9999\0' | \
    socat - UNIX-CONNECT:/var/nagios/rw/nagios.qh
```

The Nagios query handler will return `200: OK` in the case of success. A response starting with `400` indicates that the setting was not found or modified.

 The load control settings are Nagios internal settings, we do not recommend that you modify them unless needed. The previous example simply illustrates how this can be done if needed.

As a more complete example of using the `core` service, the following Ruby code queries both scheduled jobs statistics and loads control settings and prints all of them:

```ruby
#!/usr/bin/env ruby

require 'socket'

def read_response(s)
    response = ""
    while true
        b = s.recv(1)
        break if b[0] == "\0"
        response << b
    end
    return response
end

nagios_qh = "/var/nagios/rw/nagios.qh"

s = UNIXSocket.new(nagios_qh)

s.send "@core squeuestats\0", 0

puts "Squeue stats:"
puts read_response(s).split(";").sort.join("\n")
puts ""

s.send "@core loadctl\0", 0

puts "Load control:"
puts read_response(s).split(";").sort.join("\n")
puts ""
```

Introducing Nagios Event Radio Dispatcher

The query handler also includes the NERD (Nagios Event Radio Dispatcher) service, which allows you to subscribe to the service or host check results. The service name is @nerd and it accepts the following commands:

```
@nerd list\0
@nerd subscribe <channel>\0
@nerd unsubscribe <channel>\0
```

The list command returns a list of channels separated by newlines, where the channel name is the first word of a line, followed by the channel's description. The subscribe and unsubscribe commands can be used to start and stop the receipt of notifications for specified channels.

For example, to list all available channels, we can simply use the following command from the shell:

```
# echo -e '@nerd list\0' | \
    socat - UNIX-CONNECT:/var/nagios/rw/nagios.qh
```

The output will be as follows:

```
hostchecks        Host check results
servicechecks     Service check results
opathchecks       Host and service checks in gource's log format
```

The opathchecks channel for notifications can be used together with the **Gource** visualization tool to show the animated host and service check updates. This functionality is described later in the *Displaying checks using Gource* section in this chapter.

The hostchecks and servicechecks channels can be used to receive updates regarding changes in the host and/or service status. The format for the respective channels is as follows:

```
<hostname> from <old_code> -> <new_code>: <description>
<hostname>;<servicename> from <old_code> -> <new_code>: <description>
```

In the preceding command, <old_code> and <new_code> correspond to the exit codes for the check results.

For the host checks, the codes map is as follows:

Exit code	Description
0	UP
1	DOWN
2	UNREACHABLE

For the service checks, the values are as follows:

Exit code	Description
0	OK
1	WARNING
2	CRITICAL
3	UNKNOWN

Once a socket is subscribed to a channel, updates regarding the hosts and/or services are sent, separated by newline characters. To read the status updates for hosts or services, simply subscribe to one or more channels and read from the socket line by line.

For example, the following code subscribes for both the host and service updates and prints the results accordingly:

```ruby
#!/usr/bin/env ruby

require 'socket'

# mapping of status codes to textual form
svc_statuses = ["OK", "WARNING", "CRITICAL", "UNKNOWN"]
host_statuses = ["UP, DOWN", "UNREACHABLE"]

nagios_qh = "/var/nagios/rw/nagios.qh"

# connect to Nagios query handler and subscribe to channels
s = UNIXSocket.new(nagios_qh)

s.send "@nerd subscribe hostchecks\0", 0
s.send "@nerd subscribe servicechecks\0", 0
```

```
while true
  line = s.gets
  if i = line.match(/(.*?);(.*?) from ([0-9]+) -> ([0-9]+): (.*)$/)
    # chek if this is a service check status
    status = i[4].to_i
    status = 3 if status < 0 || status > 3
    status = svc_statuses[status]
    puts "Service #{i[2]} on #{i[1]} is #{status}: #{i[5]}"
  elsif i = line.match(/(.*?) from ([0-9]+) -> ([0-9]+): (.*)$/)
    # otherwise check if this is host check status
    status = i[3].to_i
    status = 2 if status < 0 || status > 2
    status = host_statuses[status].to_s
    puts "Host #{i[1]} is #{status}: #{i[4]}"
  end
end
```

The code uses regular expressions to parse the lines. It first tries to parse the result as service status updates and then checks if it matches the host status expression.

Please note that the code is mainly meant for demonstration and is far from being a complete example. A final application that uses NERD to receive notifications should handle the case when the socket is closed and retry connecting back to Nagios to handle cases such as the restart of Nagios.

Displaying real-time status updates

The first and most common use case for the NERD service is in the applications that display the host and service status in real time. This requires you to connect to the Nagios query handler, send a subscription command, receive updates, and show them.

We will now write such a tool using Tcl as the programming language. The reasons are that it comes with an easy-to-use GUI Tk framework and uses event-driven programming, which makes it easier to handle the reading of events.

First, let's start off with creating the GUI elements—a `treeview` widget (documented in detail at `http://www.tcl.tk/man/tcl/TkCmd/ttk_treeview.htm`) and a scrollbar—and configuring all of the columns using the following code:

```
#!/usr/bin/env wish8.5

set nagios_qh "/var/nagios/rw/nagios.qh"

wm title . "Nagios real-time status"
# create a treeview widget
set t [ttk::treeview .1 -height 40 \
  -columns {status time info} \
  -yscrollcommand {.scroll set}]

# configure columns and colors
$t column #0 -stretch 0
$t column status -width 100 -stretch 0
$t column time -width 160 -stretch 0
$t column info -width 200 -stretch 1
$t heading #0 -text "Name"
$t heading status -text "Status"
$t heading time -text "Time"
$t heading info -text "Details"

# create background mappings for each state
$t tag configure bgOK -background "#00ff00"
$t tag configure bgWARNING -background "#bbaa00"
$t tag configure bgCRITICAL -background "#00ff00"
$t tag configure bgUNKNOWN -background "#00ff00"
$t tag configure bgUP -background "#00ff00"
$t tag configure bbDOWN -background "#ff0000"
$t tag configure bgUNREACHABLE -background "#999999"

# create an associated scrollbar
ttk::scrollbar .scroll -command {.1 yview}

pack $t -side left -fill both -expand 1
pack .scroll -side right -fill y
```

The preceding code will initialize a `treeview` widget and configure three columns in addition to the default one to show the status, the time at which an event was received, and the event details.

The `treeview` widget and many other widgets in Tk use tags to indicate how an item should be displayed. The preceding code creates tags with `bg` prefixes and the names of all known states and changes their color. For example, all items with `bgOK` have their `-background` option set as `#00ff00`, which is green.

Next, create a code that handles communication with Nagios and stores the state of currently known hosts and services:

```
# load ceptcl package for Unix domain sockets
package require ceptcl

set s [cep -domain local -type stream $nagios_qh]
fconfigure $s -translation binary -blocking 0
puts -nonewline $s "@nerd subscribe hostchecks\0"
puts -nonewline $s "@nerd subscribe servicechecks\0"
flush $s
```

The preceding code creates a socket to the Nagios query handler to read the host and service check updates. Next, create a code that will handle the reading of data from Nagios:

```
# variable that will store map for hosts and services
set results [dict create]

proc readdata {} {
  global s results
  if {[gets $s line] > 0} {
    set now [clock format [clock seconds] \
      -format "%Y-%m-%d %H:%M:%S"]
    if {[regexp \
      {^(.*?);(.*?) from ([0-9]+) -> ([0-9]+):\s+(.*?)$} \
      $line - host svc old_status status info]} {
      set status [lindex {OK WARNING CRITICAL UNKNOWN} $status]
      dict set results $host $svc [list $status $now $info]
    } elseif {[regexp \
      {^(.*?) from ([0-9]+) -> ([0-9]+):\s+(.*?)$} \
      $line - host old_status status info]} {
      set status [lindex {UP DOWN UNREACHABLE} $status]
      dict set results $host @ [list $status $now $info]
    }
    updateWidget
  }
}

fileevent $s1 readable readdata
```

The preceding code uses the global `results` variable that stores all the host and service results as a dictionary data type. It will use the host name as a key and keep a dictionary for the host information and services.

The subdictionary for each host will keep a mapping of service names (where `@` will be used as a key to store the host information) and the value will be a list that consists of the status, update time, and details—the same as the columns in `treeview`, since it will allow us to pass the same information to the widget directly.

The `fileevent` command specifies commands to run whenever data can be read from the socket. The command then uses the global variable `s` to access the Nagios socket. It tries to parse each line using regular expressions and if it matches the pattern of the service or host check notifications, it is stored in the dictionary. The regular expression syntax in Tcl is documented in detail at `http://www.tcl.tk/man/tcl8.5/TclCmd/re_syntax.htm`. It also calls `updateWidget`, which will add or update the items in the tree.

Look at the following code:

```
array set id {}

proc updateWidget {} {
  global results t
  global id
  foreach host [dict keys $results] {
    # check if host status is known; if not
    # then assume unknown status
    if {[dict exists $results $host @]} {
      set info [dict get $results $host @]
    } else {
      set info [list UNKNOWN "" {No data}]
    }
    set status [lindex $info 0]

    # create item in list if it does not exist yet
    # use host name as identifier for storing ID
    # of the item in the list
    if {![info exists id($host)]} {
      set id($host) [$t insert {} \
        [getInsertIndex $t {} $host] \
        -text $host -open true]
    }
```

```
# update values for columns and tag for color
$t item $id($host) -values $info -tags bg$status

set hostSvc [dict get $results $host]
foreach svc [dict keys $hostSvc] {
  # skip host information if set
  if {$svc == "@"} {continue}

  # use host,svc as identifier for storing
  # ID of the item in the list
  set svcid ${host},${svc}
  set info [dict get $results $host $svc]
  set status [lindex $info 0]

  # create item in list if it does not exist yet
  if {![info exists id($svcid)]} {
    set id($svcid) [$t insert $id($host) \
      [getInsertIndex $t $id($host) $svc] \
      -text $svc]
  }

  # update values for columns and tag for color
  $t item $id($svcid) -values $info -tags bg$status
  }
 }
}
```

The preceding code iterates through all keys in the results variable, which are the host names. It then tries to get the host information by checking whether the @ key exists; if it does, it gets the host information from the dictionary, otherwise, it takes a reasonable default value that the host status is UNKNOWN and the description is No data. Then, it checks if the host was already added to the treeview widget—if it wasn't, the host is added. Next, the remaining columns' information and tags are changed to reflect the latest status.

Next, the same is done for each host's services. The code iterates through all known services for the host. If the name is @, which stores the host information, it is ignored, otherwise, a check is made whether a service with this name was already added to the treeview; if not, the service is added. Then, status of the tags and the remaining columns' information is updated.

The code uses the global array id to store the mapping of hosts or services to IDs for the treeview items. For hosts, the key for the array is the host name. For services, it is hostname;servicename, such as gateway;PING for the PING service on the gateway host.

Information about hosts and services may be updated in a random order. While inserting, the `getInsertIndex` command is used to determine at which index the new item should be inserted. The code is very simple and is as follows:

```
proc getInsertIndex {t parent text} {
   set idx 0
   foreach o [$t children $parent] {
      if {[string compare -nocase $text \
         [$t item $o -text]] <= 0} {
         return $idx
      }
      incr idx
   }
   return end
}
```

It takes all the children of the specified parent and compares the new item's text with the current item's text. If the item to be inserted is lexicographically less than the current item at the index of the `idx`, then the new item should be inserted at this point. If there are no children or all current items are lexicographically less than the items to be inserted, the special index `end` is returned, which indicates that a new item should be added at the end.

The application should now work properly. After opening it, the list will show as empty, but after leaving the application running for some time, it will receive notifications about new check statuses, and the GUI will show a more complete list of hosts and services.

The application should now look similar to the following screenshot:

Name	Status	Time	Details
▽ gateway	UP	2013-12-29 19:39:25	PING OK - Packet loss = 0%, RTA = 6.12 ms
PING	OK	2013-12-29 19:41:44	PING OK - Packet loss = 0%, RTA = 1.33 ms
▽ linux1	UP	2013-12-29 19:45:10	PING OK - Packet loss = 0%, RTA = 3.76 ms
APT	OK	2013-12-29 19:46:23	APT OK: 0 packages available for dist-upgrade (0 critical updates)
bind	OK	2013-12-29 19:38:07	PROCS OK: 1 process with UID = 106 (bind), args 'named'
dhcpd3	OK	2013-12-29 19:47:01	PROCS OK: 1 process with UID = 105 (dhcpd), args 'dhcpd3'
DISK-exports	OK	2013-12-29 19:43:03	DISK OK - free space: /exports 339712 MB (39% inode=99%):
DISK-root	OK	2013-12-29 19:39:55	DISK OK - free space: / 303789 MB (35% inode=88%):
PING	OK	2013-12-29 19:42:28	PING OK - Packet loss = 0%, RTA = 2.36 ms
Reboot Required	CRITICAL	2013-12-29 19:35:38	File /var/run/reboot-required found
SSH	OK	2013-12-29 19:38:52	SSH OK - OpenSSH_5.3p1 Debian-3ubuntu7 (protocol 2.0)
▽ linux2	UP	2013-12-29 19:40:52	PING OK - Packet loss = 0%, RTA = 2.95 ms
APT	OK	2013-12-29 19:36:34	APT OK: 0 packages available for dist-upgrade (0 critical updates)
DISK-root	OK	2013-12-29 19:43:35	DISK OK - free space: / 40319 MB (42% inode=98%):
PING	OK	2013-12-29 19:37:24	PING OK - Packet loss = 0%, RTA = 4.92 ms
Reboot Required	OK	2013-12-29 19:45:45	File /var/run/reboot-required not found
SSH	OK	2013-12-29 19:44:13	SSH OK - OpenSSH_5.3p1 Debian-3ubuntu7 (protocol 2.0)

The precious code is not a complete application to display updates, but rather a demonstration of how such an application can be written.

The main issue is that it does not try to reconnect to the Nagios query handler, so it will not handle the restart of Nagios properly.

Handling the restart of Nagios properly can be done if you move the socket creation to a command and retry if it fails, as shown in the following code snippet:

```
proc connectToNagios {} {
  global s
  # catch errors connecting to Nagios
  if {[catch {
    set s [cep -domain local -type stream $nagios_qh]
  }]} {
    # retry after 10 seconds
    after 10000 connectToNagios
    return 0
  } else {
    fconfigure $s -translation binary -blocking 0
    puts -nonewline $s "@nerd subscribe hostchecks\0"
    puts -nonewline $s "@nerd subscribe servicechecks\0"
    flush $s
    fileevent $s1 readable readdata
    return 1
  }
}
```

Now, whenever connectToNagios is invoked, it will try to connect, and if it fails, it will try to connect again. It also returns whether the connection succeeded. As only the readable event handles the data from the channel, the rest of the code can stay the same.

Next, we need to run the connectToNagios command at the application's startup, which will also report an error if the first attempt to connect fails:

```
if {![connectToNagios]} {
  puts "Unable to connect to Nagios query handler"
  exit 1
}
```

Printing the error and exiting will make it easier to troubleshoot cases where the application cannot connect to the Nagios query handler due to permissions or an incorrect query handler path.

Finally, we need to change the `readdata` command to detect end-of-file events and reconnect after 10 seconds, as shown in the following code:

```
proc readdata {} {
  global s results
  if {[gets $s line] > 0} {
    set now [clock format [clock seconds] \
      -format "%Y-%m-%d %H:%M:%S"]
    if {[regexp \
      {^(.*?);(.*?) from ([0-9]+) -> ([0-9]+):\s+(.*?)$} \
      $line - host svc old_status status info]} {
      set status [lindex {OK WARNING CRITICAL UNKNOWN} $status]
      dict set results $host $svc [list $status $now $info]
    } elseif {[regexp \
      {^(.*?) from ([0-9]+) -> ([0-9]+):\s+(.*?)$} \
      $line - host old_status status info]} {
      set status [lindex {UP DOWN UNREACHABLE} $status]
      dict set results $host @ [list $status $now $info]
    }
    updateWidget
  } elseif {[eof $s]} {
    # if EOF was detected, try to close the socket
    # and reconnect after 10 seconds
    catch {close $s}
    after 10000 connectToNagios
  }
}
```

With the current approach, the application will start showing the host and service statuses when new updates are sent by NERD. A possible improvement is to read the `status.dat` file when the program is first run to get current information on all hosts and services. The check could be done whenever a connection is made to the Nagios query handler. It should also remove all hosts and services that are no longer present in the `status.dat` file in the `treeview` widget. However, as this code would become much more complex to maintain, it is beyond the scope of this book.

Displaying checks using Gource

An interesting feature of NERD is the `opathchecks` channel, which sends out updates that can be used in conjunction with **Gource**. The application and more details about it can be found at `http://code.google.com/p/gource/`.

It is an open source application that was originally designed to show the animation of source code changes for specific files. It also supports the animated and/or real-time display of any set of changes using a custom log format (documented in detail at `http://code.google.com/p/gource/wiki/CustomLogFormat`).

The `opathchecks` channel provides updates about hosts and services in a format that matches the custom log format for Gource, so it can be passed directly to it. Each notification about the check status is sent as a separate line, similar to the `hostchecks` and `servicechecks` channels.

Each line consists of the following fields, separated by a vertical bar (`|`):

Field	Example	Description
Timestamp	1388339291	This is the Unix timestamp at which the change took place.
Username	Core Worker 12701	This is the name of the user who made the change.
Type	M	This is the operation type and can be one of A - added, M - modified, or D - deleted. Nagios always reports M type.
Path	linux1/bind	This is the oath of the updated file/object; for Nagios, it is <hostname>/_HOST_ or <hostname>/<service>.
Color	FFFF00	This is the color in the hex (FFFFFF) RGB format.

While the fields were originally meant to view changes in the source code, the way Nagios works can also be visualized as shown in the preceding table's **Example** column.

For example, a sample set of updates looks like the following output:

```
1388339291|Core Worker 12701|M|linux1/bind|AAAAAA
1388339295|Core Worker 12701|M|linux1/PING|AAAAAA
1388339304|Core Worker 12698|M|linux1/Reboot Required|AAAAAA
1388339491|Core Worker 12698|M|linux2/_HOST_|FFFF00
```

As the notifications for the `opathchecks` channel match the format for Gource, it can simply be passed as a standard input. In order to use Gource to view the results in real time, we can simply run the following shell script:

```
# (echo -e '@nerd subscribe opathchecks\0' ; sleep 10000d) \
    | socat - UNIX-CONNECT:/var/nagios/rw/nagios.qh \
    | gource --realtime --log-format custom -
```

The first line of the preceding code will write the command to `@nerd` to subscribe to the `opathchecks` channel. It will then wait indefinitely (`10000d` means approximately 27 years, which is a safe value) so that the `socat` command does not assume it should close the connection.

After running the application for some time, it will show how the Nagios worker processes perform the monitoring along with the groups of hosts and their services, as shown in the following screenshot:

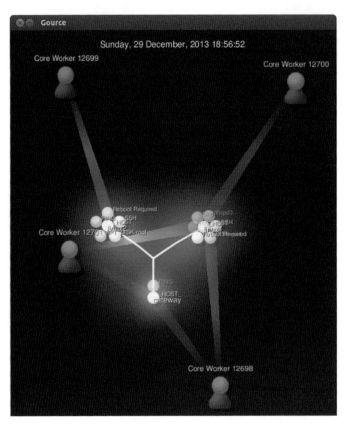

The application will show a 3D animation of the updates for the status checks in real time. The GUI can also be controlled using the mouse—the wheel to zoom in and out, and left/right-click buttons to pan and rotate the view.

It is also possible to store a history of notifications and replay it later with the Gource application. To store the output from the `opathchecks` channel, simply run the following command:

```
# (echo -e '@nerd subscribe opathchecks\0' ; sleep 10000d) \
    | socat - UNIX-CONNECT:/var/nagios/rw/nagios.qh \
    >/path/to/output.txt
```

At any time, we can break it by pressing the *Ctrl + C* keys.

Next, in order to replay it with the `gource` command, simply run the following command:

```
    | gource --log-format custom /path/to/output.txt
```

In this mode, it is also possible to pause and resume the animation as well as move the time of the animation back and forth using the timeline at the bottom of the window.

Summary

Nagios 4 provides a query handler, which can be used for two-way communications with Nagios. It is used internally by Nagios worker processes. It can also be used by external applications for getting and setting data

In this chapter, we learned what the query handler is and how to communicate with it using the Unix domain sockets. We also learned about the services that the query handler provides in Nagios 4.

We learned how to query the Nagios scheduled tasks queues and load control settings. We also found out how to change the load control settings, although we do not recommend that you do so, as they are internal settings.

We also learned how to use NERD to receive notifications about changes in the host and/or service status. We created a sample application that shows the changes in real time. In addition, we connected Nagios and the NERD notifications with the Gource application that can be used to show animated, real-time visualization of the changes in status.

This chapter concludes the book. You are encouraged to run examples that were shown throughout as well as experiment on your own with Nagios. We hope that the book will be the beginning of your journey into IT monitoring and, in particular, into Nagios.

Index

Symbols

@core squeuestats command 357

A

active checks 317
  about 195
  benefits 197
ActiveState
  URL 313
ActiveTcl 313
  URL 294
adaptive monitoring
  about 190
  using 190-193
ADD_HOST_COMMENT command 181
ADD_SVC_COMMENT command 181
administrative user
  creating, for web interface 73
advanced configuration, Nagios
  custom variables, using 158, 159
  dependencies, defining 147, 148
  file structure, configuring 145, 146
  flapping 160
  host dependencies, creating 148, 149
  maintainable configurations,
    creating 144, 145
  multiple templates, inheriting
    from 155, 157
  service dependencies, creating 150, 151
  templates, creating 154
  templates, using 152, 153
Advanced Packaging Tool (APT)
  about 134
  used, for checking updates 134

AIX (Advanced Interactive eXecutive)
  machines 145
alert histogram report 93
Amazon Web Services. *See* AWS
Ansible
  URL 301
autoie package 327
availability report 93
AWS
  monitoring 331-336

C

C/C++ 313
CentOS 236
Central Perl Archive Network (CPAN)
  URL 168
ceptcl package
  URL 355
cfengine
  URL 301
CGI (Common Gateway Interface) 70
CHANGE_CUSTOM_CONTACT_
  command 184
CHANGE_CUSTOM_HOST_VAR
  command 184
CHANGE_CUSTOM_SVC_VAR
  command 184
check_by_ssh plugin 220
  using 225
check_dummy command 308
check_http plugin 326
check_ifoperstatus plugin 277
check_ifstatus plugin 277
check_interval 184
check_linux_services_by_ssh 230

check_mrtg plugin 283
check_nt command
  syntax and options 290
  used, for performing tests 290
check_snmp command 274
check_swap_by_ssh command 228
check_swap_nrpe command 246
Chef
  URL 301
CLIENTVERSION variable
  using 292
clouds
  about 329
  private 329
  public 329
CloudWatch 331
commands
  comments, adding to hosts and services
    181
  custom variables, modifying 183
  host and service checks, scheduling 182
  sending, to Nagios 180, 181
  writing, for sending notifications 336, 338
comments
  managing 89, 90
Component Object Model (COM) 327
Concurrent Versions System (CVS)
  URL 300
configure command 25
connectivity
  testing, TCP and UDP used 110, 111
connectToNagios command 367
core service
  using 356, 357
CPULOAD variable
  using 291
cron 312
custom active checks
  creating 317
  local time, monitoring with time server
    320-322
  MySQL database correctness,
    testing 317-319
  plugins, writing 323-325

customizations
  Nagios 311
custom variables
  used, for performing checks 309
  using 158

D

database systems
  databases, checking 126
  monitoring 121
  MySQL, checking 122, 123
  Oracle, checking 124, 125
  PostgreSQL, checking 123
data objects, SNMP 259
data types, SNMP
  Counters32 and Counter64 259
  gauges 259
  Integer and Integer32 259
  IP address 259
  string 259
  time tick 259
decryption_method 212
DEL_ALL_HOST_COMMENTS command
    182
DEL_ALL_SVC_COMMENTS command
    182
DEL_HOST_COMMENT command 182
DEL_SVC_COMMENT command 182
DHCP protocol
  verifying 116, 117
disk space, storage space
  checking 128, 129
disk status, storage space
  monitoring, SMART used 127
distributed monitoring
  about 296
  freshness checking, performing 302-304
  Nagios instances, configuring 300-302
  obsessive notifications 297
  obsessive notifications, setting up 299, 300
  templates, using 304
downtimes
  managing 87
  scheduling 88, 89
  statuses, checking 87, 88

Thank you for buying
Learning Nagios 4

About Packt Publishing

Packt, pronounced 'packed', published its first book "*Mastering phpMyAdmin for Effective MySQL Management*" in April 2004 and subsequently continued to specialize in publishing highly focused books on specific technologies and solutions.

Our books and publications share the experiences of your fellow IT professionals in adapting and customizing today's systems, applications, and frameworks. Our solution based books give you the knowledge and power to customize the software and technologies you're using to get the job done. Packt books are more specific and less general than the IT books you have seen in the past. Our unique business model allows us to bring you more focused information, giving you more of what you need to know, and less of what you don't.

Packt is a modern, yet unique publishing company, which focuses on producing quality, cutting-edge books for communities of developers, administrators, and newbies alike. For more information, please visit our website: www.packtpub.com.

About Packt Open Source

In 2010, Packt launched two new brands, Packt Open Source and Packt Enterprise, in order to continue its focus on specialization. This book is part of the Packt Open Source brand, home to books published on software built around Open Source licences, and offering information to anybody from advanced developers to budding web designers. The Open Source brand also runs Packt's Open Source Royalty Scheme, by which Packt gives a royalty to each Open Source project about whose software a book is sold.

Writing for Packt

We welcome all inquiries from people who are interested in authoring. Book proposals should be sent to author@packtpub.com. If your book idea is still at an early stage and you would like to discuss it first before writing a formal book proposal, contact us; one of our commissioning editors will get in touch with you.

We're not just looking for published authors; if you have strong technical skills but no writing experience, our experienced editors can help you develop a writing career, or simply get some additional reward for your expertise.

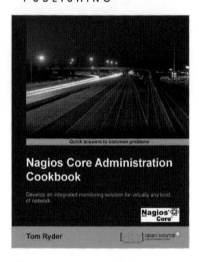

Nagios Core Administration Cookbook

ISBN: 978-1-84951-556-6   Paperback: 360 pages

Develop an integrated monitoring solution for virtually any kind of network

1. Monitor almost anything in a network.

2. Control notifications in your network by configuring Nagios Core.

3. Get a handle on best practices and time-saving configuration methods for a leaner configuration.

Instant Nagios Starter

ISBN: 978-1-78216-250-6   Paperback: 46 pages

An easy guide to getting a Nagios server up and running for monitoring, alerting, and reporting

1. Learn something new in an Instant! A short, fast, focused guide delivering immediate results.

2. Install Nagios with minimal fuss on any Unix and Linux platform.

3. Harness the flexibility of Nagios for intelligent monitoring.

4. Utilize Nagios data for reporting and data visualization.

Please check **www.PacktPub.com** for information on our titles

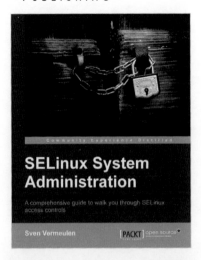

SELinux System Administration

ISBN: 978-1-78328-317-0   Paperback: 120 pages

A comprehensive guide to walk you through SELinux access controls

1. Use SELinux to further control network communications.

2. Enhance your system's security through SELinux access controls.

3. Set up SELinux roles, users, and their sensitivity levels.

Blackboard Learn Administration

ISBN: 978-1-84969-306-6   Paperback: 326 pages

Become an expert in administrating Blackboard Learn with tutorials as if a certified administrator were at your side

1. Learn both the simple and the complex skills to become an expert Blackboard Learn admin.

2. Optimize the security and performance of Blackboard Learn and create a disaster recovery plan.

3. Gain insight from an experienced Blackboard administrator using a hands-on approach.

Please check **www.PacktPub.com** for information on our titles